Palgrave Studies in Relational Sociology

Series Editor
François Dépelteau
Laurentian University
Canada

In various disciplines such as archeology, psychology, psychoanalysis, international relations, and philosophy, we have seen the emergence of relational approaches or theories. This series seeks to further develop relational sociology through the publication of diverse theoretical and empirical research—including that which is critical of the relational approach. In this respect, the goal of the series is to explore the advantages and limits of relational sociology. The series welcomes contributions related to various thinkers, theories, and methods clearly associated with relational sociology (such as Bourdieu, critical realism, Deleuze, Dewey, Elias, Latour, Luhmann, Mead, network analysis, symbolic interactionism, Tarde, and Tilly). Multidisciplinary studies which are relevant to relational sociology are also welcome, as well as research on various empirical topics (such as education, family, music, health, social inequalities, international relations, feminism, ethnicity, environmental issues, politics, culture, violence, social movements, and terrorism). Relational sociology—and more specifically, this series—will contribute to change and support contemporary sociology by discussing fundamental principles and issues within a relational framework.

More information about this series at
http://www.palgrave.com/gp/series/15100

Greti-Iulia Ivana

Social Ties in Online Networking

palgrave
macmillan

Greti-Iulia Ivana
Department of Sociology
Uppsala University
Uppsala, Sweden

Palgrave Studies in Relational Sociology
ISBN 978-3-319-71594-0   ISBN 978-3-319-71595-7   (eBook)
https://doi.org/10.1007/978-3-319-71595-7

Library of Congress Control Number: 2017964080

This Palgrave Macmillan imprint is published by Springer Nature
The registered company is Springer International Publishing AG
The registered company address is: Gewerbestrasse 11, 6330 Cham, Switzerland

For my mother, Felicia

Acknowledgments

This book discusses social networking activity and its significance in the context of users' reciprocal bonds. The bulk of the analysis is based on interviews with Facebookers about what they do, what they like and watch, but first and foremost how they intend their own actions and read into each other's within the realm of social media. I have had an interest in human communication, and in everyday life interpretative processes long before realizing it, and before being a sociologist. However, it was during my years as a graduate student when, reading Alfred Schütz, I became fully aware of it. Since then, my standpoint and my focus have shifted repeatedly. Nevertheless, my approach is still greatly indebted to Schütz, particularly for his systematic analyses of taken for grantedness and relevance and for his views on first-hand lived experience. Many other authors writing in a phenomenological vein have also served as guidance in writing this book (Merleau-Ponty stands out). Yet, the relational angle I adopt is also strongly influenced by Simmel and several symbolic interactionists, particularly Goffman and Hochschild.

As insightful as these sources have been for me as a sociologist and for my efforts of theorizing social reality, this book would have not been possible without the cooperation of my informants. For reasons of confidentiality, they cannot be named, but I do wish to thank all of them for their openness and honesty in sharing with me private aspects of their lives. Their stories and experiences are the backbone of this work.

Having said this, the greater part of the research on which this book is based was conducted through the generous funding offered by Universitat Oberta de Catalunya (UOC). For the grant without which none of this would have not been written, I wish to thank the UOC. Especially, I would like to thank Josep Llados, at the time the director of the Internet Interdisciplinary Institute in Barcelona, and David Megias, the current director, for their fairness and professionalism, which has meant so much for me. I also thank Natalia Canto Mila and Swen Seebach for their overall support and encouragement.

This book is the result of a personal project, but one which has benefited from great discussions and advice. In this regard, I would also like to thank the members of GRECS, the Group of Study for Culture and Society, especially Roger Martinez and Isaac Gonzalez, for listening to my thoughts along the way and for their valuable input. I wish to thank Martin Berg, who, despite the geographical distance, has taken the time to read my work and whose practical and well-structured ideas have been instrumental in furthering this project. Special thanks to Mary Holmes, from whom I received thoughtful and detailed comments which have brought me a new and rounder understanding of the topic of this research. I would also like to thank Calin Goina for his suggestions and Jochen Dreher for the opportunity to develop my theoretical framework with a stay at the Social Science Archive, at the University of Konstanz.

I would like to thank Patrik Aspers, whose generous advice has helped me navigate the process of writing this book and has eased the adaptation to my new academic home at Uppsala University. For comments on the Introduction, I wish to thank Alexander Dobeson, Dominik Döllinger, Peter Bengtsson, Alison Gerber, and the other members of UU's Economic Sociology Lab. For comments on the Overviewing chapter, I thank Tora Holmberg, Fredrik Palm, and the Cultural Matters Group at Uppsala University. I am indebted to François Dépelteau, editor of the Relational Sociology Series, and to the anonymous reviewers for their suggestions. At the same time, I wish to thank Palgrave editors Sharla Plant and Jack Redden for their work with the manuscript.

I am grateful to Aleksandra Wilczinska, Aleksandra Skorupinska, Maria Luisa Malerba, and Monika Kustra for the kindness and personal encouragement they offered me during the most demanding stages of this project. I thank Vlad Ceregan for his unwavering support and for the patience and warmth with which he surrounds me. Finally, my mother is the person who has been with me through every day of fieldwork and writing, through each reason of worry, each new idea, and each moment of joy. Her energy, dedication, and love continue to overwhelm me. I dedicate this book to her.

Greti-Iulia Ivana
14.08.2017, Uppsala

Contents

1   Introduction   1

2   It Happened on Facebook   27

3   Facebook and Real Life   45

4   Meaning Construction in Overviewing: "It Was Like Catching Up, But Without Talking"   73

5   Meaning Construction in Online Social Interactions   111

6   Social Networking and Emotions   141

7   The Structural Underpinnings of Online Bonds   173

8   Conclusions   197

References   205

Index   223

1

Introduction

"Any gesture—a cool greeting, an appreciative laugh, the apology for an outburst—is measured against a prior sense of what is reasonably owed another, given the sort of bond involved."
(Hochschild 1979, p. 568)

In 1939, Norbert Elias was writing, in a Simmelian fashion, about society understood as a web of relations. We are all born and raised within a group of people, we are shaped as unique individuals through our links with those around us, and we go through life weaving our purposes, wishes, and dreams in the fabric of an ever-changing, but always present relational universe. To make his stance easier to grasp, Elias invites us to imagine something as simple as a conversation between two people and to analyze the replies of one of them "as a separate unity existing with its own order independently of the network-figure of the conversation: that would be much as if one were to consider a person's individuality as something independent of the relations in which he finds himself, the constant weaving of threads through which he has become what he is" (Elias 2001, p. 25).

© The Author(s) 2018
G.-I. Ivana, *Social Ties in Online Networking*, Palgrave Studies in
Relational Sociology, https://doi.org/10.1007/978-3-319-71595-7_1

Around 70 years later, I, like most of the people I knew, decided to join Facebook and I immediately felt the first-hand experience of the imaginary scenario about which Elias talked. Every post seemed a piece of a conversation I did not know, which, in turn, was part of a relation I did not know about. Everyone seemed to be saying something to someone else and the conversation partner(s) remained undisclosed more often than not. The only posts I fully understood were my own and, sometimes, those of my close friends, but for most of the time, I was missing the context behind people's posts. The very assumption of an existing background to which the content belonged was very intriguing. I had not reflected on the relational core of that background, but there was an unshakable intuition about there being something more to what was displayed in public posts. It encouraged me to speculate about the larger situations, relations, conversations which generated the published image or text and it brought me in front of various puzzles, of which very few pieces were ever given. At the same time, these contents were labeled as "public", a term I found somewhat misleading. Publicness, in my understanding, involved an audience regarded as a whole. On Facebook, though, each and every member of one's audience had a specific relation with the owner of the profile and that added to my feeling of fragmentation.

In 2010, I started chatting to people who were using Facebook about what it meant to them, how they employed it, and how they read it. And despite receiving very diverse answers, all of them had something in common, namely, the reference to their own social bonds. A 25-year-old smiled and told me, "it's a waste of time, but I like it because it's like reading a glossy magazine about people you actually know". Several years later, someone said with mild frustration he joined "because everyone is there". In between these answers, I heard stories about romantic interests, work conflicts, old rivalries, political mobilization, and home party planning. Social bonds, and often somewhat consolidated ones, appeared to be the main underlying thread which gave coherence to this wide array of narratives.

Looking back into Norbert Elias' and others' work on the importance of social relations, my claim is that it provides crucial tools for understanding developments in social networking sites, despite the different setting specific to digital media. According to Elias, "The historicity of each individual, the phenomenon of growing up to adulthood, is the key to an understanding of what "society" is" (Elias 2001, p. 25). He goes on to elaborate on how the abovementioned individual historicity is constructed through bonds and how sociality constitutes the main precondition for the formation of individuality and unicity themselves. By pursuing this logic, Elias highlights the intrinsic interdependence rather than opposition between individual and society.

Of course, his words refer to the formation of individuals in groups that are in some ways traditional, in which people are copresent and have direct contributions on each other's lives. The online world, on the other hand, is something many associate with solitude and with disengagement from social life. It is argued people spend more and more time with their phones and laptops than with each other. Yet, in the case of social networking, and to a lesser extent in gaming, the time spent with one's phone is, from a certain perspective, time invested in the relation with the other (although not necessarily in the form of time "spent with the other", as I will show later on). Moreover, the typical Facebook practice of maintaining links with people with whom one was in contact at certain stages in one's life evokes and contributes to shaping the very relational historicity of each individual, on which Elias was insisting.

Research Approach

Despite the growing volume of research on social networking, the ways in which Facebooking practices are connected with social bonds between users are still unclear. This situation is paradoxical, as social ties are one of the main points of focus for scholars working with Facebook and new media more broadly. However, this preoccupation translates into a significant amount of work on ties and Facebook from a behavioral quantifiable large-scale perspective, and a lack of research of Facebook and ties from an in-depth subjective, phenomenological standpoint (Lambert 2016). For instance, important findings show that that intensity of Facebook use strongly predicts the number and quality of weak ties in a longitudinal analysis (Steinfield et al. 2008). On a similar note, Donath and Boyd (2004), Ellison et al. (2007), Resnick (2001), and Wellman et al. 2001 point out social networking supports loose social ties and helps users create and maintain relationships they constructed for accessing resources. As far as stronger bonds are concerned, Johnston et al. (2013) did not find a significant relationship between Facebook use and their development. However, Kwon et al. (2013) highlight a gap within this literature. Namely, they ask, "does Facebook have the same social effect on an individual who spends an hour a day composing messages and commenting and on an individual who spends an hour a day simply surfing pictures of parties that they were not at?" (Kwon et al. 2013, p. 35). They answer following a similar behaviorist approach. All this research highlights broad trends about Facebook users and their ties, showing correlations which are worth exploring. At the same time, in order to gain insight into the processes of tie construction, negotiation, or maintenance on Facebook, this work must be complemented with a qualitative approach. Kwon et al.'s question about what exactly that someone does on Facebook has an effect on ties highlights precisely that need to understand the mechanisms which lead to particular links between Facebook use and tie strength or social capital formation. The apparently simple question of how Facebook actually works in the context of social ties has been overlooked.

One reason for this is the isolated nature of Facebook within social life. There is a directly experienced limit between what happens on Facebook and what happens outside of it. So, Facebook is in this sense a predefined research field. This experiential online/offline, log in/log out switch draws attention away from the existing, underlying social bonds, which act as a background for online (inter)actions. An interesting exception can be found in discussions about dead users, where bonds are a major component (Kasket 2012; Irwin 2015). Yet, most advancements have been made in other directions. For example, Facebook scholars insist on how social network users present themselves in conformity to social expectations (Birnbaum 2008; Strano and Wattai Queen 2012; Farquhar 2013). It is often suggested people lose their genuine connections with others in an effort to display certain characteristics (Hogan 2010; Walther et al. 2008). The isolating process of self-exposure is doubled by an altered experience of togetherness and a lack of reciprocally oriented communication (Turkle 2011; van Dijck 2013; Hilsen and Helvik 2014). Although different on many levels, the perspective based on roles and normativity is equally individualizing. The user is part of a social system, which encourages, favors, rewards a series of behaviors, and sanctions others (McLaughlin and Vitak 2011; Tufekci 2008). The political impact of Facebook campaigns and mobilizations (Auter and Fine 2017; Beyer 2014; Vaccari 2017; Alduiza et al. 2014), the links between Facebook and particular consumer behaviors (Duffett 2015; Dehghani and Turner 2015; Heyman and Pierson 2013), and the construction of an identity with profound structural roots (Aguirre and Davies 2015; Micalizzi 2014; Kebadayi and Price 2014) have all been thoroughly discussed and documented.

Nevertheless, it is the links between each other that users emphasize most. Facebookers love to talk about stalking romantic interests; being judgmental of old colleagues; gossiping with good friends; getting closer to popular, powerful, and successful others; and assuming personal problems their boss might be facing. Thus, the purpose of this book is twofold:

- It explores the ways in which the exchanges of information unfolding on Facebook impact the universe of the users' social bonds;
- It looks into how the underlying fabric of social relations influences the dynamic of Facebook contents.

Speaking of Facebook's broad social background, there is no doubt about the fact that Facebook networks of friends typically consist of those with whom one has at least been acquainted. It is Facebook etiquette to have a recognizable name and/or profile picture and not to invite unknown people in one's network. In a conversation about her early experiences of social networking, a young girl explained to me, amused, about her move, as a teenager, from Hi5 to Facebook. This was a different environment, she would observe, and, if on Hi5 connecting with strangers was standard practice, it was "lame" to do the same on Facebook. Another user was bothered by a friend request he received from someone with a common first name followed by an initial (e.g. John W.), who also happened to have a cat as a profile picture. John W. never made it in my interviewee's network. Thus, besides the manner in which interactions unfold on Facebook, they are part of a larger relational narrative, to which they contribute and by which they are shaped, as we will explore, in more ways than by simple acceptance or exclusion. This being said, this book sets out to advance current debates on interpersonal relations in conditions of non-copresence, offering a relational alternative to the self and identity-oriented approaches to social networking.

Methodology

In describing the offline and online side of social relations which unfold partially through Facebook, and showing how the two levels of experience converge in meaning making, I have drawn on empirical research I conducted between 2010 and 2014. This work consisted in observation of Facebook profiles and public exchanges of information but, most importantly, 40 open-ended interviews with users about their practices and their understanding of social networking and of Facebook in particular. The interviews were conducted face to face, initially in the Romanian city of Cluj-Napoca and, after 2012, in Barcelona. The users were aged between 18 and 39; they were of various nationalities and the majority of them (36 out of 40) were either highly educated or enrolled in tertiary education at the time of the interviews. The respondents were 22 women and 18 men. The interviews were conducted in Romanian, English, and Spanish.

Illustrations for the ideas found in the book come from both participant observation and interviews with a wide scope. Namely, I began with an interest in what makes Facebook a different and successful means of communicating information in the eyes of its users. Stemming from this interrogation was the issue of what users made of their online presence in this environment, how they decided to post certain contents, and what they read into what they received from others. For instance, users were invited to talk about several things that they posted on their wall and about how they decided to share that content with their contacts. The ways in which received content was interpreted were also an important point in the interviews. Respondents were asked about identity and privacy, topics which are typically associated with social networking sites. Whenever they made general statements, inquiries were made into how the respondents reached those conclusions and they were asked about examples of concrete experiences they have had. The result was a set of rich set of data, consisting of the subjects' own attitudes, doubts, enchantment with Facebook, as well as great examples of information exchanges online and how these exchanges were lived and understood "behind the scenes", or backstage, to use Goffman's famous dramaturgical metaphor. Given the volume of the data and the variety of approaches users had when talking about what they do on Facebook, why and how they do it, delimiting the most relevant categories and finding the communalities and tensions in practices, interpretations, and motivations has proven itself to be a challenging task. However, the relational thread emerged from the data as the unanimous focus of all practices linked to or unfolding on Facebook. The respondents often talked about life trajectories and old contacts, about how Facebook users seek to increase their social status in each other's eyes, about physical and relational distance, and about the process through which they decided to post or to give feedback to another (a process which was unexpectedly laborious for many users).

At the same time, as is often the case in any small-scale analysis of social life, emotions were an important part of the respondents' discourse. More precisely, pride and embarrassment (the emotions which are most rooted in the gaze of the other) were frequently mentioned. Additionally, displays of economic and educational capital, through vacations, "check ins", graduations, and working space, are only several indicators of social class which were part of both observation and interviews. Yet, the interviews offered extra layers of understanding, especially through the constant references to the relational logic behind these elements. For instance, users would wonder about things such as: what are they hoping to achieve by flooding my newsfeed with their photos? Would my friends find it in poor taste if I share this story from my trip? The interpersonal links were always the foundation of meaning making.

Social Relations: An Overview

Insight into the networks of ties which support Facebooking practices can help clarify the relevance of social networking through the eyes of its users; it can reveal the sociological significance of how (inter)acting in this given setting is experienced and how that experience becomes meaningful in a larger relational picture. The approach I am adopting is largely distinct from the formalist methodologically oriented social networks analysis (Smith-Doerr and Powell 2005; Azarian 2010). Rather, my aim is to analyze ties outside of the form/content dichotomy, through the unfolding of everyday life situations and through subjects' experiences of those situations, with patterns and regularities emerging as elements of approximate and imperfect structuration.

Yet, when talking about concrete empirical situations, it is important to keep in mind that the exchanges of information taking place on Facebook (or elsewhere) are a recurrent element of social bonds, but they do not represent the bond as a whole. Besides these exchanges (which are sometimes direct interactions and other times a form of indirect news report), there are offline interactions which either occur alternatively with the online ones or have occurred in the past and constitute the basis of the bond. Additionally to these concrete events, the bond also includes expectations about the other in light of what is already known about them (Wolfe 1970; Weber 1978; Azarian 2010), memories about shared past experiences, projections about future encounters, emotional investment, struggles for power and control (Simmel 1950; Granovetter 1983; White 2008) as well as an understanding of the type of informal tie which binds the users and which regulates their interactions (Simmel 2009; Collins 2004; Weber 1978). The bond is neither of the online nor of the offline. It is a relatively stable frame which sums up past knowledge, shared experience, affectivity, common plans, and expectations describing the general connection between two or more people. Thus, the bond involves a mixture of reflective and emotional aspects which (1) characterize the link with the other in their absence and which (2) shape the interaction with them when it takes place. If social interactions or simple non-interactional exchanges always include a message and an act of communication, bonds are not fully graspable at the level of behavior. They have indicators and exterior manifestations, but they are also part of the wider subjectivity of the bonded individuals. It is through the stocks of impressions[1] of the subjects about each other, as well as in their understanding of general social norms and expectations, that bonds gain stability and transcend the episodic inter-connectedness from which they take shape.

The level of bond durability is not simply a given dimension to a particular exchange of information occurring through Facebook. It also constitutes the context in which that exchange is experienced first hand (if it is a direct interaction), as well as how the exchange becomes meaningful for the subjects involved in it (Argyle and Henderson 1984; Konecki 2008; Bryant and Marmo 2012). Here, meaning is understood as more than a reflective attribution of sense; it is, broadly speaking, the equivalent of value. It is also not attributed *a posteriori*, but constructed within the exchange itself. For instance, when a Facebook user sees one of his secrets exposed publicly by someone they had trusted, in a conversation with a third person, the re-evaluation of the one who divulged the secret, the deception, the embarrassment, the questions about his own understanding of friendship in general and of this friendship in particular will be part of how he experiences that event as meaningful. In this sense, the exchanges of information taking place on Facebook are inseparable from the meaning of the bonds through which they are defined and in which they find their importance.

The bonds which are behind Facebook exchanges are shaping users' first-hand experience, their emotional reactions, and their retrospective reflections with respect to any given occurrence (Keller and Fay 2012). Furthermore, the relational meaning which is inherent to exchanges also dictates their course. To continue the example above, the user whose secret was divulged may write a public angry message to the one he feels betrayed his trust. The interdependency (Tönnies 1957) in which various exchanges are rooted is of great practical importance, as it guides evaluations, but also reactions and the unfolding of concrete events.

At the same time, the episodic interactions and exchanges themselves have an impact on bonds, which are relatively stable, but not entirely fixed over time (Blumer 1969; Goffman 1971; White 2008). The user whose secret was shared publicly will read that situation in light of a particular tie he shared with the other, in light of how he was taught friends should behave, and in light of how he expects the other to feel or to behave from his previous stock of impressions about that person. At the same time, it is through this very exchange that the bond is re-evaluated and the characteristics of the other are put under question. Despite their durability, ties are still open to new interactions, to new experiences and new understandings. To be sure, it is not frequent that ties are redefined altogether, but, as we will see in the narratives of users, changes, negotiations, and adaptations are made within ties as a result of episodic interaction and exchanges of information, some of which happen to take place on Facebook.

An important aspect of bonds is the fact that while they are experienced and processed subjectively by each participant, they are at the same time in between social actors. They concern types of bonds (like friendship, romantic partnership, rivalry, etc.), roles and expectations derived from these bonds, a certain relational normativity, all of which are performed in nuanced ways by different individuals, but which are nevertheless marked by at least a roughly common social understanding. These elements do not refer to either the subject or the other with whom one establishes a bond, but to the actual bond, to that which is shared, how and why it is shared, to the actions of one social actor *in relation with* the other. Bond typologies are a common sociological preoccupation. Azarian puts it in the following terms:

> "*sociological literature is replete with schemes for classifying social relationships, varying greatly in complexity, sophistication and thoroughness. Ever since the birth of the discipline the issue has occupied many sociologists, and still continues to do so, although with much less intensity. To name only a few, Tönnies, Cooley, Durkheim, Weber, von Wiese, Parsons, Rex, Collins and White are among those who, although using different conceptual frameworks and terminologies, have tried their hands at developing typologies of social ties.*" (Azarian 2010, p. 330)

Bearing in mind this dual character of social bonds (simultaneously subjective and relational, inter-subjective), a key classificatory criterion, especially in the context of Facebook, is that of correspondence and, implicitly, of reciprocity. By correspondence, I refer to the extent in which people's evaluation of the bond they share are similar, their expectations about their own and each other's behavior converge, their emotional attachment to each other and to their rapport are compatible. It is this correspondence between those involved in a bond that, together with an orientation towards each other, results in reciprocity.

The correspondence (or lack thereof) between how the bond is lived and understood subjectively by its participants is reflected into all sorts of interactions (Adloff and Mau 2006; Harrigan and Yap 2017; Huck and Tyran 2007) including those occurring on Facebook. When a clear correspondence is not established, the interactors have to adapt to each other's framing of the interaction. However, one's subjective construction of a particular tie for him/herself is not necessarily intelligible to the other. A typical example is the relation one interprets as friendship and the other as potential romantic partnership. At the same time, professional collaboration or subordination, different levels of trust, or different interpretations of social roles are other cases where a lack of overlap between people who are part of a common tie may occur. Face to face, topics of conversation, gestures, rhythm and tone of voice are socially accepted indicators of how one person feels about the bond with the other (Blumer 1969; Goffman 1959, 1967, 1971). Among other benefits, the interaction serves for creating a similar understanding of the bond for those who participate in it. On Facebook, the possibility of a user seeing a bond differently than the one with whom they are bonded is increased. If a common relational ground was not previously established offline, Facebookers have talked to me about their confusion in finding compatible interpretations of their bonds online. Consequently, questions about appropriateness and answers found in the habitualization of specific acceptable behaviors have come up in the interviews. For instance, a young Catalan man shared a story about having read on Facebook a girl he knew had moved to a different country. However, he felt it would not have been right for him to congratulate her on this change, because even though the information was public, it would have been too forward of him to write a comment since they had not met in a long time. This is a topic I will analyze at length, in the following chapters, as potential differences in how social actors regard and experience a bond play a major part in allowing us to gain insight into Facebook exchanges, and how and why they occur.

The discussion about stable bonds and their relations with Facebook information circulation has many facets. Yet, beside the level of correspondence between those bonded, relational distance is the other main aspect that needs to be addressed from the beginning.

Distance is perhaps the most talked about topic with respect to social relations. In a strong tie, those who are tied are spatially imagined as close. The origins of this imagery can be traced back to Simmel ([1908] 2009) and his portrayal of the stranger, in the homonymous excursus from a chapter on "Space and the Spatial Ordering of Society". The concept has undergone a confusing (and confused) process since then (Levine 1985). Yet, most of the work on distance (from the Bogardus scale used in surveys to Bourdieu's proximity in the social field (1984, 1989) and to Putnam's (2000) bonding and bridging social capital) focus on how a set of characteristics correlates with certain distances between groups of people, classes, and categories. The extensive work on homophily (Louch 2000; Yap and Harrigan 2015) follows the same path. Phua et al. (2017) use a similar approach to understand the satisfaction of following particular brands through social networking. This preoccupation is a valid one and the structural organization of social bonds is something which I will tackle in due time. However, given my subjectivist standpoint and my commitment to keep the analysis as close as possible to the views and experiences of Facebook users, my approach to relational distance will be different. Namely, rather than looking into patterns of relational distance establishment, I will focus on what being close or distant from someone entails, as well as the ways in which it is symbolically communicated and interpreted interpersonally, through the lens of Facebook exchanges.

I begin by thinking of two categories: (a) people who are in the same waiting room at the dentist and share no particular interpersonal bond and (b) people who have been dear friends for 50 years. These are two poles of bonding and between them there is a continuum of different relational strengths (or distances). There is no clear-cut point between a weak tie and a strong tie, just as it is difficult to tell when people make the step from being strangers to having particular tie. In this case, the best way of conceptualizing tie strength is through its extremes. So, what is for a social actor the difference between the one with whom she has no tie and the one with whom she feels the closest? This question brings us back to impressions about the other and to the different interiorized social norms which inform them. I argue the person with whom one shares a bond is significant through one's own direct experience with them. The memories we have of the time we shared with each other, the mannerisms specific to the other, and the impression of the other as a unique human being, how we feel when we are copresent, are central in the construction of a close bond. Alternatively, with non-bonded others, our impression is typically derived directly from previously formed and taken-for-granted meanings (Ivana 2016) and from the norms through which they were legitimated. It must be said of course all our relations with others are filtered through normativities (e.g. that which the social actor must think of a certain situation or person, that which she is expected to feel, the ways in which she should move and act, etc.) (Foucault 1995; Hochschild 2012). However, with strong bonds, these multidimensional norms are used in a flexible way, adapted, and combined by the subject to match the interpersonal context and the person with whom one is in contact. In weak bonds and in contact with strangers, the same social norms are not employed in the same way to produce new impressions. Rather, they are implicit in stocks of taken-for-granted meanings, which are immediately applied to the situation at hand. Thus, the people in the dentist's waiting room will make sense of each other in these simplified terms, as "someone who has a dentist appointment", "the one who is interested in the fashion page of the magazine", "one of those who are scared", and so on. These meanings are not new or particularized; they are simple repetitions of old unquestioned ones. Considering the other is anxious, and being amused by his disproportional reaction to the situation he is in, is most likely an application of meanings about dentist visits and about those who behave like this person. This transfer of previous impressions to new situations is specific to the lack of a bond. Thus, with weak bonds, there is a certain level of generality of impressions which remain largely unaltered throughout the contact with the person and the context at hand. Simply put, people with whom one shares a close tie do not impress the subject as "one of" a group, but are meaningful in themselves. In other words, it helps to have a clear idea of what a reliable person may be like and about what it feels like to share a bond with such a person, but that sedimented construction of meaning does not imply that the close friend will be reduced to being a reliable person. This tendency of regarding the other and the bond as meaningful in themselves is fueled by interconnectedness. The shared experience of togetherness between the subject and the other confronts one with the inherent lack of overlap with any pre-given impressions formed independently of this particular bond and establishes a derived, but nonetheless separate significance for the actual tie and for the other (Ivana 2016). The bondless other is regarded through the lens of an ideal type and through the lens of a pre-established way of relating with those belonging to that type. In other words, the norms, the emotions, the expectations, the processes of meaning making in a very weak bond have a level of generality and a wider applicability, irrespective of the particularities of the context and of the other person.

Above I have been describing bondlessness and very close bonds as two ends of a spectrum of relational distances. However, most social relations are somewhere in between these extremes. Once a bond is established, be it a relatively weak one, meanings around it will be less and less shaped by taken-for-granted impressions. Those who are bonded will find an increasingly individualized significance for each other in light of their shared experiences. However, I will use the term "weak bonds" to designate those bonds where the other is meaningful predominantly still in light of impressions constructed independently of their actions. For instance, one's neighbor helps with carrying the shopping upstairs. That neighbor will be experienced in light of that interaction in a particularized way, but he will also be read at the same time in a simplifying manner through pre-given, not entirely reflective or conscious impressions about clothes or accents. In a closer tie, the proportions are reversed, with the main sources of meaning making coming from adaptation of previously held impressions and previously embraced norms to match this specific person and that which is shared with them.

This distinction I am proposing in terms of relational distances is important to make when analyzing Facebook, since users say their reactions and interpretations of content they receive are always filtered through their bonds. The answer to many of my inquiries, which was repeated many times, is "It depends who the other person is". All other things being equal, a closer and a weaker tie will think differently, react differently, construct future interactions differently as a result of receiving the same information about the same user. While this seems hardly surprising, these differences have been entirely left aside in scholarly conversations about social networking.

Social interactions have a background which is indisputably socially constructed; they are governed by the norms and expectations specific to the interaction level (Goffman 1983; Rawls 1987) and they unfold with a certain dynamic. Nonetheless, the subjective impressions of the interactors about each other, the assumed strength and type of bond being shared, the projections about the potential of that bond, their understanding of how a certain bond is established and negotiated in direct interaction are of utmost importance on Facebook, as in any interactional setting. To summarize, if the interaction is read exclusively in terms of other criteria than the interconnectedness with the subject, that interaction is tieless. If it is meaningful in terms of the interconnectedness of experiences of the interactors, it is a tie. As a parenthesis, it must be said this conceptualization of strong and weak ties is reminiscent of Schütz's scale ranging from consociates to contemporaries, with the mention that I do not assume impressions about the other (or in his terms typifications) are either exclusively a function of physical proximity, or exclusively cognitive. *Rather, they are a function of the centrality/marginality of the we-relationship in the construction of durable impressions about the other.* To illustrate, someone has a strong bond with their mailman if they regard the mailman as meaningful in light of the jokes they share every time they meet, the advice they received from this person when in trouble, and the plans of meeting them again. The bond is weak if their meaning making is primarily derived from general ideal types, such as "postman", "Catholic", "man in his 60s". This meaning is not entirely reflective, since these categories may come with a certain emotional background attached (i.e. "Catholics are frustrating because I met several who were so conservative"). In the weak bond, the a priori category of meaning overshadows the construction of new particularized meanings for instances of interconnectedness.

To go back, the unique perspective of each participant in a bond is reflected in the outer interaction through indicators of distance. These indicators are not always intended to communicate the exact strength of the tie, but the strength of the tie that one person feels the other should read them as having.

One of the cases when this happens is conflict or negative impact the other had on the subject's life. If someone made fun of my behavioral flaws, that would be a very hurtful experience for me. As a result, I would always maintain a perspective on that person as "the one who hurt me by doing that" or "the one who is capable of hurting me", in future mode. Since my perspective is defined by my own past experience of togetherness and interconnectedness with that person, that constitutes a tie of significant strength. Yet, the outer indicators present in my social interaction with that person might not look to express the existence or strength of that tie. On the contrary, I might have the intention of displaying an almost tieless interaction.

Another example of a similar discrepancy between the lived bond and the indicators one offering is, in ties based on reciprocity, the adaptation of the interaction according to the way the other's impression about the tie estimated. Thus, instead of trying to communicate the presence of what she sees/feels/understands as a strong tie with the other, one might try to express a weak tie, because of the assumption that it corresponds to the other's perspective on the tie. In ties that are not viewed as necessarily reciprocal, this tendency is not as strong.

Last but not least, this control over the indicators given off about spontaneous impressions can be a way of connecting that which is expressed with iterations and projections about the tie. If I see the other not as someone with whom I share anything meaningful, but as someone who I imagine creating a tie with, I might act in a way that indicates the desire for the projected tie, more so than the lack of the current one. If, based on my past experiences, certain experiences of social interaction have triggered in me (or I have witnessed in others) the development of a certain tie, I might feel the pressure of indicating the existence of that tie through my behavior, although the tie itself might not be present in my lived experience.

Of course, one can try to conceal or express not only the strength but also the type of tie, mirroring Simmel's forms of sociation. This is done not so much through the closeness of the interaction, but through its tone. An interaction that is intended humorous or seductive is meant to be read in terms of: "this person sees me as a friendship-type of tie/romantic type of tie."

However, neither the closeness of the interaction (as an indicator of the strength of the underlying tie) nor the tone of the interaction (corresponding to the type of tie) is necessarily intentional. As Schütz points out through his "general thesis of the alter ego's existence", one always lives either immersed in an experience or turned reflectively towards him/ herself. So, whenever someone experiences an interaction in lived durée (in Schütz's Bergsonian sense), all this control over indicators given off fades away, and mostly spontaneous expressions are left.

Although, as I have mentioned, the impressions which shape a tie and their exterior indicators are not always compatible, these indicators remain the only way for another to get a sense of the strength of the tie and the type of tie they are dealing with, if any. At the same time, even if subjective meaning of each other's inner life is not sought after, interpersonal readings and reciprocal adjustments of behaviors, emotions, and expectations will be inherent to social interaction.

This connects with the discussion about relational distance. In terms of ties, a strong tie is a close tie, whether it is conflictual, hidden, denied, even to the self, and so on. If one cannot see the other person otherwise than through their togetherness, the tie is close. In terms of the outer manifestations, social interactions linked with strong ties are marked by a socially constructed consensus. And since the strength of the tie is based on the importance of interconnectedness, the interactional indicators of strong ties which are part of this consensus often revolve around expressions of how that interconnectedness impresses the bonded subjects. Examples in this sense include remembering common memories, inside jokes, and shared secrets, all of which evoke precisely the subjective meaning of the tie itself for those who live it. On a more explicit note, some indicators may be verbal statements about the importance of the other person in one's life and about how the time spent together has impacted them. Indicators vary according to many coordinates; they are situated geographically, historically, with respect to gender, class, age, and so on. Nevertheless, they are generally intelligible for those sharing a particular social context.

On the other hand, there are also criteria according to which weak ties and tieless interactions can be read. However, they are not precisely indicators of ties, but indicators of certain characteristics in the absence of which a certain type of tie cannot grow. In other words, they are indicators of potential. Concretely, the clothes someone wears may be the criterion according to which one is impressed by another person. Clothes have cultural meanings and subjects' familiarity with those meanings will have an impact on their understandings and feelings in relation to the other. For instance, one may read clothes as the other desire for discretion or ostentation; they may read very revealing clothes as disgusting and so on. So, the potential one sees for being tied to the other is filtered through something like a choice of flashy clothing. Often, not this entire line of thinking unfolds in one's mind; moreover these impressions may not be predominantly driven by reflection. Yet, shortcuts have been created and features that have no direct link to a certain meaning have come to be indicators of it nevertheless. In other words, the analysis of bond potential, rather than of currently existing bonds, must necessarily focus (more than the analysis of established bonds) on the impressions about the other as another, as independent from the subject herself, since there is little interconnectedness to refer back to. These impressions are, as the tie is still weak, based on ideal types organized in pre-established hierarchies of desirability, prestige, and so on. Their importance in estimating tie potential must be acknowledged because impressions based on hierarchies of ideal types set the scene for particular bonds to strengthen, and for others to stagnate.

This being said, when, in weaker ties, we are reading the other without focusing on their interconnectedness with us, we are still constructing a relational image about them, but here the reference point is exterior, whether it is a group, a community, or society. Since bonds are typically not dyads emerging without any background connections, the impact of third parties is also very important. On the one hand, the other is the depositor of certain social influences, but on the other hand, he/she is part of a web of exchanges in which those influences occur. He/she is not suspended in a social void. Thus, the other is "smart as compared to most people/to most of those he/she spends time with", "a rebel from the norms I believe the majority of those around follow", "a stranger to the community he/she lives in", "the Asian—the one whose race singles him/her out from all the others present in that context". If one sees the other as a stranger only in relation to them, that is likely to result in a stronger tie than if they see him as a stranger in general and only secondarily in relation to them (which would account for a weak tie). From this point of view, the impression of the other is constructed upon the interpreter's broader understanding of the world and of a specific group or community. This impression about the other's relational background is also central to the evaluations of the potential of particular bonds to develop.

At the same time, entirely tieless interactions have indicators of distance which are as clearly socially defined as those for close bonds. "Go to" neutral topics of conversation, physical distance, and time span of interaction are several of the ways in which tieless interactions are signaled in Western societies. Furthermore, tieless interactions can also be read in a negative mode, as a lack of a tie; in this vein, the lack of indicators typical for strong ties becomes an indicator in itself. To be clear, these indicators are not always consciously communicated and they are not always consciously read, but they do constitute the established manner of conveying tie strength and form in interpersonal settings and for a socialized subject they are spontaneously experienced in embodied ways (like feeling relaxed or very controlled) and understood fairly accurately.

Some of these issues seem to touch upon the approach specific to social network analysis. However, numerous sociology scholars have signaled the atheoretic inclinations of early works within the field of social network analysis and have also made important steps in overcoming this problem (Emirbayer and Goodwin 1994; Emirbayer 1997; White 2008; Powell and Dépelteau 2013; Donati 2015). Nevertheless, these developments in the theoretical understandings of social bonds, their construction, their patterns, and their social contexts, as well as the growing preoccupation for ties beyond their formal or measurable quality, have been largely overlooked in the analysis of social networking platforms, despite their great relevance for the topic.

All these aspects are particularly important for Facebooking, because behind much of the information being communicated, the contacts within one's network have a relational background. They are ties of different strengths, with diverse levels of reciprocity, with a particular historicity and with envisioned futures. Thus, when attempting to understand what people do with this platform, how they read it, and the extent to which certain dynamics from "the online" matter outside this realm (and if so, how), the interconnectedness between certain users, the stocks of impressions one has constructed about general categories of others, and the differences in interacting with others with whom one shares different bonds are all very relevant. Furthermore, as the interviewees reveal time and again, it is within this informal relational realm that the stakes of Facebook are. During my discussions with users, they would often take out their phones and show me something they found interesting and, whenever that happened, their stories were preceded by an introduction about the bond between themselves and the others who either posted that content or who were linked with the interviewee's own decision to post that content. At the same time, for all the relational continuity between people who are networked on Facebook and outside of it, there are discontinuities between exchanges of information taking place through Facebook and other sorts of social interactions (face to face, phone calls). The concrete situations of togetherness which create ties, the situations which allow the manifestations of that tie, and which also keep it alive and constantly reshape it: this is the level where Facebook comes into play.

The Structure of the Book

The book is organized in eight chapters, including the current introduction. The second chapter is an exploration of how we can understand Facebook from the perspective of social relations. It proposes several classifications and distinctions which set the stage for the main analysis and it looks into the premise of non-copresence and its consequences on social interactions and bonds. Chapter 3 is dedicated to an analysis of the dichotomy between Facebook and "real life", from the perspective of the continuities and disruptions between the lived experience of Facebooking and everyday life in the offline life world. The fourth chapter is focused on the analysis of instances of monitoring, reading, checking content posted by someone else without engaging in any sort of conversation or feedback. Questions of entitlement, clandestinity, privacy, and the phenomenon of stalking are discussed. Chapter 5 looks into Facebook conversations and reciprocal communication. It is divided in two parts: public exchanges and private chatting. With respect to public posts and reactions, comments, or shares, several topics which are approached are the uses of publicness, the dilemma of addressability, habitualized behavior, and public insider jokes. With private chats, simultaneity, experiences of togetherness, and the production of shared here and now are discussed. Chapter 6 tackles the structural aspects of social relations, by concentrating on Facebook displays and interpretations of social class, prestige, markers of symbolic capital, and the instances of keeping up with the Joneses. Chapter 7 offers an account of emotionality in social networking. More often than not, relational narratives are intertwined with excitement, embarrassment, worries, pride, or amusement. The aim of this chapter is to bring together such narratives and to make sense of what may analytically be called "emotional component" which is dissolved into social relations in an environment many find disembodied and detached. Chapter 8 presents the conclusions resulting from this incursion into social bonds and how they are liked with the unfolding of information exchanges on Facebook.

Notes

1. Stocks of impressions is a concept I develop and use as an alternative to Alfred Schütz's stock of knowledge, by borrowing, via Sara Ahmed, Hume's notion of impression. The purpose of this replacement of knowledge with impression is to account for meaning as being constructed not only reflectively, but through embodied and emotional experience as well. The ways in which social actors make sense of their social world are not only derived from what they know as a result of their ongoing socialization, but also as a result of previous emotions and embodied experiences.

References

Adloff, Franc, and Steffen Mau. 2006. Giving Social Ties, Reciprocity in Modern Society. *European Journal of Sociology* 47 (1): 93–123.

Aguirre, Alwin C., and Sharyn Graham Davies. 2015. Imperfect Strangers: Picturing Place, Family, and Migrant Identity on Facebook. *Discourse, Context & Media* 7: 3–17.

Alduiza, Eva, Camilo Cristancho, and Jose M. Sabucedo. 2014. Mobilization through Online Social Networks: The Political Protest of the Indignados in Spain. *Information, Communication & Society* 17 (6): 750–764.

Argyle, Michael, and Monika Henderson. 1984. The Rules of Friendship. *Journal of Social and Personal Relationships* 1 (2): 211–237.

Auter, Zachary J., and Jeffrey A. Fine. 2017. Social Media Campaigning: Mobilization and Fundraising on Facebook. *Social Science Quarterly*. First published 28 February 2017.

Azarian, Reza. 2010. Social Ties. Elements of a Substantive Conceptualization. *Acta Sociologica* 53 (4): 323–338.

Beyer, Jessica L. 2014. The Emergence of a Freedom of Information Movement: Anonymous, WikiLeaks, the Pirate Party, and Iceland. *Journal of Computer-Mediated Communication* 19 (2): 141–154.

Birnbaum, Matthew Gardner. 2008. *Taking Goffman on a Tour of Facebook: College Students and the Presentation of Self in a Mediated Digital Environment.* Tuscon: The University of Arizona.

Blumer, Herbert. 1969. *Symbolic Interactionism: Perspective and Method.* Englewood Cliffs, NJ: Prentice-Hall.

Bourdieu, Pierre. 1984. *Distinction: A Social Critique of the Judgement of Taste.* Cambridge, MA: Harvard University Press.

———. 1989. Social Space and Symbolic Power. *Sociological Theory* 7 (1): 14–25.

Bryant, Erin, and Jennifer Marmo. 2012. The Rules of Facebook Friendship: A Two-Stage Examination of Interaction Rules in Close, Casual, and Acquaintance Friendships. *Journal of Social and Personal Relationships* 29 (8): 1013–1035.

Collins, Randall. 2004. *Interaction Ritual Chains.* Princeton, NJ: Princeton University Press.

Dehghani, Milad, and Mustafa Turner. 2015. A Research on Effectiveness of Facebook Advertising on Enhancing Purchase Intention of Consumers. *Computers in Human Behaviour* 49 (1): 597–600.

Donath, Judith, and danah boyd. 2004. Public Displays of Connection. *BT Technology Journal* 22 (4): 71–82.

Donati, Pierpaolo. 2015. Manifesto for a Critical Realist Relational Sociology. *International Review of Sociology* 25 (1): 86–109.

Duffett, Rodney Graeme. 2015. The Influence of Facebook Advertising on Cognitive Attitudes Amid Generation Y. *Electronic Commerce Research* 15 (2): 243–267.

Elias, Norbert. 2001. *The Society of Individuals.* New York: Continuum Publishing.

Ellison, Nicole B., Charles Steinfield, and Cliff Lampe. 2007. The Benefits of Facebook "Friends": Social Capital and College Students' Use of Online Social Network Sites. *Journal of Computer-Mediated Communication* 12 (4): 1143–1168.

Emirbayer, Mustafa. 1997. Manifesto for a Relational Sociology. *American Journal of Sociology* 103 (2): 281–317.

Emirbayer, Mustafa, and Jeff Goodwin. 1994. Network Analysis, Culture, and the Problem of Agency. *American Journal of Sociology* 99 (6): 1411–1454.

Farquhar, Lee. 2013. Performing and Interpreting Identity through Facebook Imagery. *Convergence: The International Journal of Research into New Media Technologies* 19 (4): 446–471.

Foucault, Michel. 1995. *Discipline and Punish: The Birth of the Prison*. New York: Vintage Books.

Goffman, Erving. 1959. *The Presentation of Self in Everyday Life*. New York: Doubleday.

———. 1967. *Interaction Ritual: Essays On Face-to-Face behavior*. New York: Anchor Books.

———. 1971. *Relations in Public: Microstudies of the Public Order*. Berkeley: University of California Press.

———. 1983. The Interaction Order: American Sociological Association, 1982 Presidential Address. *American Sociological Review* 48 (1): 1–17.

Granovetter, Mark. 1983. The Strength of Weak Ties: A Network Theory Revisited. *Sociological Theory* 1: 201–233.

Harrigan, Nicholas, and Janice Yap. 2017. Avoidance in Negative Ties: Inhibiting Closure, Reciprocity, and Homophily. *Social Networks* 48 (1): 126–141.

Heyman, Rob, and Jo Pierson. 2013. Blending Mass Self-communication with Advertising in Facebook and LinkedIn: Challenges for Social Media and User Empowerment. *International Journal of Media & Cultural Politics* 9 (3): 229–245.

Hilsen, Anne Inga, and Tove Helvik. 2014. The Construction of Self in Social Medias, such as Facebook. *AI & Society* 29 (1): 3–10.

Hochschild, Arlie Russell. 1979. Emotion Work, Feeling Rules, and Social Structure. *American Journal of Sociology* 85 (3): 551–575.

———. 2012. *The Outsourced Self: Intimate Life in Market Times*. New York: Metropolitan Books.

Hogan, Bernie. 2010. The Presentation of Self in the Age of Social Media: Distinguishing Performances and Exhibitions Online. *Bulletin of Science Technology* 30 (6): 377–386.

Huck, Steffen, and Jean-Robert Tyran. 2007. Reciprocity, Social Ties, and Competition in Markets for Experience Goods. *Journal of Socio-Economics* 36 (2): 191–203.

Irwin, Melissa D. 2015. Mourning 2.0—Continuing Bonds Between the Living and the Dead on Facebook. *OMEGA—Journal of Death and Dying* 72 (2): 119–150.

Ivana, Greti-Iulia. 2016. Present Contemporaries and Absent Consociates: Rethinking Schütz's "We Relation" Beyond Copresence. *Human Studies* 39 (4): 513–531.

Johnston, Kevin, Maureen Tanner, Nishant Lalla, and Dori Kawalski. 2013. Social Capital: The Benefit of Facebook 'Friends'. *Behaviour and Information Technology* 32 (1): 24–36.

Kasket, Elain. 2012. Continuing Bonds in the Age of Social Networking: Facebook as a Modern-Day Medium. *Bereavement Care* 31 (2): 62–69.

Kebadayi, Sertan, and Katherine Price. 2014. Consumer—Brand Engagement on Facebook: Liking and Commenting Behaviors. *Journal of Research in Interactive Marketing* 8 (3): 203–223.

Keller, E., and B. Fay. 2012. *The Face to Face Book: Why Real Relationships Rule in a Digital Marketplace*. New York: Free Press.

Konecki, Krzysztof. 2008. Touching and Gesture Exchange as an Element of Emotional Bond Construction. Application of Visual Sociology in the Research on Interaction between Humans and Animals. *Forum: Qualitative Social Research* 9 (3): 1–46.

Kwon, Seok-Woo, Colleen Helfin, and Martin Ruef. 2013. Community, Social Capital and Entrepreneurship. *American Sociological Review* 78 (6): 980–1008.

Lambert, Alexander. 2016. Intimacy and Social Capital on Facebook: Beyond the Psychological Perspective. *New Media & Society* 18 (11): 2559–2575.

Levine, Donald. 1985. *The Flight from Ambiguity/Essays in Social and Cultural Theory*. Chicago: University of Chicago Press.

Louch, Hugh. 2000. Personal Network Integration: Transitivity and Homophily in Strong-tie Relations. *Social Networks* 22 (1): 45–64.

McLaughlin, Caitlin, and Jessica Vitak. 2011. Norm Evolution and Violation on Facebook. *New Media & Society* 14 (2): 299–315.

Micalizzi, Alessandra. 2014. In Search of a Lost Identity. In *Identity Technologies: Constructing the Self Online*, ed. A. Poletti and J. Rak. Madison, WI: University of Wisconsin Press.

Phua, Joe, et al. 2017. Uses and Gratifications of Social Networking Sites for Social Capital: Comparing Facebook, Twitter, Instagram, and Snapchat. *Computers in Human Behavior* 72: 115–122.

Powell, Christopher, and François Depleteau. 2013. *Conceptualizing Relational Sociology: Ontological and Theoretical Issues*. New York: Palgrave Macmillan.

Putnam, Robert. 2000. *Bowling Alone: The Collapse and Revival of American Community*. New York: Simon & Schuster.

Rawls, Anne W. 1987. The Interaction Order Sui Generis: Goffman's Contribution to Social Theory. *Sociological Theory* 5 (2): 136–149.

Resnick, Paul. 2001. Beyond Bowling Together: Socio-technical Capital, HCI in the New Millennium. In *Human-Computer Interaction in the New Millennium*, ed. J.M. Carroll, 647–672. New York: ACM Press.

Simmel, Georg. 1950. *The Sociology of Georg Simmel*. Ed. and Trans. Kurt H. Wolff. New York: The Free Press.

———. 2009. *Sociology: Inquiries into the Construction of Social Forms. Vol. I and Vol. II*. Eds. and Trans. Anthony J. Blasi, Anton K. Jacobs and Mathew Kanjirathinkal. Boston: Brill.

Smith-Doerr, Laurel, and Walter W. Powell. 2005. Networks and Economic Life. In *Handbook of Economic Sociology*, ed. N.J. Smelser and R. Swedberg, 2nd ed., 379–402. Princeton, NJ: Princeton University Press.

Steinfield, Charles, Nicole B. Ellison, and Cliff Lampe. 2008. Social Capital, Self-esteem, and Use of Online Social Network Sites: A Longitudinal Analysis. *Journal of Applied Developmental Psychology* 29 (6): 434–445.

Strano, Michele M., and Jill Wattai Queen. 2012. Covering Your Face on Facebook: Suppression as Identity Management. *Journal of Media Psychology* 24 (4): 166–180.

Tönnies, Ferdinand. 1957. *Community and Society*. East Lansing, MI: Michigan State University Press.

Tufekci, Zeynep. 2008. Grooming, Gossip, Facebook and Myspace. *Information, Communication & Society* 11 (4): 544–564.

Turkle, Sherry. 2011. *Alone Together: Why We Expect More from Technology and Less from Each Other*. New York: Basic Books.

Vaccari, Cristian. 2017. Online Mobilization in Comparative Perspective: Digital Appeals and Political Engagement in Germany, Italy, and the United Kingdom. *Political Communication* 34 (1): 69–88.

van Dijck, Jose. 2013. *The Culture of Connectivity: A Critical History of Social Media*. New York: Oxford Scholarship Online.

Walther, Joseph B., Brandon Van Der Heide, Kim Sang-Yeon, David Westerman, and Stephanie Tom Tong. 2008. The Role of Friends' Appearance and Behavior on Evaluations of Individuals on Facebook: Are We Known by the Company We Keep? *Human Communication Research* 34 (1): 28–49.

Weber, Max. 1978. *Economy and Society: An Outline of Interpretive Sociology.* Berkeley: University of California Press.

Wellman, Barry, Anabel Quan Haase, James Witte, and Keith Hampton. 2001. Does the Internet Increase, Decrease, or Supplement Social Capital? *Social Networks, Participation, and Community Commitment* 45 (3): 436–455.

White, Harrison. 2008. *Identity and Control: How Social Formations Emerge.* Princeton, NJ: Princeton University Press.

Wolfe, Alvin. 1970. On Structural Comparisons of Networks. *Canadian Review of Sociology 7 (4): 226–244.*

Yap, Janice, and Nicholas Harrigan. 2015. Why does Everybody Hate me? Balance, Status, and Homophily: The Triumvirate of Signed Tie Formation. *Social Networks* 40: 103–122.

2

It Happened on Facebook

As stated in the introduction, the aim of this book is to look into the process of constructing meaning for interactions and for non-interactional content sharing on Facebook as integrated in an existing web of ties, created on the basis of a mix of face-to-face and long-distance shared experiences with the other, as well as impressions (consisting of embodied and emotional knowledge) about him/her, together with the expectations and projections of the subject based on their life course. I regard the tie as synthesizing all these elements, and it is my intention to explore meaning constructions for what happens on Facebook in connection with this synthesis. This approach is based on mediation, which rejects the break between the media and the non-media realm (Miller and Slater 2000; Silverstone 2002; Couldry 2008). At the same time, the specific moments in which bonds translate into interaction with the other unfold in an environment and in a context, and they are constituted of movements, gestures, behaviors, words, and so on. So, the facilities and the limits posed to the possibilities of communication have a very direct and non-negotiable structuring effect on the interactions and through them on actual bonds. Users can only write in a given grid, they can use a certain number of emoticons, and they can post images in a certain format.

© The Author(s) 2018
G.-I. Ivana, *Social Ties in Online Networking*, Palgrave Studies in
Relational Sociology, https://doi.org/10.1007/978-3-319-71595-7_2

From this point of view, there are distinguishable features that can be attributed to the media and can be analyzed in themselves. In this sense, it is also important to acknowledge mediatization (Hepp 2013) and discuss it as complementary to mediation. The perspective I am following in my analysis of the mediatization of exchanges through Facebook is a social constructivist one. I do not seek to identify a common logic with other media or to draw conclusions about the impact certain changes have at a societal level in an institutionalist framework. Of course, one can argue that this strict format Facebook provides is also a social product, which it undoubtedly is, but in this context it is important to note that it is experienced as a given and as an exterior-shaping element in the interaction.

When we talk about Facebook exchanges of information, about its uses, and about common practices of users, we refer to a variety of activities hosted by Facebook (Knautz and Baran 2016; McAndrew and Jeong 2012). People spend time posting something on their own wall, going through the contents they receive, "giving likes", or occasionally looking at entire albums of photos an old schoolmate posted over the years. These actions, like most of those taking place through Facebook, involve the relation with *people the user already knows* (Boyd and Ellison 2007; Ellison et al. 2009; Johnston 2009). Thus, we must consider that the context behind particular practices is always rooted in the existing bond, in past common experiences the users shared, in previous reciprocal evaluations, and/or in projections about how their relation may evolve. A man who had just changed jobs confessed to me he used Facebook to search for the profiles of all his new colleagues, not looking for a specific piece of information, but simply due to curiosity fueled by the knowledge they would be part of his life for a considerable period of time. On a similar note, a young woman explained that she would sometimes even browse through profiles of people she saw in the lunch room in her office building, but that she had no interest in a complete stranger. She needed the initial contact, as well as some familiarity with the other, before she had any desire to explore their Facebook presence. Thus, while bonds are seldom produced exclusively through Facebook, the possibilities offered to users by virtue of each other's readiness to share information online contribute to these bonds. In order to understand what Facebook brings to social relations in more detail, we shall begin with a brief discussion of what is specific about Facebooking. How is reading about one's new colleagues different from talking to them face to face and finding out almost identical information?

The great advantage of engaging in technologically mediated communication is that it links us with people who are outside of our world within reach, to borrow Alfred Schütz's (1967) term. As McLuhan (1964) famously observed, this is an extension of our senses. We hear and see things occurring in a time and/or place that are beyond our bodily capabilities. However, the other side of this extension, McLuhan argues, is amputation. We hear, but we cannot see, we see but we cannot taste or touch, and so on. There are a series options and limitations which are presupposed by Facebook's design, which immediately differentiate the experience of "Facebooking" (irrespective of the specific action undertaken) from the offline world, as well as from other online settings. However, not being in the same world within reach is not only a constraining factor which conditions our possibilities of communication. It is also a factor which reshapes communication itself in crucial ways. There are certain features specific to Facebook which make it necessary when the other is inaccessible, but also preferred when the other is accessible. Regarding the design and the available options, there is already extensive work on Facebook algorithms, and the type of structure produced through them (Bucher 2012, 2017; Tufekci 2015; Chauhan and Shukla 2016). Suggested pages, commercial content, even which posts we get to see from our friends—these are only some of the aspects determined by algorithms. However, despite their effects in other regards, these are not the elements of design which have the strongest impact specifically on shaping interpersonal exchanges mediated through Facebook.

Facebook is neither a system which establishes coordinates of action for its users, nor a platform where users act freely. What they are doing is actualizing a set of possibilities they get, in a space constructed through previous actualizations made by themselves and other users. If starting tomorrow everybody deactivated their Facebook accounts and nobody new registered anymore, there would be no Facebook to talk about, because Facebook itself exists only as a possibility which needs to be actualized. There are no empty profiles waiting to be filled, just as there are no empty exchanges waiting for the information to be poured into them.

Directionality and Facebook Options

This being said, of all the available options and design elements, I argue the ones related to directionality are particularly relevant in the context of connections between users. The content which is shared on Facebook (be it with one person in a chat or with one's entire list of acquaintances on the wall) is meant to reach one or several people and, more often than not, it does reach them. In the offline environment launching a message and making sure it was conveyed to the ones who are addressed by it is fairly straightforward. One looks at others while speaking to them, there are smiles, adaptations of the tone of voice according to how far the one who is addressed is standing, and so on. However, on Facebook, intended and achieved directionality are not always as straightforward. Thus, Weber's theory of social action, and particularly his concept of mutual orientation, reveals an interesting side of social networking. As we will later discuss in more detail, the topic of clandestinity and the experience of reading something that is not "meant for you" are very common. This concern is strongly linked with what users perceive to be their entry right into the other's private sphere (Hansson 2008). As Facebookers have repeatedly pointed out to me, many have had doubts about the intended recipients of their friends' posts and these doubts are inherent to Facebook's available options.

Facebook allows for contents to be transmitted from the wall of the user to the newsfeeds of other users grouped in one of the following categories: the general public, the user's network of friends, friends of friends, or particular people selected nominally by the user. Those who have access to the content can also see who else has access to it, except for the case when the audience consists of specific people (which appears as "custom"). The default setting is public. Irrespective of the privacy restrictions one chooses to apply, the visual organization of information is that of unilateral exposure. The grid in which the poster of the initial content writes is different from the ones where possible comments are written. The design establishes the status of the initiator and the commenter. This type of expressing oneself is aimed at groups of recipients and can be particularized. Because of the recipient being collective by default (public, friends, friends of friends), there is typically a fuzziness surrounding the issue of what is addressed to whom. This results from the fact that the categories are large enough for one to assume the sender has not considered all the recipients. As of July 2016, Facebook counted over 1 billion daily active users. According to a survey conducted by the Pew Research Center in 2013, the average number of Facebook friends was 338 among adult users. In this context, it is understandable why a user would feel like they saw something simply because they happened to be in an acquaintance's circle of Facebook friends. Having had access to private content gives them no confirmation about whether that user would readily share the same information with them personally or whether they were addressed in any way by that post.

The other option of communication, besides posting contents on one's own wall that others can see, is addressing direct private texts to one or more specific. Here, the logic is reversed. The default option is writing a personal message *to one individual* and more recipients can be added. All participants to the conversation can see who else was addressed by the same message. The initiator and the replier(s) have the same status within the exchange. By the fact that people need to actually be added to the recipients' list in order to receive the content, there is no question about the directionality of the message. Consequently, it is always clear: the sender must have selected the name of the receiver from a list of names and faces in order to send that message. It is not diffused; it is not meant for others. It is from him/her to me, maybe not exclusively to me, but certainly also to me. Interestingly, there is no readily accessible option for mass messages, so the only way to write to more people at once using private messaging is to add each of them as recipients. From this point of view, the reciprocal exchanges between users messaging each other are unequivocal social interactions. However, even in private messaging, there is the possibility for addressing collectivities as pre-existent groups. For instance, one cannot send a message to their entire network of friends at one time, but they can send a message to the group of friends they have constituted beforehand. Yet, even in this case, each of those receiving the message has been selected at a certain point by the sender himself/herself. Consequently, even when addressing groups, the directionality is clearer than in public posts, which makes the issue of whether sharing that content or receiving it is an interaction less debatable.

Due to these different features, it is useful to divide the spaces where content is shared into two categories, generically named "the public" and "the private". As I have pointed out above, "the public" has a pre-established broad group of recipients that can be narrowed down and become quite individualized, while "the private" is by default individualized and can expand to large numbers of addressees. Moreover, since in the private case the directionality is quasi-certain, I will refer to the situation of private exchanges as "private interactions". In the case of public exchanges, I will not use the term "interaction", unless there is a definite intended recipient for the shared content.

Are We Interacting?

Laura, a 25-year-old Catalan girl I interviewed about two years ago, told me one of the main reasons for her being on Facebook was to keep in touch with people, especially those she does not meet regularly offline. At the same time, she explained she rarely talks to them, but does check their profiles and stops to read their posts when they come up on her newsfeed. What stroke me as odd in her narrative was the concept of keeping in touch and the practices in which it translated. When I asked her about it, she confessed that it was something she had thought about herself and that she was concerned about the sort of connection that was being established this way.

This is an area where users and scholars alike often struggle as a result of collapsing distinct practices into one generic category such as "acting in a virtual environment", or "Facebook interaction" or "online self-display". The notion of experience does not clarify much either. It highlights the common thread of disembodiment and focuses on sensoriality and materiality. Yet, the important notion that is often missing is relational, namely directedness, or the I-Thou relation and Thou orientation, as they appear in the works of Schütz. While this aspect of online sociality is sometimes touched upon (Zhao 2004, 2005, 2007; Bakardjieva 2005; Ralon and Vieta 2011; Wegerif 2013), its implications have not been fully revealed. Despite Schütz's Thou orientation being specifically limited to face-to-face interaction, I argue it can be applied in a fruitful way to technological advancements Schütz had not foreseen. Namely, the very core of the concept is the awareness and acknowledging of the other's presence. In the case of Facebook, this presence of the other, not only in the network, but "on" the content one shares, is verifiable only through visible action with a clear address.

From Laura's and others' stories, this is the major element which transforms Facebook actions (from gazing at profiles to posting songs) into interactions. In order for person A to consider he/she is interacting with person B, he/she needs to think person B is receiving something and is reading it as directed to him/her. If an infatuated teenager is looking through photos of their romantic interest, the owner of the images is not aware of it. If she also "gives him a like", she is not only socially validating that content or displaying solidarity with the poster, but she is also establishing a reciprocal exchange with him. She is not only saying something *about* him, but also *to* him, in a deliberate manner: "I looked at this, I liked it, and I want you to know it". Such feedback is often missing and when that happens, from the perspective of the initiator, the interaction itself is uncertain. In other words, the challenge which comes with Facebook's design is often not in communicating information, but in establishing a mutual confirmation about the reciprocal directedness of the messages. As a result, there is confusion about which attempted interactions failed and which were successful. For instance, according to the findings of a small survey conducted by Facebook on over 1000 users, "when we asked users how many friends saw a particular post, the median user guessed 20 friends, while the actual median was 78" (Source: Facebook Data Science). Besides these quantitative data, there is also the issue of who exactly sees what one has transmitted. Unless other interactions occur, Facebook does not offer ways to grasp other indicators in order to answer this question. This is the case of posts that are published for groups, rather than aimed at certain individuals.

However, even in the case of private messaging, there is also an uncertainty around the issue of reciprocity. Has it been received? Did the other person see it/read it? The problem has been partially tackled by the "seen at..." text that appears to the sender when the reader accesses the message. This is a way of compensating for the lack of indicators that the message (in some form or understanding) has gotten across, so that the existence of the interaction will not be doubted.

Secondly, from the perspective of the receiver, if the content has been aimed at a collectivity (the author's friend, friends of friends, a thematic group, etc.), directionality is questioned. Instead of a social interaction, which is characterized by a reciprocal directedness (or an exchange that is read as potentially addressed to them, among others, at the very least), this context appears similar to direct observation, where one person directs their gaze at the other, without the other doing the same. Indeed, this is how this one-sided directionality is typically viewed. However, we have to keep in mind this is a situation where copresence is lacking. In direct observation, one subject has access to the other in an immediate way. They notice gestures, movements, a tone of voice, and a series of other indicators about the one who is observed as a subject in his/her own right. They can interpret this information and draw conclusions. Contrastingly, the situation I am describing is one where, on Facebook, someone receives a content which they do not know is addressed to them from a person with whom they have interacted before (in most cases) but who is not in their world within reach at that time. Since the other is only manifest through the shared piece of information and no other clues, this situation is then becoming more similar to a third-party report over someone who is absent. You receive news of their life, but you are neither interacting with them (lack of directionality), nor observing them (lack of physical capacity to do so).

Thus, when the user does not address someone in particular and/or when the recipients do not interpret the message as addressed to them, the frame of social interaction is replaced by a frame of information gathering. Going back to the question of keeping in touch, as well as the comparison with reading a magazine about one's own friends, they seem to converge in the publication and reception of (apparently) untargeted Facebook public posts.

However, when it comes to reciprocal directedness, and thus interaction, it is not only established in private chats. References to common experiences or, more directly, tags (their name and a link to their profile) accompanying public posts are some of the ways through which the person knows they are being aimed. In this case, feedback in the form of likes or comments from the ones who were being addressed directly is commonplace and typically expected. The mutual exchange becomes evident.

What is particularly interesting in this situation is not only the significant shift from a non-interactional to an interactional setting, but also the possibility of expansion beyond the dyad of initial participants to the conversation. Such exchanges are by default viewed by others, who may feel compelled to contribute and who will inevitably make sense of the tie between those who are interacting publicly. Assumed levels of intimacy, attempts at reciprocal face construction or face erosion (Ivana 2016) by those who are interacting publicly will not go unnoticed. Furthermore, they will contribute to social evaluations, acceptance/rejection from networks, and negotiations of status. At the same time, the interaction may have multiple participants from the beginning (i.e. more users are being tagged in the same post). Whether they are only linked to the author of the post or they also share their own relations is an added dimension. Nevertheless, the public character of such interactions configurates them differently than chatting.

With respect to private chatting, the element related to the design of the network which is most significant is the possibility for audio and video calling when the interaction is synchronous. This is reflected in a distinct experience of togetherness on which I will elaborate in a separate section.

To summarize, the way in which Facebook is designed allows three types of exchanges to occur between people who know each other and are part of each other's circle of friends: (1) non-interactional and non-observational transmission and reception of information, (2) direct public interactions (which is not necessarily dyadic), (3) private chatting.

Spatio-temporality in Facebook Exchanges and Interactions

Up to now, we have gone through some of the differences arising from the design of Facebook in relation to *establishing an exchange*. Now let us turn to the ways in which the lack of a shared here and now shapes the *spatio-temporal frame of the exchange*. The following considerations apply to both public and private exchanges, since they are mostly discussing the context in which they occur, rather than their particularities.

Once the interaction has been established in the understanding of the initiator (he/she sent something targeted and knows the other has seen it), that singlehandedly creates an understanding of a common "here", which is the world within reach for both of them and which is circumscribed by that which is shared. We are both "here", "in this conversation". When a user from the United States and one from Japan can contact each other on Facebook, it means that they have the possibility of constructing a world within reach for both of them in the form of shared content. This is a third "here", which is added to two separate "here's" of the interactors. In the example above there are "here in the United States", "here in Japan", and "here in our common world within reach". This common world within reach can consist of a movie they both saw, an old picture of a trip they did together, of their chat screens that look identical, or of a shared article on timeline. In colloquial terms, everyone is "on Facebook". Linguistically, Facebook is constructed in a spatialized manner. This space is the common world within reach users share with those who are not physically copresent, by means of their shared access to the same content. Just like copresent people can see the same leaf fallen from the same tree on the same alley, "copresent" users can click on the same link and view the same video and hear the same jokes and laugh together. *The computer screen as a third, common, here and now of non-copresent people is a fundamental feature of Facebook interactions.* This idea is connected to what Christiansen (2017) views as the unique deterritorialized social place of online social media.

However, one difference between sharing this world within reach and the world within reach shared in a face-to-face encounter is choice. On Facebook, one decides what will be included in the world within reach she shares with the other. If the two users from above meet and go for a walk, the fact that there is a song playing at a terrace they pass by is in their common world within reach, but it is not put there by either of them. If the song ends up in their worlds within reach via a link that one shares through Facebook, that was a decision, so the two situations will be different in terms of meaning construction, an aspect to which I will come back later on.

Furthermore, the separate "here's" are also incorporated in the form of an imaginary of each other's worlds within reach. The users located in the

United States and Japan have their screen as a common here, but they also have an unsurpassable experience of each other's absence and of their unshared here. One may witness a thunderstorm; the other will not be there to see it. And if the common experience of a shared here cannot come immediately and sensorially, it is constructed in communication. Facebook users will share narratives about the beauty, the violence, the unpredictability of the thunderstorm they lived through to help construct this imaginary about their here for others to grasp. They will take photographs or film it and share those as well, in a *constant attempt to transfer elements of the separate here into the common one.*

Yet, unlike in the case of physical copresence, the online micro-world-within-reach created through shared content is mediated by the first-hand experience of only one of the participants to the exchange. Above, I have touched upon the problem of choice; contents become shared through a selection. That which one transfers from their separate here to the common here of the computer or mobile phone screen is inevitably a representation of an experience. The moment when the recipient of the thunderstorm video watches it will not constitute for either party the same experience as having witnessed the thunderstorm together. Thus, as a related side note to Facebooking, content that is found (quasi-)exclusively on the Internet (e.g. memes) becomes rewarding to share because it constructs a common here while also eliminating the experiential asymmetry of importing elements of the users' separate worlds within reach.

At the same time, besides the issue of the common here, there is also the one of the common now. In the dynamics of face-to-face interactions, this problem is less prominent, since there is a certain pace at which the one's actions and the other's reactions happen and are interpreted. However, in an environment like Facebook, a time gap occurs significantly more often and it is linked with the specific features of "here". A typical distinction being made in the literature about Internet is the one between synchronous and asynchronous interactions (Garcia and Jacobs 1999; Pauwels 2005; Ledbetter 2009; O. Schwartz 2011; R. Schwartz and Halegoua 2015). I believe the impact of time gaps in interactions is very different according to the estimated type of interaction that is initiated. For instance, if one user writes something that does not require a reply or that they intend as the beginning of a very short objective-meaning type of interaction, their experience of the time gap is not the same as if they write something very personal to a dear friend who fails to read their message for a week. Drawing on Bergson (1910), we may say that on the level of the space-time world the two situations are equivalent, whereas on the level of durée, they are not. Thus, when interactions are expected to be asynchronous, the initiator enters in a brief imagined synchronous interaction with the other, which becomes a parenthesis in his/her flow of the "now". To illustrate this idea, let us think of the example of a parent writing a letter for their 2-year-old child to open in 30 years. The letter will be based on the imaginary about the child having become an adult and it will be written from the standpoint of a future perfect tense. This is an accentuation of the logic that occurs in interactions that are expected to be asynchronous. They happen through a jump to a future (imaginary) "common now", not through a continuation of an experienced present. If someone knows their interaction partner does not have an Internet connection the next three hours, they will not write asking them to do something in half an hour. Rather, in their message they will place themselves in the imaginary of "3 hours from now". Yet, the reason why this works as an interaction despite the time gap is the common "here" that will be accessed in different moments. In this respect, it is important to note that the common micro "world within reach" that is constructed in online interaction through shared content is *fixed over time*, which allows this temporal flexibility. The Facebook screen will look the same now as in three hours from now. Since it is a micro-world within reach made and shaped exclusively by the interactors, when they are absent, it lacks the engines to unfold, so it gets frozen. This mechanism lays at the bottom of what Dimmick and Albarran (1994) call "gratification opportunities", or the ways in which spatio-temporal constraints are overcome.

This brings me to a related topic: the one of irreversibility. Here, the private and public online interactions differ. Interestingly, the content that is shared in the space that is public by default (although it can be narrowed down) can be edited or deleted, while the one from private messaging cannot. This is an attempt at mimicking the conditions of copresence in the same "here and now" in Facebook private interactions, while the public sharing of content is not designed for that purpose. By sharing something with others publicly and by deciding what to share, you are bringing part of your separate world within reach in the common world within reach where it will be interpreted and read by the others, and so will your very decision of bringing it in the common world. If someone changes their mind, they can exclude an item from the common world within reach, in the time gap in which it has not actually been reached by the other. Thus, the expected time gap is a period of reversibility in public sharing of information on Facebook. In private interactions, this reversibility does not occur.

On the other hand, when the interaction is expected to be synchronous, the experience of time gaps is stronger. If the other is expected to communicate "in real time", it means flow is expected. Yet, in order for flow to be experienced, the interaction needs to occur on the level of lived durée. In these conditions, every gap will throw the experience out of flow and induce a state of "attention to life". Facebook used to contribute to this by displaying a measurement of the time passed between replies; right now, the elapsed time is accessible, but it is not displayed by default. Furthermore, besides breaking the flow of lived durée, time gaps also break the continuity of the "here" in the micro-world within reach. Since absence means fixity on Facebook, when one interactor goes missing, the other is trapped in a static world, out of which he/she has the possibility to escape by focusing on their offline separate, ever-dynamic world within reach. Assuming the interaction is synchronous, it becomes a flow and it is an experience of time as lived durée (Kaun and Stiernstedt 2014). Then, the only discrepancy from face-to-face interactions resides in the existence of two separate "here's" in addition to the common disembodied here.

Another aspect of online exchanges of information is this partial disembodiment specific to the alternative "here and now's" (that Facebook also allows) (Kang 2007; Young and Whitty 2010; Rodogno 2012). At the same time, a series of scholars have insisted many facets of embodiment are still present, from gender construction (Garcia Gomez 2010; van Doorn 2011), to social activism (Barassi 2013). Still, the lack of the typical bodily indicators of the other's lived experience is one aspect of embodiment which remains out of reach. So, two strategies of re-materialization have become commonplace. One is trying to find ways of capturing as much as the embodied experience as possible. In this sense, interaction has to be clear and directionality well established, time has to be synchronous, the worlds within reach have to be as similar as possible, and the presence of the other has to be grasped. This typically includes voice and video calls, where some indicators of the other's inner life become accessible, together with parts of their world within reach. The other strategy is finding other ways, specific to a mediatized environment, to transmit some of the information that would have been gathered in a face-to-face interaction, enough for the exchange to unfold without major miscommunications. This includes the use of abbreviations, such as "lol" (laugh out loud) or "rofl" (roll on the floor laughing), and conventions, such as the use of caps lock for screaming and emoticons, which typically represent facial expressions. In public Facebook posts, the emoticons are accompanied by a label about the emotional state they stand for, eliminating any ambivalence (and complexity) of interpreting indicators about the other.

Thus, to summarize, the design and the possibilities offered by Facebook as a platform directly shape the exchanges of information in several ways: (1) the different display and reach of private chatting versus public sharing of contents impact directionality; (2) the lack of copresence, combined with unilateral gazing allowed by Facebook design, favors new and very specific ways of "staying in touch", with various levels of interaction involved; (3) sharing possibilities make the computer screen of non-copresent users function as a common spatiality, additional to each user's separate here; (4) the common here of Facebook is alimented through users' conscious choices of content sharing; (5) Facebook exchanges of information come with diverse expectations of synchronicity and time flow. These aspects are all very strongly linked to what is allowed for one to do on Facebook, be it for technical reasons, or for moral or commercial considerations. They function as a frame for both interactions and non-interactional content sharing. In other words, the new input coming from Facebook into a user's bonds must be seen within these constraints; in turn, the influence of existing bonds on Facebook (inter)activity must also pass through the same structural filter.

References

Bakardjieva, Maria. 2005. *Internet Society: The Internet in Everyday Life.* London: Sage.

Barassi, Veronica. 2013. Ethnographic Cartographies: Social Movements, Alternative Media and the Spaces of Networks. *Social Movement Studies* 12 (1): 48–62.

Bergson, Henri. 1910. *Time and Free Will. An Essay on the Immediate Data of Consciousness.* Trans. F.L. Pogson. London: George Allen & Unwin.

boyd, danah, and Nicole B. Ellison. 2007. Social Network Sites: Definition, History, and Scholarship. *Journal of Computer-Mediated Communication* 13 (1): 210–230.

Bucher, Taina. 2012. Want to be on the Top? Algorithmic Power and the Threat of Invisibility on Facebook. *New Media & Society* 14 (7): 1164–1180.

———. 2017. The Algorithmic Imaginary: Exploring the Ordinary Affects of Facebook Algorithms. *Information, Communication & Society* 20 (1): 30–44.

Chauhan, G.S., and T. Shukla. 2016. Social Media Advertising and Public Awareness: Touching the LGBT Chord! *Journal of International Women's Studies* 18 (1): 145–155.

Christiansen, Martha Sidury. 2017. Creating a Unique Transnational Place: Deterritorialized Discourse and the Blending of Time and Space in Online Social Media. *Written Communication* 34 (2): 135–164.

Couldry, Nick. 2008. Mediatization or Mediation? Alternative Understandings of the Emergent Space of Digital Storytelling. *New Media & Society* 10 (3): 373–391.

Dimmick, John, and A.B. Albarran. 1994. The Role of Gratification Opportunities in Determining Media Preference. *Mass Communication Review* 21: 223–235.

Ellison, Nicole B., Cliff Lampe, and Charles Steinfield. 2009. Social Network Sites and Society: Current Trends and Future Possibilities. *Interactions* 16 (1): 6–9.

Garcia, Angela Cora, and Jennifer Baker Jacobs. 1999. The Eyes of the Beholder: Understanding the Turn-Taking System in Quasi-Synchronous Computer-Mediated Communication. *Research on Language and Social Interaction* 32 (4): 337–367.

Garcia Gomez, Antonio. 2010. Disembodiment and Cyberspace: Gendered Discourses in Female Teenagers' Personal Information Disclosure. *Discourse and Society* 21 (2): 135–160.

Hansson, Mats G. 2008. *The Private Sphere. An Emotional Territory and Its Agent*. Dordrecht: Springer.

Hepp, Andreas. 2013. The Communicative Figurations of Mediatized Worlds: Mediatization Research in Times of the 'mediation of everything'. *European Journal of Communication* 28 (6): 615–629.

Ivana, Greti-Iulia. 2016. Face and the Dynamics of Its Construction: A Relational and Multilayered Perspective. *Symbolic Interaction* 39 (1): 106–125.

Johnston, Hank. 2009. *Culture, Social Movement and Protest*. Aldershot: Ashgate.

Kang, Seok. 2007. Disembodiment in Online Social Interaction: Impact of Online Chat on Social Support and Psychosocial Well-being. *CyberPsychology & Behavior* 10 (3): 475–477.

Kaun, Annee, and Fredrik Stiernstedt. 2014. Facebook Time: Technological and Institutional Affordances for Media Memories. *New Media & Society* 16 (7): 1154–1168.

Knautz, Kathrin, and Katsiaryna Baran. 2016. *Facets of Facebook: Use and Users*. Hawthorne, NJ: Walter de Gruyter.

Ledbetter, Andrew. 2009. Measuring Online Communication Attitude: Instrument Development and Validation. *Communication Monographs* 76 (4): 463–486.

McAndrew, Francis T., and Hye Sun Jeong. 2012. Who Does What on Facebook? Age, Sex, and Relationship Status as Predictors of Facebook Use. *Computers in Human Behavior* 28 (6): 2359–2365.

McLuhan, Marshall. 1964. *Understanding Media: The Extensions of Man*. New York: McGraw-Hill.

Miller, Daniel, and Don Slater. 2000. *The Internet: An Ethnographic Approach*. Oxford: Berg Publishers.

Pauwels, Luc. 2005. Websites as Visual and Multimodal Cultural Expressions: Opportunities and Issues of Online Hybrid Media Research. *Media, Culture & Society* 27 (4): 604–613.

Ralon, Laureano, and Marcelo Vieta. 2011. McLuhan and Phenomenology. *Explorations in Media Ecology* 10 (3–4): 185–206.

Rodogno, Raffaele. 2012. Personal Identity Online. *Philosophy and Technology* 25 (3): 309–328.

Schütz, Alfred. 1967. *The Phenomenology of the Social World*. Evanston, IL: Northwestern University Press.

Schwartz, Ori. 2011. Who Moved My Conversation? Instant Messaging, Intertextuality and New Regimes of Intimacy and Truth. *Media Culture & Society* 33 (1): 71–87.

Schwartz, Raz, and Germaine Halegoua. 2015. The Spatial Self: Location-based Identity Performance on Social Media. *New Media & Society* 17 (10): 1643–1660.

Silverstone, Roger. 2002. Complicity and Collusion in the Mediation of Everyday Life. *New Literary History* 33 (4): 761–780.

Tufekci, Zeynep. 2015. Algorithmic Harms beyond Facebook and Google: Emergent Challenges of Computational Agency. *Journal on Telecommunications & High Technology Law* 13: 203–445.

van Doorn, Niels. 2011. Digital Spaces, Material Traces: How Matter Comes to Matter in Online Performances of Gender, Sexuality and Embodiment. *Media, Culture & Society* 33 (4): 531–547.

Wegerif, Rupert. 2013. *Dialogic: Education for the Internet Age*. London: Routledge.

Young, Garry, and Monica T. Whitty. 2010. In Search of the Cartesian Self: Intentional Disembodiment within 21st Century Communication. *Theory & Psychology* 20 (2): 209–229.

Zhao, Shanyang. 2004. Consociated Contemporaries as an Emergent Realm of the Lifeworld: Extending Schütz's Phenomenological Analysis to Cyberspace. *Human Studies* 27 (1): 91–105.

———. 2005. The Digital Self: Through the Looking Glass of Telecopresent Others. *Symbolic Interaction* 28 (3): 387–405.

———. 2007. Internet and the Lifeworld: Updating Schütz Theory of Mutual Knowledge. *Information, Technology & People* 20 (5): 140–160.

3

Facebook and Real Life

Thinking of Facebook as a network of ties between its users, who typically know each other face to face before adding each other to their circle of contacts emphasizes the continuity between the online and the offline realm. Facebook is never *just Facebook*, it taps into an underlying relational web, into existing bonds, sometimes very strong ones, into hopes, curiosities, complicities, anger, or disappointment between users. In light of these considerations about bond continuity, it seems like the partial mediatization of certain bonds has become naturally incorporated into the relations between people/users without disruptions. The specificities of Facebook appear like temporary limitations in communication which, although frustrating at times, have otherwise little bearing on interactions and exchanges of information.

However, there is a particular aspect which questions such a position. Facebook users often refer to their interactions, their posts, and their reactions as "on Facebook" or "in real life". This classification of the two realms highlights the fact that, despite its continuities and connections with the offline, Facebook is experienced and understood differently than the rest of our everyday life. Thus, instead of either taking for granted this separation between social networking and real life, or, alternatively,

© The Author(s) 2018
G.-I. Ivana, *Social Ties in Online Networking*, Palgrave Studies in
Relational Sociology, https://doi.org/10.1007/978-3-319-71595-7_3

dismissing the formulation used by interviewees as an unfortunate metaphor, I propose a systematic analysis of how and why this distinction is made. The outcome of this analysis will be a better understanding not only of the border between online and offline, but also a better understanding of the extent and the manner in which social bonds go beyond this border.

As it is perhaps expected intuitively, many users have mentioned Facebook information exchanges and interactions as "less than" real life, as replicas which are missing significant parts of face-to-face experience with another. Paradoxically, some of the interviewees also talked about ways in which sharing certain contents on Facebook was a way of making them real. However, there are some differences between these two types of realities. On the one hand reality is seen as equivalent with publicness; on the other, it is depicted as non-mediatized.

The Public-Private Axis

Let us take a look at what several users have said regarding the much discussed public-private axis (Papacharissi 2002; Aarseth 1997; Trepte and Reinecke 2011; Bateman et al. 2010). Furthermore, one of the topics explored at length is the reconfiguration of the very notion of publicness in the context of social networking (Ito et al. 2008; Boyd 2010; Baym and Boyd 2012). Namely, given the multi-layered audiences, the blurred boundaries, and the characteristics of social networking (like searchability and replicability), publicness has transformed into a set of networked publics. In this context, I begin the exploration of the links between publicness and reality with a few examples of affirming or confirming events happening offline through online actions:

> I do it a little bit to force myself to be present in the new ways of being; I do it for professional reasons, since I am working with the media and stuff. I am not a crowd person. I feel more comfortable as a bit of an outsider, sit in the corner, but nobody cares about you. So, I did it in a way for professional reasons, as a person who has to earn a living in that segment, so it's better for me to know what the things that happen in those spaces are.

Sometimes I go to a seminar and tweet a little bit about it, just to make sense of what it is to be there. I think that is why I participate more on Tweeter than Facebook. (**SB11**)

INT: Can you think of something that someone posted that triggered a positive emotion in you?

SB13: Yes, it's easy. After the last barbeque that we made, I don't know who, but one of my friends, took a picture and it was a very nice picture, a group picture and when they uploaded it on Facebook and they tagged me, I felt happy to be part of that, the feeling of the group being there and remembering that moment; calçotada (note: Catalan gathering where grilled green onion is eaten) in fact, not barbeque. (**SB13**)

In the first example, the interviewee feels that he is giving reality to his action of participating to a seminar by tweeting about it. In the second case, although the respondent had been part of that group gathering and definitely had some memories of it, it took someone posting that photo on Facebook, for him to feel happiness and belonging to the group. In these two cases, the very fact that the information was on Facebook is highly relevant. However, the perception of more reality is not given by passing the information through the filter of the media. The disembodiment, the ambiguous directionality, the spatio-temporal specificities have no importance whatsoever for them here. Rather, the content becomes real through its public character. If one is to imagine ways of making information public without the use of the media, this would equally result in the increase of reality of that information. So, here, Facebook stands for public, not for mediatized.

When talking about the changes that occurred with industrialization, secularization, and the concentration of the population in the big city at the end of the seventeenth century, Sennett (1992) points out to the distinctions between the public and the private realm and the ways in which the boundaries between the two have softened as a result of the need for reading the other, for attributing meaning to the (limited) information that was available about the other and for evaluating his/her credibility. And the means for answering these questions was looking beyond the mask, in Sennett's terms, or looking at the private life. The information from the private became the tool to evaluate the public. Thus, the consequence of this process is a more careful protection of the private from the public eye, a greater control and selectivity over what is displayed. That is the information according to which others will make sense of you; that will shape your interactions with those around you; so that is why that information is real. When users are willing to share something with their network, they accept that information to become real. In the quotation about being tagged at a reunion with friends, the interviewee felt that sort of exposure more real because it meant the tagger was willing to admit to others the fact that they are friends and spending time together. He was willing to allow that information on Facebook, which was equivalent to agreeing to be evaluated according to it. The tagger had no issue with being viewed by others as the friend of the interviewee and it is because of this that the interviewee himself feels more included in the group than he would have if he had just participated to the party privately. In this logic, the sense of reality is tied with publicness, but also credibility, confirmation of worth and expected scrutiny from those receiving the content.

Confusingly, but interestingly, the opposite view is expressed by another user. He points out the lack of importance of Facebook's publicness in relation with reality. I will quote a segment of our conversation:

INT: But you said your relationship status appeared on you wall. How did that happen?

SB6: I have no idea. It was just I don't know… it just happened. It was not something on purpose, for others to see, it was just for me and her. It was something between us.

INT: But did you feel it as being more official because it was on Facebook?

SB6: Hmm, to a certain extent it was more public, but being more public was not the purpose of it appearing on my wall.

INT: Then is it ok if I ask what the purpose was?

SB6: Hmm, I have no idea. It probably didn't have a purpose. It was just between me and her: ok, let's do this/oh, let's do it. As far as I remember, I think she was the one who decided to make it public. I didn't care about that.

INT: And why do you think she did that?

SB6: Hm, I have no idea. It's not something important. Of course having a relationship with someone is important, but having it on your

Facebook account, well it doesn't actually matter, at least for me. It's not like "ok, I am gonna brag about being in a relationship with him or her ". From my perspective, you cannot have a purpose in that. (**SB6**)

Here, the interviewee does not see the any reason for wanting to publish his relationship status on Facebook, but at the same time has no reason to keep it private. Although one might argue that being seen as single or committed will be reflected on the interviewee's social life and that the reality of his relation will be different and so will the reality of how he is generally perceived, he does not consider this to be the case. On the other hand, an issue that concerns him is bragging. In other words, the fact that he shared that piece of information may lose its relevance in the eyes of the others as a result of the suspicion that the reason for posting it on Facebook was particularly to impress, and this suspicion neutralizes all the other conclusions that might have emerged from the information itself. In this sense, his position on the publicness of Facebook gets closer to the two examples mentioned above. The same issues of credibility and expected scrutiny are central, but the conclusion differs. One explanation for this difference derives from the actual content being made public, as the respondent feels his romantic status should not be something of great relevance in potential evaluations. His skepticism highlights the idea that the increased sense of reality which comes together with publicness is also strongly dependent upon expected consequences of particular information being made public, as well as upon estimated criteria according to which evaluations occur. At the same time, his repetition of the idea that, despite the accessibility of the information about his relational status, this was something between himself and his partner highlights the tension in demarcating the private from that which will stand as ground for assessment. He does not wish to brag. Put differently, he wishes to make clear he did not make this information public in an attempt to have a positive impact on how he would be publicly evaluated in the future. He may be aware of that result, but he does not actively pursue it.

In all the examples mentioned above, users make a distinction between Facebook (as an environment of publicness) and their offline lives. However, despite this distinction, what happens on Facebook and what happens outside of it are not in contradiction. Through its public character, the online information is seen as confirming, accentuating, or bringing new light to (often private or lesser known) aspects of the offline. Yet, the discourse where Facebook is depicted as opposed to "real life" is also present in various ways in the interviewees' positions. In order to explore the instances where the reality of the content is not enhanced by the network, I will start with the distinction many users make between Facebook and the real life:

> (after being asked what were the reactions she received after posting photos she did not like) Most of the people commented on the pictures where I looked fine, they liked it or made a comment, saying you look gorgeous or you're pretty. On that occasion, when I chose the bad one, they refused commenting. They preferred not to comment and to tell me in real life "What are you doing? Why did you choose that picture?", but they didn't comment, they told me in real life. (**SB5**)

This respondent feels Facebook and non-Facebook are two different worlds, but the distinction between the two is still given, in my interpretation, by the fact that the others commented in private, not by how that communication was conditioned by technical means. What is also important to note in this context is that while reality and publicness seem to go hand in hand for the interviewees mentioned above, there seems to be a tension between them in this case. At the same time, this quotation is also distinct because it reveals the specific sort of publicness of Facebook. The audience is made of direct contacts, who share personal bonds, and this makes for a relational dynamic. The "viewers" do not simply watch and evaluate, they may also meet or call the author of certain contents and say "what were you thinking?" Besides publicness, the emphasis falls on the underlying exchange. Being seen attending a seminar, participating to a gathering of friends and being in a romantic relationship were all strongly unilateral cases, which evoke the type of publicness of earlier modernity. Yet, as soon as the situation requires it, the anonymous audience morphs into identifiable individuals. And the fact that the respondent posted "an ugly picture" is enough of a violation of Facebook normativity to encourage such answers. To be clear, all audiences may react in one way or another towards what is presented to them. However, here the reaction is private, and the user finds it more "real" precisely because it speaks of the bonds behind what appears to be personal display and one-sided image management.

Another example around the issue of publicness is the following:

> INT: And the place where you work, or your studies, you said you mentioned those, but religion, politics, why didn't you fill those in?/ SB1: Because they are not appropriate, at least in my opinion, in this context. They don't have, I don't know, I didn't feel like writing me on a social network, I mean, not as a public profile. (**SB1**)

The formulation "writing me" is very clearly connected with the sense of reality. It suggests exposing what she feels is her "real self" and she explicitly says she would not do that on Facebook, on the public profile. So, it is precisely the public character that is making her decide to limit the openness she invests in her profile. This statement is connected to a theme to which the user talking about his romantic relationship also eludes. Namely, the problem of which contents one feels should be in the public eye and which should not constitute criteria for general social evaluation. Both this woman and the man above used the notion of appropriateness to the context. Furthermore, she, like many others who discuss Facebook's publicness, has an accurate idea of who is part of her network and to whom certain information she posts is available. In this respect, besides context suitability, there is also an appropriateness in relation to various people. For instance, the presence of parents and former school teachers is seen to limit appropriateness. Also, conflicting views with close bonds generate doubts about what is appropriate for users to share publicly. One person confessed to me she wanted to post an article containing a very serious critique of the pope, but considered it inappropriate towards a number of close bonds who were ardent Catholics. Several interviewees explained they "know the best practice" of separating contacts into different networks and making different contents accessible to different people, but the overwhelming majority of them did not (only one exception). Again, here the so-called audience each user has gets broken down in the mind of the subject, into very specific groups or individuals. Thus, the appropriateness of information made public on Facebook is shaped by the normativity of the interpersonal bonds of different strengths one gathers in their network. In this sense, the type of publicness of Facebook profiles is similar to that of a pre-urbanized community, a virtual village in which those with whom you are connected are the people you know and some of whom you have known your entire life. This idea is clearly captured by the concept of the networked self (Papacharissi 2011).

The Mediatized-Non-mediatized Axis

However, the two worlds, the inside and outside of Facebook, can be conceptualized not only as public/private, but also as mediatized/non-mediatized. Here is an example of an interviewee talking about it that way:

> SB10: You know, on Facebook you have some really close friends, who are your close friends in real life (…) INT: But earlier you made this distinction between Facebook and real life. I am curious to know why you made this distinction or why don't you feel Facebook as being real life?/ SB10: Because, I don't know. There are some people I don't talk to in real life, I mean outside of Facebook. And on the other hand, there are some people, close family, or work colleagues who I talk to every day and don't talk to them on Facebook. (**SB10**)

This interviewee comes back to the relational core of Facebook. However, while she acknowledges ties being at the center of her own activity on the platform, she signals the fact that the overlap between the online and the offline is only partial. The main reason for that is the mismatch between the strength and importance of a bond and its Facebook manifestation. This consideration is, I believe, emblematic for understanding the necessity of research about social media that goes beyond the analysis of online behavior, into how that behavior is connected with broader bonds. Having said this, I am linking this quotation to the notion of mediatization, because it is the design of the network which may explain the gaps between bond closeness and disproportionate Facebook reflection of the bond. Namely, particularly with very weak ties, the lack of directedness of information and the possibilities of silent overlooking have an impact on the difference between the online and the offline facets of a bond. At the same time, the lack of accessibility of particular people who are "not on Facebook" is an issue of mediatization which has not been overcome.

SB3 also shares the feeling of a different nature of the mediatized and the non-mediatized environment when it comes to social interaction. To her, the differences come from the different capabilities allowed by the two environments:

> INT: You make this distinction between what is on Facebook and in real life and I'd love to know why you make that difference./ SB3: I can't even think of when I made it. It probably just came naturally. Well, why do I make this distinction. Because there are certain aspects that I think are more obvious in the face to face interactions and there are certain other aspects that are more obvious on Facebook. And maybe Facebook is not as telling as real life because I think everything you can grasp on Facebook you can also get in real life. But what you do have on Facebook is time to put it together. Because in real life you miss things.(…). (**SB3**)

This user talks about the limited information available on Facebook as compared to a situation of face-to-face interaction. The lack of availability of particular cues from the other is one of the typically signaled consequences of disembodiment in literature about the non-copresence (Waskul 2002, 2005; Miller 2011; White 2006). She also mentions the lack of synchronicity as time for a more reflective approach to the exchanges. The lack of synchronicity is another common topic in analyses of social media, particularly in the scholarship on the use of social media in educational purposes (Pullen Mark and Snow 2007; Borup et al. 2015). Thus, this interview fragment pinpoints precisely the features of mediatization as the key to what distinguishes Facebook from "real life". However, her words maintain the same focus as the previous interviewee: the bond with the other.

It is important to note that for most respondents, including the examples above, the weight of the offline is significantly higher and it is the main indicator for making sense of what is happening within the network. Additionally, as subjects socialized in the offline world, many feel the architecture of the mediatized environment does not always allow the expressions they wish to transmit, which is precisely the aspect which is emphasized in analyses of how bonds change with the online setting (Turkle 2011):

> INT: And in the statuses, do you look more for factual information? What they did? Who they were with? Or are you more interested in the emotional side? If they had a bad day/ SB2: Let me think I think... what they do mostly. Because with emotions you had a bad day, so what? What do you want me to do about it? What should I say? Hey, it's ok, here's a virtual hug? I don't know. (**SB2**)
>
> I just don t like Facebook chat. I just go on Facebook if I want to see something, have some news about my friends or related to the events or groups that I have created, so see where I am supposed to go, but personally I don t like to speak through this chat and to get in touch with my friends using this chat. (**SB13**)

For these two interviewees, the problem lays in the possibilities and limits of the network. In the first example, the respondent feels he cannot have a significant interaction with the other person, because through Facebook you cannot do much else than send a virtual hug. Moreover, he is bothered by the other person who does not acknowledge or accept this and acts as if real relations could unfold within Facebook. The second interviewee limits his interactions on Facebook to exchanges of practical information, even when it comes to private conversations, like the chatting option. Consequently, he is not entirely satisfied with the way the interaction changes by becoming mediatized. In this respect, additional research into generational gaps may highlight whether and to what extent the anchoring of interactional expectations into the offline experience is also specific to users aged under 20, whose socialization may have included different means and patterns of interaction. However, for users over 20, the offline frame of reference clearly guides their experience and understanding of online exchanges.

A Little Less Conversation (Typify Me)

Until now, I have identified two main axes respondents invoke as important with respect to the distinction between the online and the offline: publicness and mediatization. The two axes are typically brought up in connection to "real life" and what makes Facebook separate from it. Having said this, it is interesting to note references to the public and respectively mediatized character of the network have different logics behind them: in the first case it is the logic of the construction of an imaginary about the world that is within reach for only one of the participants to the exchange, while in the second it is the logic the construction of a common world within reach that would compensate distance for those telecopresent. In the former, we have diffuse directionality, while in the latter the addressee is well established. In this respect, I would like to make the distinction between posts inviting other to view/read/listen something *of me* or *with me*. When asked whether he thinks public posts are released by Facebook users with the intention to reach particular people, an interviewee talks precisely about this distinction and puts it in the following words:

> I don't think they are for his friends, I think they are for himself, for his necessity to make things public, not for the others, not these things. If I publish some news, yes, it's for the others, but if I publish a photo, I just wish the others to see the time I am having. That's just how I see it. (**SB23**—translated from Spanish)

The "of me" perspective involves my world within reach to be imagined by the other, either as a snapshot, or as a plot. But, besides whether I am offering information for a snapshot or a plot, the key for how Facebook information will be interpreted also lays in the bond itself. Namely, if the bond is weak, the other's impression of me is derived from an ideal type; thus, sharing my experience will add new information to the same typification. If the other has a sedimented impression of me according to our interconnectedness (memories, shared beliefs, emotions) rather than through reduction to an ideal type, they will read even a snapshot of experience as part of a plot with which they are not fully familiar. Neither of these will have a direct impact on the experience of togetherness I have with them. Whether we are talking about a static or a dynamic imaginary of me, this is not an experience of growing old together. If such experience has already occurred previously, users point out, the extra information gotten through Facebook is not of much use for redefining ties and stable impressions. However, when the ties are weak enough that the other is interpreted as isolated rather than in connection with the subject, information becomes central for constructing new impressions. In this case, someone's Facebook activity is a valid way of gathering knowledge about them.

However, if I am constructing a common world within reach, that sets the scene for a "with me" approach and a thou orientation. That world within reach can be simultaneously experienced in lived durée, although the other will remain out of reach in this common experience.

Going back to the issue of reality as it results from the interview fragments, the distinction between "knowing of me" and "being with me" appears very clear-cut in the users' discourses. Namely, the *information* about the other as someone who is not accessible is considered real, the *interaction* with the other is not. According to the interviewees, the network excels in knowledge diffusion, but not in online interaction. Thus, Facebook becomes a generator of reality in the sense of constructing a projection about the other's world within reach and lived experience in a here and now that the interpreter does not have access to. What I call a "him/her orientation", or what Schütz regards as the subtype of the they orientation that has the most concreteness, is the manner of relating to a particular (known) other in the times of physical distance and lack of interaction. That is reality because it will enter in the general framework according to which the other will read the author of the content and because their stock of impressions will be updated. By being public, the information is expected to be assimilated by those who are exposed to it and shape further interactions between the poster and these persons. Or, if one is not the author of the post, but just tagged, it is a way through which the author of the post is presenting the tagged one, for others to make sense of. And the main way in which one can make sense of another who is not in the same world within reach and with whom I do not share a strong previous bond is through their own world within reach (their interactions, their taste, their location, etc.). For instance, when asked about his habit of making a short video of himself from all the places he visited and posting it on Facebook, an interviewee explained:

> Oh, it's just something I want to share with my friends, to make them jealous (laughs). They already think I have this fantastic lifestyle and that I'm a womanizer: "You are the most exciting person we know", they tell me. (**SB40**)

Thus, he was trying to make that image real by putting it in the others' projections about him and their projections of his world within reach that they were not part of. The aim was not constructing a common here and now with those who were far away, or bridging experiences, but encouraging the construction of a certain imaginary for the others about what must have been his world within reach. That imaginary, in turn, will come back in the interactions with the author of the posts. These respondents are expecting to be the professional in media, the one with the great social life, the guy with the great girlfriend, or the one traveling to all those beautiful places for the ones who view their posts. These exchanges of information do not create a common here and now because they are (or have been) experienced in lived durée by the author of the post, while the one who is far away only has the experience of reading, watching, looking at representations of what the author lived. For instance, another respondent describes how he chooses his profile pictures:

> I can't really post my worst picture. I don't want to make a fool of myself. I post photos where I look relatively ok, but I post especially with what is happening around me. It's not like oh, look how well I came out in this one, let's post it! I have started posting more pictures where what is behind me or what I am doing is more interesting. My current profile picture is a picture of me (you can barely notice me in a corner) on a rock in Meteora. The rock was incredibly high and abrupt. I went to a dangerous spot, where if I moved an inch, I'd fall (…). I looked down and my legs were shaking. My girlfriend was far away and trying to also capture the landscape in the picture. If you look at the picture, I seem very relaxed (…) but I kept thinking oh, please take the picture so that I can go! Take the picture because I am dying here! (**SB32**—translated from Romanian)

This fragment shows how the focus of the user is not on directly projecting an image about himself, but trying to construct an imaginary of his world within reach and his experience of that world within reach for those living in a different here and now. That imaginary is, in turn, expected to be integrated into how he will be typified by those who saw the content. It is also important to notice the dissociation from the practice of choosing photos to post based exclusively on aesthetic criteria. He prefers sending a message about his world within reach than directly about himself. In other words, he prefers framing the action of posting a profile picture, which is per excellence an action "of me" in such a way that it looks as if it was a "with me". This attempt has no chances of success, since the experience that is evoked is one that the user alone has had access to. Thus, it will construct by default an imaginary about his world within reach rather than a common space of interaction. The interviewee himself is aware of the picture's limited potential of constituting a common world within reach, since he explains how different his lived experience has been from what he is projecting through his post.

But, since one can choose what to share (or what to allow), the projected world within reach of that person by someone who is not in the same here and now becomes a reflection on the one who made the choice. It ceases being a question of what the world within reach tells about the subject to whom it belongs. It is a question of how one is willing to construct an imaginary of his/her here and now for those who are away to use in typifying him/her. That is why several of the interviewees mention many of the things they read as inappropriate or unflattering in others posts are things they do themselves, but they are different in choosing not to share them. So, the poster is not evaluated (exclusively) according to his/her world within reach (as that world appears in the imagination of the viewer), but according to what he/she has decided is worthy of entering the others imaginary of his/her world within reach. One respondent makes the following statement:

I find nothing worse than posting a song by Salam (note: Romanian singer). Even if you listen to it, I will not throw stones at you if you listen to it at home where nobody sees you and you're in your own corner. That's it; maybe you had too much to drink that night. Go and listen, but do not post it. (SB21)

So, put differently, what was being evaluated was not only the taste or how the other constructed parts of his/her world within reach, but the choice of sharing that and allowing it to give rise to a certain imaginary about his/her here and now for those who were not around and whose stock of knowledge in relation to him/her, he/she has control over.

Furthermore, the content that is shared is passed through a filter of consciousness, as we have seen in all the quotations above. Yet that filtering is known to everyone, so what results is a snapshot of the world within reach of the other as he/she wishes it to be imagined. In respect to the question of reality, there is a certain concern derived from this consciousness. Namely, it is the bias in providing information for the others construction of an imaginary about the poster's world within reach. In relation to this issue, most interviewees claim to have noticed a strong tendency from other users to inflict an idealized version of their world within reach on the imaginary of people in their network.

> I think every social network is mirroring the reality, but it is also a place where you can go and be more interesting or sort of… twist things. It is not as good as being in reality. (SB34)

From this perspective, the posting of the other or the tag is seen as more desirable. It displays an image about one's world within reach without that person having had a say in it. So, some of the possible suspicions of overly favorable representations are eliminated. This is an excerpt from another one of the interviews:

> INT: But what you are saying, if I understand it correctly, it was not the same whether you posted those pictures or someone else posted them and tagged you in them. Did it have a different meaning for you? Was it more exciting if someone else posted them?/ SB15: Oh, yes! Definitely! Because if you post a picture of yourself I posted a few pictures of myself and maybe I tagged myself, maybe I didn't. I usually don't tag myself, only if I really like myself in that picture. I want to show the best side of myself, of course.

So, the fact that someone else uploads pictures of you makes you feel that other people appreciate you (?) I don't know/INT: But have you ever thought about the fact that other people in your network will see that you have been tagged by someone else and that would increase in a way your social status?/SB15: Oh, yeah! I have thought about it (laughs). So, for example I go to a birthday party with my school friends and someone from work sees the pictures and he tells me oh, I see you did this, I think that's cool (laughs). (**SB15**)

So, on the one hand, tags are interpreted as a form of acceptance from the ones that have shared a here and now with the interviewee and who are willing to display that by sharing a content that will be added not only to the projected world within reach about the interviewee, but also to the projected world within reach about the one who posted. To make it clearer, let us say the person who posted certain content is person A, while the interviewee is person B. By having posted a content where he tagged person B, he is not only contributing to the construction of an imaginary about person B's world within reach, by person B's friends. He, person A, will also contribute to the projection of his world within reach by his own friends. That is why for person B that would be a confirmation of person A's high opinion of him.

On the other hand, it is a question of expected (or experienced) effects the posted information has for those who have access to it, but who are not in the world within reach that the status, photo, video is referring to. In the quotation above, it is the construction made in the mind of the work mate about the lifestyle of the interviewee, based on photos where he was tagged. Another interviewee says, in relation to the topic of being tagged (especially in photos):

There are different kinds and ways of doing this, because I have friends who would like frequently go and delete the photos of them and just have these 5 pictures showing them from a point of view or what they want to be seen. Some people want like loads of pictures and some of them are really careful about it. (...) I have more than 600. Most of them are really ugly and really silly, so it's not like I actually wanted to sort them out, but many of them show me in situations I like or enjoy, so in that way it might be OK. (**SB28**)

So, in other words, she interprets the variation in the amount of shared pictures as a conscious decision of those tagged, a decision based on that according to which they want to be typified: what they want to be seen as.

This him/her orientation, resulting from the construction of an imaginary about the world within reach of those with whom one does not share a here and now, is typical for the "of me" category, and it can only be obtained through public undirected sharing of information. When directionality occurs, even if the content that is exchanged is of me, rather than with me, the existence of the interaction already means to the construction of a common world within reach, however limited. This middle ground is represented by interactions, be they public or private, with specified recipient, which are still focused on the imaginary of the separate worlds within reach of the interactors, but in which something that is ours is created as well through interaction. In this situation, whether the focus is on the constructed experience of togetherness and the common micro-world within reach created by it or it is on the imaginary of the here and now of each other is a question of interpretation and of how those involved read the interaction. Some of the possible sources of variantion are the type and strength of tie and the past interconnectedness between the interactors, but that is an issue I will return to later.

As we have seen, it is the "of me" mode that generates an experience of reality, while the directed interaction does not. So, we might ask ourselves why that is the case. I believe this can be explained by the fact that the construction of an imaginary for your world within reach for the others is a process that has never been based on a common here and now. Knowledge of someone, the him/her orientation, is, in any context, based on someone who is absent and of whom an imaginary is developed. That happens when someone tells a story or shows pictures from their vacation, which evokes a different here and now, when two people are talking about an absent third party or when one simply thinks of what a friend who is not around is doing. All these ways of knowing of another function similarly to what happens on Facebook. At its core, any story telling is a construction of an imaginary about a different here and now. Thus, subjects have been socialized in a way that allows them to find patterns to apply for this type of information exchanges. You read it as if they were showing you photos from their vacation, you read it as if someone else told you the other got a new job, you read it as if you imagined what they did when they were away just by the previous experiences you had with them. Or, if you are at the other end of the communication chain, you expect it to be read in those ways. Consequently, reality in this case comes from the incorporation of the new information in the stock of knowledge about the other and the use of that information in creating an impression of him/her; and the expectation on the part of the information provider that this process would occur.

The Difficulty of Togetherness and the Constantly a Posteriori Experience of Interaction

Yet, when it comes to generating realities in interaction and to constructing togetherness and a common shared micro-world within reach, Facebook has limited potential. However, before going into details, there is one aspect that needs to be clarified. I have been making the distinction between inviting people to get information with me and of me and I have made an equivalence between the "with me" category and interactions. Now, since the focus is on interactions, it is important to mention that constructing a common micro-world within reach means experiencing something with me, but that implies also experiencing me. If knowing of the other helps construct the imaginary of each other's distant worlds within reach, being with the other helps construct experiences of togetherness. Thus, clearly *directed interaction means experiencing with the other and, through that, experiencing the other*. In this sense, the actual conversation with the other, as opposed to the non-interactional exchange, is particularly relevant. This is an issue which Turkle's (2015) recent book on the importance of conversation in the digital age tackles in a detailed and convincing manner. However, her analysis places conversation mostly outside technologically mediated communication. Through the distinction between being with the other and knowing of the other, I attempt to reveal particular nuances to the online experience. Thus, I claim, the construction of the common micro-world within reach can be realized through the experience of togetherness and through interconnectedness. By having an influence on my experience of certain here's and now's, the other brings me in his/her reach and reciprocally. And the area where interconnectedness of experience can be achieved is this common constructed world within reach for the two interactors. It is a world where they share things and have access to each other. The topic of online shared experience and virtual togetherness has already been analyzed with respect to online communities (Bakardjieva 2003) and romantic partnerships (Ben-Ze'ev 2004; Holmes 2014). Building on this work, I propose a parallel analysis between such instances of togetherness and the very common practice of "keeping in touch" in the absence of online moments of togetherness.

Simply by addressing another person on Facebook, one is initiating a sphere of interconnectedness, by suspending their here and now and entering into the here and now of an interaction, where they are also pulling the other out of his/her here and now into that interaction. In contrast, knowing of the other does not trigger this togetherness, as it is not aimed at a common or reciprocally directed experience. Yet, if knowing of the other does not require, by default, physical presence, interaction traditionally does.

In order to know of me, the others can receive information in their there and then, but in order to experience me, in order for interconnectedness of experience to occur, we need to be in at least a particular form of the necessarily common here and now. I have mentioned above that the situations where the other is directly addressed, but when the content that is exchanged is about the separate worlds within reach of each interactor, as being the middle ground between the knowing of me and the interaction with me. On the one hand, by addressing one another, the interaction and the experience of togetherness will emerge, but so will the image of the world that is/was within reach for the other and not me. Whether the aspect of sharing or the aspect of constructing an imaginary for the absent is predominant depends on the key in which it is intended by one and interpreted by the other. I might tell someone about the great restaurant I have been at because I am thrilled about the restaurant and I would like to be imagined there by the other, while they might read it as a moment of connection we are having in the current conversation by that which is shared. Yet, Facebook users argue that sinking into a common here and now is not easy to achieve in this environment. From this point of view, users often talk about interactions happening on Facebook as unreal.

For instance, when asked if he sees having someone as a friend on Facebook is a way of maintaining contact with that person, one interviewee affirms:

> It's a parche, as we call it in Spanish, a supplement. Now, for instance, I have many friends who remained in city S. and the only relation we have now is through Facebook and I know that with time, many of them will disappear. Because it is something that is not real, I mean you cannot do Skype or something more interactional, I mean more Facebook is good so that from time to time you know something of that person, but you cannot maintain a relation with a person over Facebook. (**SB23**—translated from Spanish)

Correlating this quotation with the previous statements about the unreal feeling of Facebook interactions, a few elements appear as central. The timing of interactions is different and so is the selection of interlocutors. At the same time, the range of opportunities of interpreting the other as well as the possibilities of being interpreted and having an impact on them are different than in face-to-face interactions. This connects to the issue of disembodiment and to the relation between written dialogues and audio/video calls.

With respect to the timing of the interaction, one of the interviewees above was talking about the fact that in exchanges happening on Facebook, the dynamic is different from face to face, allowing for the interpretation of the other. So, in other words, it allows for the interaction to be interpreted mostly reflectively rather than becoming a flow in lived durée. Flow is a notion which the scholarly literature on social networking has begun focusing on increasingly over the course of the last three years, in order to capture the dimension of the lived spatio-temporal experience of the users (Kaun and Stiernstedt 2014; Kwak et al. 2014; Kaur et al. 2016). To continue, the absence of flow means that the exchange does not immerse the participant in a different here and now than the one he/she had been living in. It is a form of *constantly a posteriori experience*. From the very moment in which a user receives information from another, they are after the interaction rather than in it. This shift from the offline environment to Facebook is primarily linked with pace and temporality. As flow breaks down, one gets the chance to interpret the other because they find things of them rather than experiencing them in lived durée, like it would happen in a face-to-face interaction. This would also explain why the same respondent mentions that the information from Facebook is more scarce (due to the lack of experienced togetherness), yet easier to interpret for a synthetic, but reductionist impression of the other (due to the lack of flow). At the same time, the issue of having more time to put it together, as well as the lack of fluidity, is also related to the written form of the interaction. Although Facebook has a function that allows a video and audio call, the interviewees associate Facebook interactions with a written format. None of the respondents has mentioned anything about the audio/video call function of Facebook. Furthermore, in the fragment I quoted in the paragraph before, the user makes a distinction between Facebook and Skype, by associating Facebook with written content and Skype with visual and spoken interaction.

This written character that Facebook has established for itself is directly linked to the unfolding of the interaction. On the one hand, the pace is different, even in synchronous interactions, than face to face. On the other hand, everything is recorded and can be accessed at all times. Thus, instead of a flow, the result is an accumulation. Access to the past is not mediated through memory, selective gazes, and first-hand experiences, but gained directly through archives. As a consequence, the experience of time is transposed in a spatial and timeless manner. The answer to the question of what happened at a certain time is to scroll down and look.

Moreover, one limit users' mention about Facebook interaction, which is partially overcome by audio and video calling, is the embodied experience of the other. If the things which happen in an interaction are, for one participant, indicators of the inner life of the other, individuals who have been socialized in interactions where the other was present in their world within reach have learned to interpret indicators from the information they received sensorially. As a result, an interaction where the inflections in the other's voice, the tone, their look, their smile, and their

gestures are missing is very difficult for many. For instance, one interviewee explains:

> Because it is not the same talking to a person and having a chat. I don't
> know if you know this, but only 10% of our interaction is what we actually
> say. 70% is body language and 20% is the way we say things. So, on
> Facebook you only have that 10%. (**SB22**)

From this point of view, this affirmation is very similar to the one of
the person above who believes Skype is more suitable for long-distance
interactions. But one of the key elements behind this access to the other
and gathering as many indicators as possible in order to read them is
the construction of togetherness, which ultimately lies in interconnectedness of experience, in the reshaping of one's flow of lived durée by the
influence of the other. Above, SB2 was saying it makes no sense to
comfort someone with a virtual hug. Another interviewee has similar
concerns:

> But then again, I had someone in my class, for example, in high school,
> who would be like posting these posts about being really sad and writing to
> their cousin who just died, or something, and this is really serious and it
> makes me feel uncomfortable, because I would like to help them and be
> there for them, but when they go and post it on Facebook it's taking some-
> thing really personal which you should discuss with your closest ones and
> making it like an unimportant event.(…) I would never go and comment
> because I wouldn't know what to say. I couldn't really support them by
> using Facebook. It would be a face to face conversation. (**SB34**)

The lack of reality of these interactions lies in the incapacity to have an
impact on the lived experience of the other or, in other words, the incapacity to construct a common micro-world within reach in which our
here's and now's converge, making us accessible to each other. Users have
not been prepared in their socialization to read another based solely on
written information, let alone to reshape the lived experience of another
with the tools of interacting offered by Facebook. In that sense, the
exchange of information happening through Facebook communication
is interpreted by some of the users as unreal interaction, even if it meets

the conditions of an interaction. In the quotation above, the respondent is talking about her feeling of uselessness as a result of the insurmountable out-of-reach status of the other. He/she is in a there and then where the subject cannot have any impact on their experience. There is no interconnectedness, and where there is no interconnectedness, there is no real experience of each other. In the example above, the interviewee felt the original public post invited an "with me" rather than "of me" approach, and this framework made her acutely aware of the impossibility of actually engaging in a significant flow shared with the author of the post. However, when feelings are triggered, when certain ways of attributing meaning are challenged and reshaped, so when that interconnectedness of experiences occurs, the common micro-world within reach may be lived as real. This appears in the discourses of the users with whom I have discussed not explicitly, but through the disappearance of the Facebook real-life separation. Instead, the continuity of their narrative gained priority over the setting of the exchange.

There is, nevertheless, an amendment to this interpretation of reality. It is, just like interpretations of face-to-face interactions, dynamic and subject to shifts. An interviewee who did not agree to being recorded and whose story I am reconstructing on the basis of written notes told me she met a guy at a party and they talked briefly. Afterwards, they started chatting on Facebook for hours over the course of a few weeks. She thought she was very in love. Yet, when they met face to face again, she said: "He was so annoying! I couldn't stand him! I couldn't stand being in the same room as him! I didn't know him and I had just gave him qualities that I would have liked and imagined he was like that. So Facebook is not real at all!" (**SB39**).

So, in this case, despite having had a shared lived experience with the other, she qualifies it as unreal. However, we must note that at the time when those interactions occurred and for as long as their initial interpretation was considered valid, those experiences were very much real life. Hence, she talks about having been in love as a consequence of the long conversations which have given her a sense of togetherness. During their conversations, her world within reach must have included him since he was having an impact on her experience as lived durée. Yet, when meeting him again, she had access to additional indicators in order to read him and these indicators told her a different story than the written interaction had told. Since it was based on more information and an undeniable presence in the same world within reach, this interpretation gained prevalence over the way in which meaning was attributed based on the written interaction. As she mentions, the indicators she could grasp over Facebook were not enough to offer a holistic image of the other (Baker 2008, quoted by Baym 2010), but in the absence of any other readable input, she constructed an ungrounded fiction in the frame of which she understood the interactions. In the face-to-face interaction, she got access to indicators according to which she could fill in the gaps. So, when she experienced him in the same physical here and now, her interpretation of him changed. Furthermore, she retrospectively reconsidered her initial reading of the Facebook interaction as well. Just as in face-to-face interactions new information can deconstruct an entire previous understanding of a situation or impression of a person, new inputs are even easier to be acquired and to function the same way when going from online to offline. So, previous events will be brought back into memory (or looked at by scrolling the chat tab on Facebook) and reinterpreted in light of new indicators and new evaluations of the other. The discrepancy between what is taken out of the face-to-face interaction and the understanding that had been generated through Facebook chatting made the respondent dismiss the common micro-world within reach created in online communication as an illusion, since it had given her a limited (and susceptible to distortions) experience of the other. From this point of view, even the interconnectedness in that past lived experience is questioned. The ways in which the other has influenced her experience might have not even anything else but her own interpretations of scarce clues that she imagined to be indicators of something they were not.

Another issue that needs to be approached in the discussion about interacting as experiencing the other and exchanges of information as knowing of the other is interactions through feedback in public posts. If the posts are, although public, particularly directed at someone or if the author hints to an experience of togetherness with someone, that is a tentative construction of an interaction and a common here and now. In this case, feedback (in the form of likes and especially comments) is contributing to the construction of within reachness. It is a confirmation that the author's message has had an impact. On the other hand, if the message was not particularly aimed at someone, it can only be meant to construct an imaginary about the author's separate world within reach. In that case, likes and comments are the actual beginning of the interaction, since they are the first contents sent with an identified recipient in mind. They can either be an attempt at establishing togetherness or a signal that the information launched publicly has been received and will be used, one way or another, in the future assessments of the author.

The aim of this section has been to underline the ways in which interaction on Facebook is different than other interactions and to justify the decision of analyzing it as a separate category. Thus, up to now my focus has been on mediatization, or, in other words, on the disruptions occurring especially between Facebook and face-to-face interactions or, more generally, exchanges of information. However, these interactions and exchanges of information do not happen spontaneously and unconnected with anything else. On the contrary, they are often continuations of face-to-face interactions or various manifestations of previous ties. They are linked to the strength of ties, to the ways in which the other has already been read, to objective and subjective meaning contexts, to social constructions of habits, expectations, roles, and so on. At the same time, through new experiences of interconnectedness, through new accumulations in stocks of impressions, through negotiations of meanings and tie strength, Facebook exchanges also contribute to the relational universe that they were born of. So, besides mediatization, we are equally witnessing mediation. That is to say an analysis of Facebook exchanges needs to take into account the continuities with the offline. This is also the theme I will focus on in the following chapters.

References

Aarseth, Espen J. 1997. *Cybertext: Perspectives on Ergodic Literature.* Baltimore and London: JHU Press.

Bakardjieva, Maria. 2003. Virtual Togetherness: An Everyday-life Perspective. *Media, Culture & Society* 25 (3): 291–313.

Baker, Andrea. 2008. Down the Rabbit Hole: The Role of Place in the Initiation and Development of Online Relationships. In *Psychological Aspects of Cyberspace: Theory, Research, Applications*, ed. A. Barak, 163–184. Cambridge: Cambridge University Press.

Bateman, Patrick J., Jacqueline Pike, and Brian Butler. 2010. To Disclose or Not: Publicness in Social Networking Sites. *Information Technology & People* 24 (1): 78–100.

Baym, Nancy K. 2010. *Personal Connections in the Digital Age*. Cambridge: Polity Press.

Baym, Nancy K., and danah boyd. 2012. Socially Mediated Publicness: An Introduction. *Journal of Broadcasting & Electronic Media* 56 (3): 320–329.

Ben-Ze'ev, Aaron. 2004. *Love Online: Emotions on the Internet*. Cambridge: Cambridge University Press.

Borup, Jered, Richard E. West, and Rebecca Thomas. 2015. The Impact of Text Versus Video Communication on Instructor Feedback in Blended Courses. *Educational Technology Research and Development* 63 (2): 161–184.

boyd, danah. 2010. Social Network Sites as Networked Publics: Affordances, Dynamics, and Implications. In *Networked Self: Identity, Community, and Culture on Social Network Sites*, ed. Zizi Papacharissi, 39–58. London: Routledge.

Holmes, Mary. 2014. *Distance Relationships: Intimacy and Emotions Amongst Academics and their Partners in Dual-Locations*. Basingstoke: Palgrave Macmillan.

Ito, Mizuko, Heather A. Horst, Matteo Bittanti, danah boyd, Becky Herr Stephenson, Patricia G. Lange, C.J. Pascoe, and Laura Robinson. 2008. *Living and Learning with New Media: Summary of Findings from the Digital Youth Project in The John D. and Catherine T. MacArthur Foundation Reports on Digital Media and Learning*. Cambridge, MA: MIT Press.

Kaun, Annee, and Fredrik Stiernstedt. 2014. Facebook Time: Technological and Institutional Affordances for Media Memories. *New Media & Society* 16 (7): 1154–1168.

Kaur, Puneet, Amandeep Dhir, Sufen Chen, and Risto Rajala. 2016. Flow in Context: Development and Validation of the Flow Experience Instrument for Social Networking. *Computers in Human Behavior* 59: 358–367.

Kwak, K.T., S.K. Choi, and B.G. Lee. 2014. SNS Flow, SNS Self-disclosure and Post Hoc Interpersonal Relations Change: Focused on Korean Facebook User. *Computers in Human Behavior* 31: 294–304.

Miller, Vincent. 2011. *Understanding Digital Culture*. London: Sage Publications.

Papacharissi, Zizi. 2002. The Virtual Sphere: The Internet as a Public Sphere. *New Media & Society* 4 (1): 9–27.

———. 2011. *A Networked Self: Identity, Community, and Culture on Social Network Sites.* New York: Routledge.

Pullen Mark, J., and Charles Snow. 2007. Integrating Synchronous and Asynchronous Internet Distributed Education for Maximum Effectiveness. *Education and Information Technologies* 12 (3): 137–148.

Sennett, Richard. 1992. *The Fall of the Public Man.* New York: WW Norton Publishing.

Trepte, Sabine, and Leonard Reinecke, eds. 2011. *Privacy Online: Perspectives on Privacy and Self-Disclosure in the Social Web.* Dordrecht: Springer.

Turkle, Sherry. 2011. *Alone Together: Why We Expect More from Technology and Less from Each Other.* New York: Basic Books.

———. 2015. *Reclaiming Conversation: The Power of Talk in a Digital Age.* New York: Penguin Press.

Waskul, Dennis D. 2002. The Naked Self: Being a Body in Televideo Cybersex. *Symbolic Interaction* 25 (2): 199–227.

———. 2005. Ekstasis and the Internet: Liminality and Computer-mediated Communication. *New Media & Society* 7 (1): 47–63.

White, Michele. 2006. *The Body and the Screen: Theories of Internet Spectatorship.* Cambridge, MA: MIT Press.

4

Meaning Construction in Overviewing: "It Was Like Catching Up, But Without Talking"

As have seen in Chap. 3, unaddressed public posts tend to favor knowing of the other over experiencing the other in lived durée. Access is gained to segments of the other's world within reach, but no common here and now emerges between the sender and the receiver. However, the tie between the sender and the receiver is, as users point out, an important part of how the content displayed will be read. Yet, first of all, it is an important part of the decision about whether it will be read at all. One of the first things that are visible from the interviews is the discrepancy between a focus on the posts of close friends and the posts of ties that are weaker. The following two quotations illustrate the two approaches:

Also, I disabled the notifications of the majority of my friends. I mean I don't receive notifications from most of the people, because I sometimes for me it's a bit silly posting kittens, children, kittens. I mean, I have nothing against it, but again, with the majority of my friends, I am not close friends. I mean I met them in university in the country A or in country B or in country C, we are not close friends and I don't think that... Firstly, it's not very interesting for me to look at their personal private life and secondly, maybe I am not supposed to look at it. So I only left the news

© The Author(s) 2018
G.-I. Ivana, *Social Ties in Online Networking*, Palgrave Studies in Relational Sociology, https://doi.org/10.1007/978-3-319-71595-7_4

feed for some people, like close friends and also like, news agencies, magazines, blogs. (**SB12**)

Ok, so let's say if they are close friends, maybe I check them, maybe I don't and if they're not that close, I don't know why, but with some people you feel like, even if you don't really talk to them… It's like ha, ha, I am looking at your private stuff and you don't know or maybe you are not aware (laughs). (…) The fact that it's someone you don't really talk to that much makes you want to see what they are doing. I don't know why. (**SB15**)

The former interviewee is only interested in those with whom he feels he has a connection, while the latter focuses on those with whom he does not have a strong bond. There is a clear difference in levels of interest for weak ties between the two, but what is more interesting is the communality in the two quotations. Namely, both of them note the assumed expectation of the other about who should see the content: "maybe I am not supposed to look" and "I am looking at your private stuff and you are not aware". They have different positions about how to deal with this problem, but they both get a sense of clandestinity about reading/looking at/ listening to contents published by weak ties. I will analyze the issue of clandestinity in more detail at the end of this chapter. Right now, what I believe is important to keep in mind is that there is an assumption that even that which is public and not addressed is, in fact, addressed implicitly to certain people, namely the ones who have a close link with the author. At the same time, an issue which is visible here and which is recurrent throughout the interviews is normativity. More specifically, the norms associated with various types and strengths of ties are the main concern of interviewees. The words of SB12 about his disinterest in weak ties point to a level of normativity, as he mentions that such disinterest is actually legitimate for people who one does not know too well. SB15's interest in weak ties alludes to the same normativity, as he believes the tie itself does not legitimate the curiosity; he regards his overviewing is an act of mildly breaking a social norm.

Some of the subjects are, however, less discriminate in their interest. When asked whether he browses for profiles of his ties, one respondent says:

Nooooo, because I get seriously lost. I won't get out of there, because I really have this tendency./ INT: And is it aimed more at certain people or can it be anyone?/ SB29: No, it can be anyone. Once I'm in, I'll just go through their whole Facebook. I mean it./ INT: And are you looking for anything in particular?/ SB29: No. Any information. I just assimilate a lot of information. (**SB29**—translated from Romanian)

This is an example of a user whose curiosity extends to strong and weak ties alike and who is interested in knowing as much as possible about any of his contacts. Nevertheless, his understandings about those he gathers information about and the interpretations of the information itself will vary. In the following pages, I will explore this variation.

Meaning Construction for Public Posts by Close Ties

As for the actual content others post, interviewees insist content posted by close friends is interpreted differently than the one posted by average contacts within the network. A 25-year-old woman I interviewed after work at her office job in Barcelona talked about this topic fairly at length. Namely, she explained many of her friends and former university mates posted photos which were revealing their bodies. She found that problematic not because she would have a negative evaluation of those people as a result of seeing those pictures; she makes it very clear her bond with them is strong enough not to depend on such evaluations. However, she fears they will get negatively evaluated by others who are not as close to them. Negative assessments, she highlights, are probable not necessarily in situations of the physical exposure itself (a group photo at the beach would be ok), but when exposure is actively and transparently pursued (selfies or photos in front of a mirror).

There are a series of interesting aspects to discuss regarding this interviewee's point of view, such as the preference for photos depicting experiences over physical self-disclosure. This is connected with the issue I have analyzed in the previous chapter about the sharing of content as a way of constructing a common world within reach as opposed to encouraging the other to produce an imaginary about your here and now which for them is out of reach (but which will trigger certain typifications). However, now I will focus on her explanation about not minding something that in principle bothers her, only because the authors are her friends. The formulation she uses, "they are still my friends", refers to the fact that an impression has already been constructed with respect to those people, according to their impact on the subject's life, through what they lived together and through how the other has shaped her experiences. She also has a generic knowledge about a type of people who post selfies and photos of themselves in bikinis. Yet, the persons in question will not fall into this category, because this would be a general typification used as a hint for making sense of the other in the absence of more personalized indicators. Here, more personalized and varied indicators exist already and exceed the knowledge derived from a type, so that typification does not matter anymore.

Another interviewee, a boy in his early 20s, agrees. When asked about whether he feels one's Facebook activity guides him in making sense of that person, he mentions this is sometimes the case, but not always:

> But I have a really good friend, she is in country A now, and she really loves shopping. If I saw her profile, I would have had a bad impression about her, but I know her and we talk a lot, we have great chemistry when we meet, so that doesn't matter anymore. (SB2)

This girl is already meaningful to my interviewee according to the impact she has had on his lived experience. He thus constructs their connection as a quite strong tie, so he does not need to interpret her Facebook posts. However, the interviewee in the first example above expresses her concern over how those posts would be interpreted by others, who do not find themselves closely tied with the poster of the bikini pictures. She is worried just as she typifies some of her contacts according to ideal types more than reading them through the lens of shared experience and interconnectedness (as limited or extended as it might be), others will also typify her friend the same way. Thus, she disagrees with her friend's practice, not because it changes her tie with her friend, but she expects it to change the tie her friend has with others. In SB2's example, the profile is also a collection of information that can be used for fitting the other in an ideal type, but not always accurately. Also, since these are public posts, at least formally not directed to anyone in particular, they are by design only contributing to an imaginary about the world within reach of the other rather than to the construction of a common here and now. Yet, in the case of close ties, that imaginary about the other's world within reach, just like the understanding, emotions, and bond of the other person, will also be shaped by information coming from other sources than what is shared in Facebook. When asked about whether she interprets the posts she sees on Facebook (the public ones, not those addressed to her) as indicators of what the author of the post might be going through at a certain point, one respondent answered:

Yes. With close people, because with others, I don't know why they are posting that, but when it is about close friends, yes I can make that deduction. (**SB5**)

Another user emphasizes:

Yes, but I don't think it is so much about the indicators within the content, it's just that you know the person a little, so from a starting point which is what I know of them and what they publish, I think you have the elements to consider what is going on, or at least you have your hypotheses. (**SB11**)

These are just two out of countless examples where Facebook users talk about the ways of attributing meaning to the other while showing the actual presence of the other or the interaction (as specifically directed content) is not necessary for subjective understandings to emerge. In the two quotations above, the interpreter and the interpreted are not physically copresent and they are not addressing each other. They are in contexts I have described in the previous chapter as knowing of one another. Thus, in terms of Schütz's distinction between those who are present in one's world within reach, on the one hand, and those who are absent and who we only know of, on the other, the exchanges of information in the Facebook public wall fall into the second category. They are similar to hearing a story about a third person. Yet the attribution of meaning can be subjective, because the impression about the other may be constituted according to the general interpretative frame of how the user experiences the tie with the author of the post. In turn, that frame emerged from previous concrete situations lived with the other (as it is the case in the quotations above), rather than from an ideal type. In this case, meaning is built upon what we know of a certain him/her, and how we feel about that person in light of a multifaceted bond, not on cold detached information about people like him/her. In the two fragments above, the interviewees use their own past experiences of togetherness, as well as the stock of knowledge they have of the other, in order to construct an imaginary about what the other's lived experience must have been and to derive an understanding starting from there. Both of them mention that they need a close relationship with the other to have this subjective reading despite their absence from the world within reach.

Thus, when the tie is close, the other has already become meaningful in certain (quite particularized) ways before entering the exchange on Facebook; he/she is already meaningful for the subject mainly in terms of how they impacted each other's' lives and of their shared experiences. That produces a round impression cumulating emotions, reflections, memories, and expectations which in quotidian language is referred to as "knowing someone" with whom a strong bond is shared. So, when the tie is close enough, the subject feels he/she knows the other, not people like the other, but that precise person. That is the reason why the interviewees above state if they have a close relation with the author of the post, they can interpret the post more accurately. At the same time, they might also have more than an understanding of the other according to the unique impact he/she had on the subject. They might also have concrete knowledge about a particular course of events. They might already have an imaginary of what the other might be living when they are apart, which is typically constructed largely through exchanges happening outside of Facebook. In that case, the personalized impression of the other that comes from the close tie, coupled with an existing imaginary about his/her world within reach, grounded on previous information, will form a certain construction of meaning, to which the contents shared on Facebook are only an addition, a piece of a puzzle. Above, we have seen that this addition is not substituting or even completing the impression based on interconnectedness. Yet, it is relevant for making the imaginary about the other's world within reach dynamic. Thus, instead of identifying, categorizing, or evaluating the other, in the case of close bonds, Facebook exchanges of information serve for putting together a narrative. As a consequence, the other will also be imagined in movement and, thus, in his/her unfolding experience. It is similar to the principle of animating cartoons. When the subject has access to more captures from a flow of the other's experience, he/she is able to reconstitute that flow with approximation. One interviewee explains this using an example about the ups and downs of her romantic relationship and how she shares these situations with her close friends who live in a different country:

> The more in love and enthusiastic I am, the more I post about romance, for instance. The angrier I am because maybe we had a fight 5 minutes before, the more I post things like men are pigs. And statuses, yes, when I am upset I post it as a status, you know? And probably my best friend (who I have just told about him) will understand, and he will understand because he feels in the wrong. (…) Maybe I don't have time to be on the phone with my best friend for half an hour daily, so then she sees what happened from my posts. Many times, she called or messaged me asking "Hey, what happened? I saw that on your profile… Did you break up again?" (**SB7**—translated from Romanian)

Here, the interviewee insists she expects her best friend to understand her posts because she had already told her friend an entire story before that post. So, the information contained by the post would represent for the friend not so much something according to which to make sense of the author of the post, but a new sequence in a plot. That is why the Facebook public post becomes part of an imaginary about a dynamic world within reach in which the subject's close tie must be living. In other words, it favors a very particular orientation, where, besides impersonal typification of others in categories of diverse levels of generality, there is also a form of flow. This imaginary about the other's world within reach in a dynamic form is still in the "of me" rather than "with me" mode of interpretation, but it is "of me" as more than an exponent of a type. This "of me" recreates flows and imagines experiences, because it is "of me" with whom you share a bond, "of me" who you already know well and care about, and "of me" of whose life you are a part. The same phenomenon, but from the perspective of the other participant, is described by another interviewee when he is asked about examples of overexposure on Facebook. In this context he mentions women who publicly write about their boyfriends leaving them, or saying they are sad without explaining why, which bothers him even more. In such situations, he explains he would not react in any way, unless they were close friends; then he would send them a private message.

In other words, if the tie with the poster is weak, the interviewee will read the content as a means of seeking attention and he will find it irritating, whereas if he has a strong tie with the author, the message will be interpreted as serious enough to deserve a private message as a response. Like in the case of the interviewees who discarded the information they received through Facebook about their friends in a bikini or being overly concerned with shopping, this user would also read his close ties according to other criteria, namely evaluations drawn from previous experience with the other, an experience in which the other has made an impression and which serves as the ground for new meaning construction. Certain motivations or meanings are read as uncharacteristic to that person and, often unreflectively, ruled out of the interpretative process or are tolerated in light of other considerations about him/her. Then, the content from Facebook is just an update on the changes in the other's world within reach, changes of which the interviewee becomes aware, as the result of the posting. An important element here is, once again, the normativity which shapes informal ties, and especially strong ones. It is expected of someone's behavior, or on Facebook, their posts, not to be under constant scrutiny by their close friends, as the unwritten social rule is that friends do not engage in detailed evaluations resulting in categorizations of each other into ideal types. Given Facebook's relational fabric, it follows that it is only acceptable for contents posted by close friends will be meaningful within the frame of the bond, with the norms it implies. In this respect, reconstructing events of a friend's life when they are apart, "catching up", "learning what's going on", or in other words recreating flow, is not only socially acceptable, but also desirable.

However, since the public message is not specifically addressed, very often no actual social interaction is initiated. Thus, since the content is not regarded as aimed at the one who happens to read it, the dynamic aspects of the life of the author of the post have little bearing on the bond with the receiver of the post. The interpreter and his tie with the poster of the content was not under negotiation in any of the previous quotations talking about strong ties and Facebook posts. In the case of the last interviewee, the actual bond of the interpreted with the interpreter entered in the scenario only when the subject decides how he should react about the situation his close friend is going through, but not in the actual reading of the content his friend shared.

Furthermore, close ties can be part of the decision about what someone posts publicly or they can be accomplices to a plan. One interviewee gives an example in this sense:

> With my best friends, when I see what they post, I am never surprised, because I know what they like or who they want to impress. And they also know about me. For instance, once some friends posted pictures with me and I didn't want a guy I liked to know where I was that weekend because I wanted to keep him guessing, so I told my friends: 'Look, you can tag each other if you want, but don't tag me because I don't want him to see this'. So then they posted the pictures and commented, but they didn't tag me and I didn't comment and they all knew what was going on. With other friends, if we do not talk all the time, I don't care about a song or an article they post, because I know their style anyway. But if it seems to be something personal or a hidden meaning and I get curious, I have a chat with them in private to catch up. (**SB26**)

In this case, that which appears publicly had already been discussed with close ties, so they will not need to construct an imaginary of the poster's world within reach, because they were in the same here and now. This means for them the information of the post will have a very clear interpretation. The only way in which that content can still be novel to them is reading it through a different lens. Namely, the friend can take an outsider perspective and try to ignore the background information to construct an estimation of how that post might be understood by someone who sees it without knowing other details.

There are, however, situations where the public information from Facebook is interpreted neither as a part of the dynamic of the other's experience and his/her moving world within reach, nor as a ground for evaluation.

For instance, in the excerpt below, information which is directly relevant for the tie is left aside only because it is gathered online as opposed to taken out of a shared experience. The respondent says:

> 2 years ago I fell in love with this guy and he was really different from me because I like to be with one person and see each other and chat and be friends at the same time when you are dating the person, and he would be like more easygoing and his approach towards this would be very different. So, if I started following him on Facebook, I am sure I would see many pictures that I didn't really like, but it's ok, because it's just his way of doing things. This would disappoint me a lot, but I think it is difficult, because it is the same with text messages, that you can't really… it's not the same as being face to face and most of the time you should try to calm down and if you have any doubts about something, just go and ask because it's easy to misunderstand. (**SB34**)

In her explanation, the interviewee shows she doubts the information she gets from Facebook because, in the absence of lived experience together, the reconstitution of the other's experience apart might be faulted by the lack of details. So, the possible grounds for failed expectations would not be actions occurring on Facebook, but actions that happened in an inaccessible here and now and that would only be put together through information from Facebook. Then, the subject is more reserved in reshaping her impression of the other on the basis of imagined plots about what is not within her reach. Yet, despite being wary of misunderstandings, she also acknowledges the potential of public Facebook information to have an influence (in this case disappointment) on how she saw a close tie in relation to her, if that which was posted came against her prior sense of interconnectedness with the author of the posts. While this example is not precisely a close bond and the way in which content is interpreted is somewhat different, I am invoking it here especially with respect to bond questioning and how it may link with Facebook information.

At the same time, as I have mentioned before, ties differ in terms of strength, but also in terms of types. Not all close ties are friendships. As we have seen, Facebook users often feel strongly linked to (former/possible future) romantic partners, or to people with whom they have had major (irreconcilable) conflicts. One respondent exemplifies this by talking about how he has put his current girlfriend in a Facebook group of close friends where she is the only member. The reason for doing so is to keep track of everything she likes and comments. He concludes by saying he spies on her.

This user has made particular settings in order to effortlessly monitor his girlfriend. In my understanding of his words, his motivation for doing so is gaining information about the situations that do not occur in their common here and now, but during the times when they are apart. Moreover, it is a way of reconstructing the experiences she might have had and might not want to share with him. The information he gets from this source can potentially change his impression of her only if some of the things he learns will contradict his interpretation of the bond on which that impression is based. He would not see her differently if he discovered she likes a different style of music, but he would re-evaluate her if his view of her was based on how considerate she has always been to him and he reads a post where she publicly talks about something he had confessed to her. In a strong tie, unless the new information attacks the very foundation of the bond of the other, it will not be relevant.

From another perspective, unlike in the cases where the close ties were friends of the user, here the interviewee is not interested in getting information to continue a plot that had started in a previous interaction, because the tie is close enough that the imaginary about the partner's experience would not need to be fed with public Facebook posts, but with depictions of that experience by the partner in direct interaction. So, here is sought the reconstitution of an alternative course of events lived by the partner.

> Maybe you don't love somebody, but you have the need to know what he or she is doing. It's an obsession, it's like when you eat you think oh, I have to check it. It's not because I am interested, it is because of habit and I am worried about this. If you do that without even liking the person, when

you really love someone, it can become very bad. (…) Sometimes, when I have an ex-girlfriend I want to check on, I see who she is with. I check the pictures, the comments, who made the comments, then I check the profile of the person who made the comment. I am thinking of leaving Facebook because of this, because when I have some free time, I might waste it doing something like that. (**SB38**)

In this case, the subject talks about romantic interests which, irrespective of whether they are maintained or they fade away, favor a close monitoring of the other on Facebook. The tie is close enough for the other to have already been interpreted based on past lived experience. So, this is an example of monitoring with the defined purpose of grasping as much as possible from what is shared publicly in order to reconstruct the dynamic of the other's world within reach and, ultimately, the course of the other's experience. She wants to know what her ex-girlfriend had been doing despite not spending time in the same here and now and despite not communicating enough to construct an imaginary plot about the other's here and now. In this sense, the mechanism of meaning construction is not very different from the above examples of interpreting posts from close friends. However, unlike in the case of close friends where the imaginary of the other's experience is built to an important extent on the information gathered from other sources that the public posts, in this case it is only the public posts. Thus, the effort of approximating the right plot is greater. Furthermore, in the case of close ties with friends, none of the interviewees mentioned going to such great lengths as checking who comments on the friends' posts and browsing for the profiles of the commenters to reconstruct the experience of their friends. Yet, this happens because the interviewee knows that if she is to reconstruct daily experiences of her ex-girlfriend, she needs to do so relationally. She also bases her reconstitution on certain institutionalizations of interactions that already exist on Facebook and that I will approach later. For now, if we are to put it briefly, let us say she knows it is likely that those who post comments have a close tie with her object of interest and it is also likely that the tie has emerged in shared experiences. *Thus, this scrutiny into the details of Facebook posts appears to be a good way (if not the only sustainable one) of receiving news about another without interacting with them.* This characteristic makes Facebook very important in certain relational scenarios, like conflicts and tensions.

The situation of conflict between friends is similar to the situation of ended romantic relations, because the starting point is in the same lack of contact and in the same limitations of imagining someone's experience and dynamic world within reach without being in touch with them, exclusively on the basis of public messages:

> We were, during high school and in the first year at the university, a group of girls who did everything together. And at a certain point, some of us lived together and things started to deteriorate. We started to argue. So eventually the group of 7 split in small groups. I am not speaking to 3 of them at all, with some I am still good friend, but they are not friends with each other. But sometimes I like to look. For instance, one of them has been chubby before and she has lost a lot of weight. I love to take a look and see what she looks like now. They are the ones I search for and I wouldn't want them to know I looked and they probably do the same thing with me. (**SB7**—translated from Romanian)

However, comparing this statement with the affirmations about interpreting the information posted by close friends, romantic partners, and ex-partners, in the case of conflicts the interest for actually reconstructing the experience of the other is weaker. His/her here and now, what he/she did, with whom, and how it unfolded are not deduced in great detail. A general view of the other's life and the changes from the last time the interpreter and the interpreted shared an experience are the main focus.

So, to summarize the section on public posts published by strong ties, I believe it is important to point out that interviewees rarely mentioned evaluations of their strong ties based on information they got through public Facebook content. Moreover, some of them insisted that due to the strength of the tie, this does not constitute a criterion for assessment. The situations where public information from Facebook reshaped the interpretation of a close tie were when the information was read as having direct repercussions on the tie itself. Secondly, those who are closely tied with the author of posts will find it easier to read the input they get in a way they feel confident is similar to what the poster had in mind.

Thirdly, they interpret public content in light of knowledge obtained from alternative sources about the other and/or a given situation. When the author of the content is not in the same world within reach as his strong ties, the post will be used to complete an imaginary about the author's experience and the dynamics of his/her world within reach. When the author and the contacts with whom he/she has a close relationship have a common world within reach, the public display may be a result of previous social interactions between them. If the tie is a romantic relationship, the information that is sought in Facebook public posts doubles, rather than continues, the other's depictions of his/her separate experience. If the tie is an ended or conflictual relationship, the reconstitution of the others experience does not benefit from a ground of previous information and is mostly done on the basis of information from the profile. In the case of close ties marked by conflict, the interpretation of public posts is not detailed enough to actually recreate the other's experience, but follows only major changes happening in the other life. Nevertheless, not all of these ties are of the same closeness and as a general rule I believe it can be said that the stronger the bond, the more one is interested in reconstructing the other's separate lived experience in imagination (whether he/she only has the means of public Facebook information or many other sources at his/her disposal) than to generate new impressions.

Meaning Construction for Public Posts by Weak Ties

In this section, I will continue the discussion about public unaddressed posts, but I will focus on their interpretation by weak ties, which I regard as the core of the flowing web of exchanges occurring on Facebook. Despite my formulation of this as a unitary topic, we have to keep in mind, on the one hand, the lack of a clear-cut distinction between strong and weak ties (they both result from fluid experiences and interpretative processes) and on the other hand the variety of modes in which weak ties exist. Thus, the purpose is not to generate a one-size-fits-all explanation, but to explore the ways different understandings develop about the other and his/her in relation to the subject. In order to do so, I will make some distinctions between weak ties, namely: weak ties from one's past (old colleagues, neighbors, people with whom contact has been lost for a period of time and re-found on Facebook), new ties (people one has just met and added on Facebook), and weak quotidian ties (people whom one meets occasionally, but with whom they have yet to become closely connected). These categories are very similar to the ones proposed by Hiller and Franz (2004), in the context of discussing the uses of the internet in diaspora. I will begin with the discussion about old ties.

Overviewing Old Ties

> I remember from the beginning I looked for old class mates, by names, by nicknames. I sometimes still search for them, by town or by high-school also, because many of them got married and changed their names. (...) I look for their photos, because it is faster. I don't want to waste time finding out too much, just some photos, some comments and that's all. I just like to know some things about people I haven't kept in touch with, what they do, where they are (...) family events, if they got married, if they had kids. (**SB8**—translated from Romanian)

This is just one example of a user talking about having old ties in their network, but similar statements were made by most Facebookers with whom I talked. Yet, these are weak ties because even if they were read according to past interconnectedness with the subject, they are even more strongly typified according to an objective category: in these cases, having attended the same school as the subject. As a consequence, the interviewees describe them not according to certain shared experiences or interactions that had an impact on them, but according to this generic quality. Furthermore, in the first excerpt, the user emphasizes the old schoolmates are people she has not seen in ten years and she places them in the same category with people you rarely meet, in other words, those who are not a central presence in one's relational universe. The second person also highlights that she tends to take a quick look over photos, because her curiosity is limited to finding out general information about whether they got married or about their job. But, as general as this interest might be, it is present, since she explains she is interested in finding out whether they got married or had children and what their current cities were. These interests are recurrent in many of the interviews. To illustrate, I will cite another user who says the following:

> I wanted to see what kind of adult people they had become. How they looked like, whether they were sort of having families, whether they settled themselves and they're happy (smiles), how they actually evolved in life. (**SB4**)

I believe there are two important aspects in the exploration of how public displays from old colleagues are interpreted. It must be said these are people together with whom the subjects have spent significant amounts of time in the past and with whom they shared many experiences. So, we can expect the subject to have at least a schematic image about almost all of them (especially the ones he/she looks for). So, from one point of view, the interpretation of Facebook public information would be as an update of that old impression. In the case of strong ties respondents often said Facebook public information does not constitute a criterion for typifying the other, because he/she has already been left a nuanced and vivid impression on the subject according to past lived experience together. However, in the case of old contacts, even if the initial impression had been very potent and based on strong interconnectedness between the subject and the other, that impression is still not as unquestionable as with current close ties. One of the interviewees illustrates this with an example:

> A colleague from secondary school, who, poor guy, was one of the… He barely passed his evaluations every year and I am talking about secondary school here. And, you know, at the end you leave with a certain opinion about each of them. Anyway, I went to a different high school, we didn't keep in touch. Finally, I added him on Facebook and saw how he has changed. It's unbelievable. He posts really cool music, only rock… I really think he changed. And the statuses or the comments to the pictures… he is funny, he makes jokes with subtext, very cool! And he also looks great! (**SB7**—translated from Romanian)

In this case, she makes a detailed description of how her impression of her old classmate changed through the other's Facebook public posts. He had never been a close tie to her, so her initial impression was mainly developed from an ideal type, rather than from interconnectedness, but it was nevertheless a well-cemented typification. Yet, as a result of the content he posted, he re-evaluated him and placed him in a different box.

However, in the case of the subjects above, who said they were interested in how the other turned up to be, in what he/she did in life, there is one other aspect than the updating of an old typification. Namely, it is a way of understanding the social world at a structural level by identifying patterns of life courses unfolding in correlation with the typifications of individuals. The old colleague is already typified and that typification is not always negotiated or changed. When there is no re-evaluation, what is of interest is, like in the case of posts from strong ties, what happened to them. Yet, since here the ties are weaker, the other is typified more in terms of ideal types, rather than read through meaningful shared experience. In turn that allows for the potential of developing a life course pattern for people like them. Allow me to clarify this idea starting from another interview fragment:

> It was a former colleague of mine from primary school, she was a fabulous student, one of the best in our group and also a great girl, I mean I've always thought highly of her. (…) Somehow we got to be friends on Facebook. I hadn't seen her in 7 or 8 years.(…) She probably invited me and when I went on her profile I was very surprised to see how she ended up. I mean she has a very ostentatious look, heavy make-up and tight clothes and listens to a certain type of music that I wouldn't expect her to listen to, like music I would consider of bad quality, like stuff that teenagers or kids listened to in mid 90's and I had this idea that you get over that stage at some point in your life and apparently she hasn't gotten over it. And what else… Apparently she is dating a guy with no higher education. (**SB3**)

In this case, the interviewee maintains the old typification about the other being a great, intelligent girl of whom she thinks very highly, but is surprised of how the life course of someone with those qualities has unfolded. On the basis of the initial typification, as well as a general knowledge about the life course of people like her colleague, she had constructed a projection about how the other would have grown up, what her taste in music would be, who she would be dating. Yet, what happened is that these extensions expanding from the initial typification and the subject's life experience with others who had been typified similarly turned out to be inaccurate. So, although the core typification might still stand (unlike in the case of the former colleague of SB7 who did poorly in secondary school), the whole chain of deductions made from that typification is broken. As a consequence, this will raise a question mark about the connection that the subject was making between the initial typification and the subsequent ones. In other words, it will contribute to the subject becoming doubtful about connecting, for instance, one's intelligence with his/her dating choices. In more general terms, having projections about the other's life course contradicted this way can change the understanding of the regularities with which life courses unfold. It will provide examples of individuals achieving things that the subject thought were against the odds and it may reshape their understanding of what it takes to achieve that. Furthermore, the peculiarity of old ties and especially old schoolmates are that, borrowing from physics, T0 of the typification occurred in an incipient phase of his/her life and T1 is very far from T0. From this perspective, the subject gets a panoramic view on the other's life course. This is, in fact, the most common key in which posts by old ties are understood and only if very flagrant contradictions of the initial typification of the person occur, the typification itself would also be readdressed. Thus, the two modes of reading public posts (recreating life courses and re-evaluations of others) are often present at the same time, but in fluctuating proportions.

Following a thread which was also often present in the discussion about overviewing strong ties, I believe it is important to point out once again normativity. The ideal types according to which typifications are carried out have a series of moral and emotional implications which reverberate in concrete evaluations. For instance, the notion of "a friend" does not simply comprise of a set of characteristics which can be captured reflectively. It includes certain moral expectations, projections about how the experience of togetherness should feel, and so on. Additionally, different types may include features like aggressiveness, snobbery, superficiality, to name just a few attributes. In this case, associating someone with such types becomes intertwined with particular normative attitudes in relation to them. Thus, perhaps even more clearly than in the case of the strong bond, where new evaluations were not being generated, with weaker bonds social norms are central, as they function as a compass for what is significant about the other and in which ways. Another facet of this normativity refers to circumscribing what is an acceptable reading of the other in light of the tie involved. So, when the tie is weak enough, the social rule deems it "normal" and "understandable" to seek for particular cues or to develop evaluations different than with strong bonds.

At the same time, it is also worth noting that unlike in the case of strong ties, where the receiver was trying to reconstruct the dynamic world within reach of the sender, as well as his/her experience within that world, nothing of that sort is mentioned in the case of old ties. The interviewees do not try to imagine specific events or life experiences of these contacts. Moreover, the actual tie between the subject and his/her mate is never brought up. The information exchanged is read mainly in confronting actual events in the other's life and the subject's projections about life course regularities. At the same time, given the abovementioned panoramic view on life course offered on Facebook, to which is added a perceived flat starting point (all were students of the same age, in the same class, although much can be said about background inequalities), estranged mates become a great reference for comparisons of life trajectories. However, this is not an interpretation that is limited to old schoolmates. One interviewee puts it in the following words:

> Anyway, I would say that there is an issue with authenticity, because there are so many identical news feeds, like with the same trips, eating, gatherings, so I suppose it is just stating that you are not worse than the others who are posting that. I also have a social life! (**SB12**)

The issue this subject addresses is the possible motivation why users would post very similar contents. However, the underlying assumption here is that users read each other's posts in terms of comparisons, which would trigger the need to reaffirm their own life choices. Yet, these comparisons are somewhat specific, as opposed to the panoramic life course evaluations discussed before, where only major events were of interest. And in all the interviews that touched upon life trajectories, the topic emerged in discussions about old ties with whom contact had been lost for a number of years.

At the same time, with the people from one's past there is a lack of any recent shared experience and any interconnectedness. There is, also, a lack of a projected future shared experience or an imagined growing closer. These elements point, in the end, not to a weak tie, but to an absence of the tie altogether (if the link from decades ago was not enough to fuel a connection). That is why, if an overview of life courses is the only interpretation given to public information on Facebook, once that overview has been finished, the interest in the other ends. One subject says:

> I have them (note: old acquaintances) in the network. But it's true that I am starting to delete them because in the beginning you enjoy it: Hey, look! and you see their photos, you see them changed, but afterwards it just wears off (…) I look at their photos, to see them, if they changed a lot physically, and I also look at their life, because if you look on their profile you can see perfectly if they live with their lover or not, if they have kids, because through photos and everything, you can know their life. And you just look to see what life they have. (**SB19**—translated from Spanish)

Once the general picture about the other's life has been completed, the additional information gathered through new posts becomes irrelevant. In the case of lifestyle comparisons, interest never fades away, but if only life trajectories as a whole are at stake, the subject had rather not receive most public posts which happen on a quotidian scale of magnitude.

An intermediate interpretative process (derived from an intermediate tie) between the attempt of imaginarily reconstructing the other's lived experience and the very general interest in their life trajectory is keeping a constant moderate interest in the other's life. For instance, one interviewee affirms:

> Well, a friend of mine… When I was an exchange student (note: two to three years before), I met this girl, I thought she was really cool, she lives in country A., so we didn't have much contact afterwards. I mean, if we were in the same place, I'd definitely be friends with her again, but in these terms, it's complicated. I remember a while ago she went to country B. and she posted some pictures and I was like oh, it's person X! and I looked at

her pictures and then I went to her profile and I saw what she is studying and where, just to get a general view of what she was up to. It was like catching up, but without talking (laughs). (**SB15**)

In this case, what the interviewee describes is not a reading of the other's public posts as a close friend. He does not try to construct an imaginary about her actual experience and the dynamics of her here and now. He had not kept enough contact with her through other channels to have additional information to use in assembling a plot. He just wanted, in his own words, a general view of what she was up to, but still with a higher level of specificity than the interest most users have for people they have not known anything about for periods longer than three years. For instance, he was not only looking for major life events, her family, or her job but also for her pictures from a recent trip. This, I believe, comes from an awareness of the other's transformation while they are not part of our world within reach. The other leads a parallel existence that will continue to unfold when they are apart. In this case, receiving some information about the other's experience, while they are not in the same here and now as the subject, is a way of keeping up with the changes in the other and his/her world within reach. For this to be of interest, the subject needs to interpret the other as someone with whom they are still connected, even if not very strongly. Thus, to conclude, it follows from the last quotation, as well as the ones above, that the level of detail in which the dynamics of the other's life is relevant is proportional with the strength of the tie. The stronger the tie, the more detailed image of the other's experience while apart will be sought. When the tie is weak and the other is only typified based on an ideal type, the experience will be interpreted in a frame of generality rather than specificity.

At the same time, what is interesting to note here is the way in which relational normativity establishes acceptable online exchanges. In this case, the intergender friendship seems to come with its own norms. This is something Felmlee et al. (2012) were analyzing using an experimental design regarding friendships unfolding in traditional settings. Furthermore, the topic is not new in the literature (Booth and Hess 1974; O'Meara 1989; Werking 1997). For the respondent above, the intuitively grasped norms about intergender friendship have a direct translation in online behavior which must signal his faithfulness to the pre-established frame of the bond.

New Acquaintances

Another type of weak ties who have access to one's public posts and whose interpretations have certain particularities are the new acquaintances. It is typically considered and documented through research that the formation of new ties is favored by the online environment (McKenna et al. 2002; Ellison et al. 2006; Baym 2010). However, in this respect social networking platforms and Facebook in particular do not closely follow that pattern. All of the users I interviewed stated they do not have any contacts they do not know at least indirectly in their networks. They do have, however, what Baym (2010) calls latent ties. Many mention the fact that it has become habitual to add people one has recently met to the network of Facebook contacts. I will provide a few quotations to illustrate this:

> From the beginning I had a large group of friends. I was the administrator of a Facebook group of lesbians from the city V., so most of the lesbian girls from our city added me and I felt great, like oh, I am the administrator (…) I believe it was [a position of power]. (**SB38**)

When asked about her privacy options, another interviewee responded:

> It's available only for friends. For all 507 of them and I don't even know half of them. (…) No, I mean I have met them at least once in my life or we have had a five minutes' conversation or we have been in the same context, at an event, but we never shared anything other than that. I don't even know why I added them, but I am a lot more selective now. This was happening two years ago. (**SB1**)

Thus, as it can be seen in these users' experiences, it takes very little connection for someone to qualify for becoming a contact on Facebook. Yet, as SB1 remarks, the threshold for adding someone has shifted over the years. As West et al. (2009) have shown, the so-called public realm of the Facebook wall does not fall into the classic private-public dichotomy. Thus, the need the keep the access restrained and manageable enough has become more and more urgent. Another subject talks about this issue:

> I mean I don't add people that I just meet for a short period of time. If it is people I am getting to know more, I will add them. But I am trying not to get too many friends again. Especially now that I am in a new place and I keep meeting new people I don't want to add people I will just end up deleting anyway. (**SB2**)

Like the interviewee above, SB2 also constructed his habit of adding on Facebook only certain people based on his past experience with the issue. The public access to his profile must remain compatible to the level of publicness of the information he shares. He says he does not want to have too many friends again, so he is trying to avoid the practice through which he believes he got in that situation before. That practice had been adding everyone with whom he had been in the same context and he had interacted briefly, that which SB1 described as the five-minute conversation. Thus, that person will not be above the privacy threshold. In this respect, possibilities for clandestinity are becoming somewhat narrower. The strategy of both interviewees is to include not necessarily people with whom they interact more, but particularly people with whom they are developing a tie (although the two often overlap). Furthermore, SB2 mentions he does not want to end up deleting people anymore, so there is also a component of projection for the future tie with that person to be strong enough that he would not need to delete them. This means that, unlike in the case of people who are added by virtue of a tie in the past, but with whom the projection of future interconnectedness is very weak, in the case of new Facebook contacts, the existing tie is the ground for the projection of the tie in the future. Once having added the new contacts, the meaning given to the public content the other shares will vary according to this projection, as well as the nature of the tie already created. On the one hand, if the tie is very weak, that information can be used to typify the other starting from an ideal type. I will provide two slightly different examples to illustrate this idea. One is referring to new ties in general, while the other is focused on new ties with romantic potential, as online communication is increasingly important in pursuing romance (Rosenfeld and Thomas 2012).

> INT: But do you check others profiles and timelines?/ SB23: If I have just added them, yes./ INT: And what are you interested in?/ SB23: I am interested in I don't know what it is called, but on the left side, what they are studying, what they are working and then the photos./ INT: What about likes in movies, music?/ SB23: I've never been big on movies, but if they list some literature, I'll also check that. (**SB23**—translated from Spanish)

Here, the subject mentions that he would check the public information posted by the other when he has just added them. Then, the actual elements that are of interest are mostly those that can produce a static typification of the other (their studies, their job, the books they read), rather than to construct an imaginary about the dynamics or the narrative happening in the other's life at a particular point. As Ellison et al. (2014) point out, Facebook interaction constitutes a resource in social capital formation, and I argue it is precisely this weak tie resourcefulness which is evaluated and aimed through bondless typifications of the other according to hints about their structural position.

Another subject goes through a similar meaning attribution process, and in the fragment below he explains the situation where he is romantically interested in the new contact:

> Oh yeah! Let's say I might find on Facebook things that make me think maybe this person is not that attractive, but it.../ INT: Such as?/ SB15: Oh, I am going to come across as incredibly demanding and a horrible person, but if she likes music that I think is awful, I might reconsider my interest in this person. I like lots of different music, but I think there are signs that might tell you how a person is. (**SB15**)

As I have mentioned in the chapter on ties, strong ties are to a greater extent based on an impression constructed in shared experience, while weaker ones are predominantly typifications based on sets of characteristics, behaviors, and tastes of the other. I have also argued that the typifications made in weak ties often serve in evaluations for the potential of stronger ties. This is exactly the train of thought that both SB23 and

SB15 follow in the quotations above. Thus, when SB15 adds a new contact, the tie is very weak and based on changeable typifications. Acquiring information from Facebook does not provide new shared experiences, so it cannot encourage the organic formation of an impression of the other and the sedimentation of a meaningful bond. However, it can and it does offer grounds for a more detailed typification of the other as a separate bondless entity, which, in turn, results in a certain projection about the potential future interconnectedness. Namely, in this case the information the new contact has published about the kind of music she enjoys constitutes the basis for SB15 typifying her in a broader sense: There are signs that might tell you how a person is. Starting from this typification, he developed a certain projection about how strong would a future tie possibly be and the potential decreased as compared to before this information was known.

Yet, in cases where the subject has a clear projection for the future of the tie, or at least a clear idea about what would be a desirable future for that tie, content would be interpreted close to how it is interpreted in strong ties, despite the weakness of the current connection with the other. Below, there is an example:

> This is embarrassing, but for example if I met a boy I liked, I am going to check. You could say that I am stalking this person, but yes, I would check out his friends and who wrote on his wall and yeah, maybe see if he is together with someone, who are his best friends, but of course I prefer to go and ask and have a chat and meet them, but sometimes it's just easier to go on Facebook and have a look. (**SB34**)

In this case, the subject is not trying to typify the other, like the person in the example above, but there is a difference in the level of stability of the tie at the moment of viewing the profile. In the case before, there was no solidified impression and the future of the tie with the other was uncertain, whereas in the latter case, the subject had already decided she liked the boy and was projecting a tie of certain strength. In light of that projection, the interviewee is interpreting the information from the profile as a source for reconstituting his experience on the one hand and as data directly relevant for their tie, on the other hand. The interest in who writes on his wall and who his best friends are is part of the attempt to create an imaginary about his experience and the dynamic of his world within reach. The interest in whether he is dating another person is directly linked to her projection about the future of their tie. In the case of strong ties, information on the other's profile had an impact on the tie if it was interpreted as affecting the interconnectedness between the owner of the profile and the overviewer. Here, in weak ties, there is little typification of the other based on passed interconnectedness, but there is an imagined future strong tie and present situations and events that can restrict that imaginary. In this case, such a situation is if he is in a relationship with someone else. *So, the interpretation of public information is not only a continuation of an existing plot or the reconstitution of an inaccessible one, but the projection of a future plot.*

At the same time, not all users are as attentive to the public information shared by their new weak ties. Furthermore, some of them make a specific point of not reading into any of that information. When asked about why he decided to have very high level of privacy for the contents he shares on Facebook, one interviewee says:

Because I don't want anyone to have preconceptions about me. I just want them to meet me and see who I am, not expect someone better or worse than what I am like, because you can't know a person through their profile. You can see some things about them, but you can't really know them. (**SB2**)

Someone else has a similar opinion:

This is the bad thing about Facebook profiles, that you are allowing the person to know you without having talked to him/her. This scares me. It scares me in the sense that if you are with a girl in a disco, you meet her and she adds you to Facebook, she just takes a look on your profile and you don t have to tell her anything more. She already knows in what field you work, if you like music, if you play an instrument... In this sense, I don't like it at all. I'd rather she had my phone number, but not my Facebook profile. (**SB23**—translated from Spanish)

Both these subjects express their concern with being evaluated in a detached artificial manner, based on the limited information they shared on Facebook. As we have seen in the quotations above (one of which belonged to the same SB23), a common interpretation of what the other publishes is the categorization of the author of the content in a static category. Then, as a result of that classification, the future tie is bound within certain limits of closeness. So, they don't want the interconnectedness from shared experience to be altered by previous typifications according to ideal types. In my understanding, that is what SB2 is talking about when he says that one cannot be known through their profile. He means that the interconnectedness that would occur in a shared experience is not predictable by a categorization of the other according to an ideal type constructed using information from Facebook. That is also why SB23 does not want to make his Facebook profile available to new contacts. Yet, it is important to notice that the concerns of both of the subjects occur in relation to themselves being typified, rather than to the practice of them typifying others. Moreover, I believe their concern with having their information interpreted this way comes from an assumption of typicality of their own practice. Of course, the processes of constructing a new tie through face-to-face interaction will often have the same evaluative dimension, but that is blend in a shared experience and read together with the experience. Consequently, the subjects prefer to be known in interaction, although, as SB23 points out, he would probably share the same information about what he does and what he likes, as he shares on Facebook. Yet, that would be bonding because of the interconnectedness of experiences, whereas the acquisition of Facebook public information can only produce a typification of the other through deposits of knowledge. It must be said the evaluative mechanisms through which the information about the other is read by the receiver involve a mix of reflections, emotions, beliefs, and so on. Nevertheless, the input comes strictly in the form of stocks of factual information, devoid of the shared experience.

Having said this, we need to keep in mind that these distant and static typifications of the other may function in different directions with respect to the tie:

I wouldn't say it's a huge surprise, but just a matter of interest in... for example I remember I added one friend, I mean when you meet people, you have an idea, or just guessing what this person likes.(...) That happened with one of my new friends and she liked, for example Nabokov and I thought hm, that's strange, because I also like him and for me it was quite surprising./ INT: But does is change the opinion about that person?/ SB12: Well, it always changes at least to a certain degree. At least you know this person a bit better and it changes your perception of this person a bit. (**SB12**)

This quotation illustrates that evaluations done through Facebook also produce a green light for the possibility of a tie with the other. Another interesting aspect signaled by this interviewee and which has been pointed out repeatedly by other subjects as well is the fact that even in weak or new ties typifications are made in advance. Afterwards they may turn out to be more or less accurate, more or less stable. These typifications also shape the meaning construction around that which is learned through Facebook. They will have consequences on the further development of the bond. However, this element is stronger in ties that have already developed a certain strength, or at least stability in a weak connection.

Another facet of this normativity emerges here, and it refers to circum-scribing what is an acceptable reading of the other in light of the tie involved. When the tie is weak enough, the social rule deems it "normal" and "understandable" to seek for particular cues or to develop evaluations different than with strong bonds. It also deems it acceptable to have what appears as a "rational" approach to the relation with the other, which these typifications reveal. As Parsons (1951) had argued through his notion of affective neutrality, emotion is suppressed in secondary institu-tions and expressed in primary ones. In this case, the weak bond is closer to a secondary institution, which means a rational state is predominant, a state which is not unemotional, but one where emotions remain in the background (Barbalet 1998). Thus, evaluations like the one above, based openly on cognition are part of the normative handing of the unsedi-mented tie. The possibilities of non-interactional exchanges of informa-tion offered by the network also contribute to leaving non-cognitive mechanisms of making sense of the other in the background.

In this subchapter, I have explored the understanding given to unad-dressed information by weak ties from one's past and by weak recent ties. Now I will focus mainly on weak ties that have a somewhat constant pres-ence in the subject's life, but with whom the bond never became stronger.

Quotidian Weak Ties

Most of the remarks about interpreting the contents posted by new weak ties can also be applied for older ties that have maintained themselves below a threshold of closeness. Yet, there are also a set of elements that distinguish older and newer ties of comparable strengths. One of them is the abovementioned role of previous organic impressions that are sedimented and grounded in a longer period of interaction. In case the interactions have been scarce enough that those impressions still have a provisional character, we may still speak of a certain (although paradoxical) novelty of that tie, despite it dating from a moment before the immediate past. In this case, information from one's public activity on Facebook can trigger new categorizations or evaluations, like they do in new ties. Furthermore, also similar to what happens to new weak ties, when the other is somewhat closer or a certain potential for strengthening the tie is noticed, the contents will be read through the lens of experience reconstruction, more than life course approximation.

These differences between the ways in which newer and older weak ties are interpreted tend to reoccur in other contexts as well. Asked about whether he has any concern about the authenticity of profiles, one respondent elaborates through an example of what he believes to be lack of authenticity from someone in his network and concludes by saying:

> What I told you was just a small part of the profile activity, but it also connects with what you know about the person in the non-digital environment. So, I think in the end it's the people that you don't like, you don't like in the online as well. (**SB11**)

Someone else explains it in the following words:

> I think there is always a suspicion of posting what looks good for certain target groups or your circle of friends, so yes, credibility is an issue. I mean I have my own suspicion of two or three people constantly doing it. (...) It's probably a mixture of what I see them doing on Facebook and what I know about them on real life. (**SB3**)

In both of these examples, the content in itself was not enough for them to typify the other in a certain way (compared to the cases above where, for new ties, their taste in music or their job would be considered). These two subjects, however, were interpreting information that they did not necessarily see as solid criteria for classifying the other, but it nevertheless added a new argument to the existing impression by reading that content in light of that very impression. It is a circular mechanism by which the other is re-evaluated with the old evaluation as both the underlying premise and the achieved conclusion. Thus, the purpose is not challenging how the other has been regarded, but reconfirming it. Moreover, some of the respondents derive a certain satisfaction out of this confirmation of previous impressions. One of them talks about it:

> I had a friend who hooked up with a girl. I heard the girl was not a saint. I added her on Facebook just out of curiosity, to see what's her deal. Meanwhile, they broke up and theoretically I had no connection with the girl anymore. She posts such stupid things! She is a veritable bimbo. She makes grammar mistakes and things like men are pigs and look how cool we are on the beach! I haven't unfriended her because I am curious what she will do next. I just want to laugh a bit. (**SB32**—translated from Romanian)

In this case, the subject had typified the other very fast after having added her, but he explains that he enjoys having his typification restated through the contents she posts time and time again. However, this is an atypical scenario, because most of the interviewees affirm they would periodically delete very weak ties if the past experiences have not created enough of a bond between them and no future interconnectedness with that person is foreseen.

> Yeah, because those people that I think we added each other just by being for example in the same class, but we never ever had a conversation or the only thing I know about this person is that he studied in the same university and the name. So, there is no point of interest. Sometimes I see them in the news feed and I go and delete them. (**SB12**)

These users highlight the fact that, in the decision to delete someone on the basis of the weakness of the tie, two elements are considered. One is the current strength of the tie, which is correlated with the bond that has been established between them through past shared experience, and the other is the projection about the potential of the tie. So, as discussed earlier on, besides the categorizations according to ideal types or the possibility of imagining someone else's experience through gathering information about them, in the end, that which gives the strength of the tie is the interconnectedness with the subject. The other has to be anchored in the user's life by past or future ropes, because otherwise any exchange of information is not read as part of a tie. It is by following this line of understanding that another respondent reached the conclusion that eliminating someone from Facebook is like eliminating them from your life. Namely, when asked about instances when he deleted people from his network, one user explained he did when he knew there is no future relation there and he would never be in contact with that person again. Furthermore, he admitted conflicts triggered exclusion from his circle of friends: "You cross me, I eliminate you" (SB19—translated from Spanish). He insists he was also eliminated from other people's networks and he found the experience hurtful precisely because it clearly meant exclusion from the everyday life of the other. Yet, his words rather seem to point to the reverse scenario, namely, the others are seen as not being part of your life (or in the case of conflict, not being a desirable part of your life), so there is no interest for knowing what they have to say and making sense of it.

Stalking

Last but not least, when talking about ties of different strengths and the meaning attribution to content they post, perhaps one of the most common issues that I have also briefly touched upon earlier with new ties (but that is not limited to new ties) is stalking. By stalking, I am referring to the activity of constantly monitoring any accessible change occurring in another user's profile without initiating an interaction or admitting to have been involved in a detailed process of overviewing them. The topic has been taken up particularly from the perspective of psychological well-being (Marshall 2012; Lyndon et al. 2011; Chaulk and Jones 2011) or threats and strategies of protecting privacy (Young and Quan-Hasse 2013). Surprisingly, little attention has been paid to the phenomenon by the branch of sociology dealing with interactions and social bonds. In this regard, I come back to the initial issue of the sense of clandestinity in viewing contents posted by the other, as a result of an assumption that those contents, despite being public, were addressed to ties of certain strength for the author. There is a question about whether one is at the level of closeness where they are expected to look.

The processes users describe are similar to what Cooley calls the looking glass self, but they apply to ties. Cooley's ([1902] 1964) theory, also used by Mead, points out the construction of the self according to three stages:

1. One imagines how he/she appears to the other.
2. They imagine how that appearance is evaluated.
3. They construct themselves according to (1) and (2).

I believe the same steps can be identified in the words of the Facebook users to whom I have talked, but in relation to ties. Namely:

1. The user imagines how close the relationship appears to the other (what the user thinks the other sees). For example, I think X does not see us as very close.
2. He/she imagines how that level of closeness is evaluated by the other (what the user thinks the other sees as ideal as compared to (1). For example, I think X is happy with us not being very close.
3. He/she constructs the tie according to the two premises above. For example, I should try to maintain this level of closeness.

In other words, the level of displayed closeness reflects the imaginary about, firstly, the other's view of the actual closeness and, secondly, the imaginary about the other's desire for closeness. Nevertheless, there is the level of how close the subjects themselves feel/want to be to the other. One's own account of the relationship and the imaginary about the other's position are of course dependent upon each other. I believe phrases like "it is not interesting for me to look and maybe I am not supposed to look" capture that process perfectly. In the interviewee's view, the tie is weak, he does not want it to be any stronger and he expects the other also perceives the tie as weak, so he does not find any reason to overview that contact.

Even when the expectations of the other are not mentioned explicitly, they are intertwined in the ways in which users motivate their own actions and create their own view about closeness. That is also why SB11 feels that it is appropriate to contribute to conversations about actions he had been part of. This gives him the confirmation that the level of closeness he has attributed to the relation, based on previous interactions and based on the estimations about the other's account of the strength of the tie, is accurate. He explains it further in these lines:

> If it's people that are not part of my daily life, but they post something that I enjoy and let's say I want to, not give my approval, because they don't need my approval for anything, but send a positive vibe, well maybe a like is enough, because otherwise you might be participating in conversations that are not yours. If someone you are not close to publishes something that you want to support, but in the conversation there are others who are not in your circle, a like is enough. (**SB11**)

The user is aware of the ways in which his actions are read as reflecting a certain level of closeness that the other might or might not share. Feedback is, consequently, the expression of the level of closeness not that one necessarily assigns to a relation in a certain moment, but the level of closeness one is willing to claim he/she has assigned to the relationship, which is, as I have described above, dependent upon the imaginary about the other's assigned level of closeness. Since this is a chapter about the interpretation of public posts by ties of different strengths, I will not insist upon the issue of feedback right now, but rather on the opacity of the process of overviewing and how meaning is attributed to that process on the basis of tie strength, and imagined tie strength for the other, respectively. This constant negotiation is clearly captured in the following quotation:

> Now I am into a guy and we don't know each other too well, so we are not Facebook friends, but I browsed for him and some of the information on

his wall is public. So, I check his profile very often, although with my limited access, there is not much to see. I just see if he added a new friend or what event he said he would attend I don't go to the same events or do anything about it, but if he ever found out somehow that I do this or worse, that I do it daily, I'd die of shame.(…) Yes, if I also found out he was checking mine just as much, that would be great! (**SB26**)

This respondent admits her tie with the other is, for the time being, weak. In fact, it is weak enough that they are not even connected with each other on Facebook. Nevertheless, she has a projection about this tie gaining strength. At the same time, she would feel ashamed if the other knew she saw the contents which he posted publicly, with no restrictions, and which were, at least formally, addressed to anyone who is interested enough to look. The reason for that is that she suspects a discrepancy between her level of interest in reconstructing as much as possible of his experience and his assumed lack of interest in her. That is why, when asked what she would feel if reciprocity was established, her interpretation of the whole situation would be entirely different.

Thus, the conditions leading to stalking are, at least based on the statements used in these instances:

1. the user believes the other sees the existing tie as weak and has no desire of strengthening it;
2. the user's own ideal tie is stronger than the current tie;
3. the user acts in ways that are consistent with his/her own degree of ideal closeness, which goes beyond the level of closeness they estimate the other considers ideal,
4. the users keep their actions undisclosed, so that the other does not gain awareness about what they assume is a discrepancy between their own and the other's ideal levels of closeness.

Facebook is one of the few environments designed in such a way that it allows for that to happen. Since knowing of the other through their public posts is completely lacking transparency, there is, especially with weak ties, a constant thrill and guilt of acquiring information in a way in which nothing is given in return and in which actions can be taken according to the subject's wishes, without requiring a negotiation of meanings or an agreement with the other.

However, between the weak tie that gets deleted because it is projected as non-existent in the future and the tie for which the user has a projection of strength, there are the weak ties that are projected as remaining constant. They might not be framed primarily through shared experience and interconnectedness, but there were nevertheless some shared experiences, over mixed with an overarching static typification. These ties are, as users have pointed out and as I have briefly mentioned before, materials from comparisons. These comparisons are different from those focusing on life trajectories, since they are mainly focused on lifestyle and taste.

On the News Feed I just take a brief look and I see the majority posts things like I love you, I miss you, I can't live without you and these things bore me and then I go and play something./ INT: But do you block them? (because you can do that if you don t want to see what they post)/ SB25: Oh, no, I don t block them, because I still like to see what they say. (**SB25**—translated from Romanian)

For example, if someone joins a club that is really stupid, like some sentence that is trying to be clever, but it's not. It makes me think: Dude, you're so stupid! I am not going to say anything, because it's just me getting upset, but it's also fun to think this way. It's like: I'm so smart and clever! Ha ha! I only like smart jokes! (laughs)./ INT: So would you say you compare yourself with other people?/ SB15: Oh, definitely, all the time: *I wouldn't do this. I am better than this person, because I do that instead. (**SB15**)

In these two fragments, the interviewees talk about posts by ties that are weak enough to be typified almost exclusively according to Facebook posts, rather than becoming meaningful through shared experience. No reference to an underlying tie between the interpreter and the other is mentioned, since the subjects do not need that aspect to explain their understanding of the content. Furthermore, the respondents both confess to drawing a positive emotion from generating a negative typification based on the information they receive. In the case of SB25, she only says that despite being bored by a type of posts, she still enjoys receiving them.

SB15 talks about a similar ambivalence, namely, he states it upsets him when viewing content he classifies as stupid (together with the author of the content), but he also finds it fun. In contrast to what SB25 affirmed, he is also explicit about the reason behind enjoying such typifications, and that reason is self-validation. Thus, seeing posts from other users that are weak ties and that one can typify as stupid, boring, attention seeking, and so on without having to deal with other nuances of their behavior that might indicate anything different helps some of the subjects reaffirm a sense of self-worth. At the same time, if we go back to the fragments discussed at the beginning of the chapter when referring to the attribution of meaning for posts by strong ties, respondents did not use Facebook posts to typify people with whom they had strong bonds, irrespective of their possible disagreements with the contents published. Thus, it is mainly the strength and type of underlying tie between the author of the post and the interpreter that favor one attribution of meaning or another. At the same time, even looking at two comparable weak ties, not all posts from both will be read in the self-validating mode by the overviewer. When the tie is weak enough to allow typifications through Facebook public contents, only then does the nature of those typifications vary according to content itself. And evaluating something as interesting or boring, stupid or clever, and so on (while bracketing tie strength) is not random either. This is a topic I will tackle in more detail in a different section.

To conclude, this chapter has been aiming to shed light over the issue of how meaning is attributed to public posts in relation to tie between the author and the interpreter of the content. I have firstly looked into meaning construction for various strong ties (close friends, romantic partners, and ties overshadowed by conflict) and how the underlying tie favors certain readings of public posts. Then, I have turned to different types of weak ties (old colleagues, new acquaintances, and stagnant weak ties) and analyzed their relations with meaning construction in public posts. Some of the main processes identified were static typifications according to ideal types, attempts at creating an imaginary about the other's lived experience in a dynamic world within reach, panoramic views of life trajectories, projections about tie strength, and lifestyle comparisons.

References

Barbalet, Jack. 1998. *Emotion, Social Theory, and Social Structure: A Macrosociological Approach*. Cambridge: Cambridge University Press.

Baym, Nancy K. 2010. *Personal Connections in the Digital Age*. Cambridge: Polity Press.

Booth, Alan, and Elaine Hess. 1974. Cross-Sex Friendship. *Journal of Marriage and the Family* 36 (1): 38–47.

Chaulk, Kasey, and Tim Jones. 2011. Online Obsessive Relational Intrusion: Further Concerns About Facebook. *Journal of Family Violence* 26 (4): 245–254.

Cooley, Charles. 1964. *Human Nature and the Social Order*. New York: Schocken Books.

Ellison, Nicole B., Rebecca Gray, Cliff Lampe, and Andrew T. Fiore. 2014. Social Capital and Resource Requests on Facebook. *New Media & Society* 16 (7): 1104–1121.

Ellison, Nicole B., Rebecca Heino, and Jennifer Gibbs. 2006. Managing Impressions Online: Self-Presentation Processes in the Online Dating Environment. *Journal of Computer-Mediated Communication* 11 (2): 415–441.

Felmlee, Diane, et al. 2012. Gender Rules: Same- and Cross-Gender Friendships Norms. *Sex Roles* 66 (7–8): 518–529.

Hiller, Harry H., and Tara M. Franz. 2004. New Ties, Old Ties and Lost Ties: The Use of the Internet in Diaspora. *New Media & Society* 6 (6): 731–752.

Lyndon, A., J. Bonds-Raacke, and A. Crattty. 2011. College Students' Facebook Stalking of Ex-partners. *Cyberpsychology, Behavior and Social Networking* 14 (12): 711–716.

Marshall, Tara C. 2012. Facebook Surveillance of Former Romantic Partners: Associations with PostBreakup Recovery and Personal Growth. *CyberPsychology, Behavior & Social Networking* 15 (10): 521–526.

McKenna, K.Y.A., et al. 2002. Relationship Formation on the Internet: What's the Big Attraction? *Journal of Social Issues* 56 (1): 9–31.

O'Meara, Donald. 1989. Cross-sex Friendship: Four Basic Challenges of an Ignored Relationship. *Sex Roles* 21 (7–8): 525–543.

Parsons, Talcott. 1951. *The Social System*. London: Routledge.

Rosenfeld, Michael J., and Reuben J. Thomas. 2012. Searching for a Mate: The Rise of the Internet as a Social Intermediary. *American Sociological Review* 77 (4): 523–547.

Werking, Kathy. 1997. *We're Just Good Friends: Women and Men in Nonromantic Relationships*. New York: The Guilford Press.

West, Anne, Jane Lewis, and Peter Currie. 2009. Students' Facebook 'Friends': Public and Private Spheres. *Journal of Youth Studies* 12 (6): 615–627.

Young, Alyson Leigh, and Anabel Quan-Hasse. 2013. Privacy Protection Strategies on Facebook. The Internet Privacy Paradox Revisited. *Information, Communication & Society* 16 (4): 479–500.

5

Meaning Construction in Online Social Interactions

In Chap. 2, I have discussed the condition under which I will consider an exchange of reciprocal actions and effects to be a social interaction. Namely, social interactions were those reciprocal actions and effects characterized by (1) a dimension of consciousness, (2) where the interacting subjects took each other for granted as meaning makers and (3) in which the actions were directed at one another or interpreted as such. In the context of research about exchanges of information occurring on Facebook, I believe the third point in this conceptualization is the most challenging, since the observable indicators for directionality are fewer than face to face (or, in some cases, they are missing entirely). In the previous chapter I have explored those exchanges of information that unfold in an undirected (and thus non-interactional) manner. Yet, there are a set of options available to establish directionality and social interaction in exchanges on Facebook. The most obvious is sending someone a message on the chatting option, where the receiver has to be selected from a list of contacts. I have referred to these situations as private social interactions. At the same time, there is the category of public social interactions. They consist of feedback to public posts (not only comments but also likes and shares), as well as posts on another user's timeline and tags and indirect

© The Author(s) 2018
G.-I. Ivana, *Social Ties in Online Networking*, Palgrave Studies in
Relational Sociology, https://doi.org/10.1007/978-3-319-71595-7_5

references to shared experiences (i.e. jokes with subtext), where the intention of the author of the post is for the one who is addressed to interpret the post as an interaction.

The aim of the current chapter is to shed light on the meaning construction of contents exchanged in interactions, while keeping in mind the underlying tie between the interactors. Firstly, I will look into public interactions unfolding between users who are bond by strong ties and weak ties, respectively. Secondly, I will turn to private interactions, also focusing separately on social interactions between strong and weak ties. What needs to be said from the beginning is that strong and weak ties on the one hand and the decision for privacy and publicness of an interaction on the other are strongly linked. At the same time, it is important to keep in mind that especially in the case of interactions constructed around public posts, the meaning constructions discussed in the chapter before still apply. They are not replaced, but complemented with new meanings and new shared contents as an interaction begins.

Strong Ties and Public Interactions

Entitlement to Interact

There are many ways in which strong ties correlate with public interactions on Facebook, but I will start this discussion with perhaps one of the most common and generalized affirmations made by interviewees. It refers to giving feedback on public posts. Below, there are two examples:

> INT: But do you ever like or comment on other people's posts?/ SB25: Only if they are very close friends, who I feel I am on good grounds with, who I talk daily with, yes, I give them a like, post a monkey that smiles or something. (**SB25**—translated from Romanian)
> I think that if they posted something interesting, for example an article or something, I would go and read it and I would get the point even if I don t comment, but if it's a friend, I go and say "Hey, this is great!" and the comment is not really important, it would just be a way of saying that I read it and share something with your friends that I wouldn't share with

everybody. I wouldn't do that with someone I don't know that well, even if I would still get the same from that post. (**SB34**)

These are only two fragments illustrating the connection between the strength of the tie and the public interactions, but all of the interviewees have confirmed the same consideration given to the bond they have with the other before initiating a public interaction. There are many elements involved in this relation between the construction of the interaction and the underlying tie by which it is framed, but one of the central ones is the idea of entitlement. Let us go back to the discussion in the previous chapter about the (non-interactional) exchanges that occur in viewing and attributing meaning to a public post by someone from the subject's network of contacts. As I have showed then, despite the lack of explicit addressability for the contents posted, the interviewees typically interpret those contents as being for someone. Moreover, that someone is assumed to be a person (or a group of people) who are in a close bond with the author of the post. That is why the idea of clandestinity appeared when the subjects looked on the profile or the contents posted by someone who they imagined would not expect them to look because of the weak tie. Conversely, in the cases where the tie is strong, the subject feels he/she is one of those addressed, or at least one of those with whom the author of the content would not mind sharing that content. Both of the interviewees above explain this very clearly. They would initiate an interaction because they feel if would not be against their own or the other's understanding of the strength of the tie if they did so. SB25 explains that if the author is someone very close, to whom she talks daily, she would feel it would not be inappropriate if she commented on his/her post. SB34 even makes a parallel between very similar contents posted by two people with whom she has ties of different strengths. If the tie is weak, she would not say anything, even if the content impressed her in some way. Yet, when the tie is stronger, she would. Although, as we have seen in the chapter before, information about weak ties is often acquired and interpreted on Facebook, an interaction is a way of acknowledging that practice which is, although very common, regarded as transgressing boundaries previously established for that bond. One of the interviewees explains how she feels about receiving comments from contacts with whom she has a very weak tie:

There are people who do this (note: comment on posts despite not being close to the author of the post), and it also happens to me, and that is really really annoying, because there is no connection, they just come out of nowhere. (**SB1**)

My problem is, I don't know how it is for the others, but I've got friends who love to comment. So even if they don't get it, they will comment and probably their comments would do more harm than good. (**SB4**)

I am using these quotations about weak bonds here (despite the fact that this is a section about public interaction between users who have a strong tie) to illustrate the type of situation that the interviewees above wish to avoid when saying they would only comment if they thought the tie was strong enough. Furthermore, they show why the feeling of entitlement is so important in initiating a public interaction on Facebook. As the users above highlight, the publicness does not mean all feedback is welcome. SB1 says she is bothered by users who come out of nowhere despite the lack of connection. So, she is openly bothered by the other's lack of consideration for the strength of the tie when initiating the interaction. In the case of SB4, it is not precisely the tie strength itself that she'd like the others to take into account. She is bothered particularly by those commenting although they did not understand the intended meaning of the post. This indirectly touches upon the same tie strength, because the ones who are likely to "get it" are typically the ones who have enough information to place the post in a contextual setting, which are those strongly bonded with the subject.

However, entitlement also has other forms of manifestation:

For instance, my work colleague… when I have a picture with my sister or something and my sister posts the photo over the weekend, on Monday my work colleague tells me I already know what you did this weekend. I saw it on Facebook, because your sister posts it all. But it's true that sometimes you just don't know how someone found something out, but they say you posted it on Facebook and someone else saw it and it just went from mouth to mouth from there. (**SB19**—translated from Spanish)

Here, the work colleague is a close enough tie of the subject's and she feels she is entitled to receive the information she is receiving through

Facebook. If it was not for that post, she assumes she would have gained access to that information anyway in an alternative way (the interviewee would tell her about how she spent last weekend on Monday). Thus, in the colleague's understanding, she can be open about having seen that information and about having paid attention to it.

The axis of entitlement and clandestinity is also very interesting from a different angle. I will begin with an interview fragment and discuss it afterwards:

> So, if I had 10 Facebook profiles with 10 people in each of them, it would be a lot easier. The audience is too mixed for me. There are some options for creating groups and I guess I could do that, but I never bothered to. (**SB9**)

This incompatibility between different areas of her social life that the interviewee is talking about is avoidable by the organization of Facebook contacts in certain groups, but that is an option most of the respondents have considered too laborious to understand and to use. However, the resulting space reunites individuals with various expectations and processes of meaning attributions, hence the awareness of some of the users about the difficulty of posting something that would be compatible with all of them. The solution for many of them is to focus certain groups of contacts with which they wish to interact or whose impression they are actively attempting to manage:

> I support gay marriage because I have a few gay friends, I think it is morally correct, whatever (...) If my group of friends doesn't have a problem with that, but people that I am not so close to would be offended, I don't care. It's fine. (**SB15**)

Coming back to the theme of feedback and entitlement, overviewers are also Facebook users, so they already have an understanding of the interactional space in which they are functioning. They already know about the collapsing of contacts coming from different areas of one's life and different tie strengths, so they construct the interactions in a way that mimics the divisions functioning outside of Facebook. That is the reason why, often times, the publicness of the post is not immediately interpreted as entitlement to like or comment, irrespective of who you might be in relation to the author of the post, and that is also why, despite the accessibility of information, the sense of clandestinity persists in monitoring especially weak ties.

Institutionalization of Interaction Habits

Furthermore, users who have a strong tie with each other do not only interpret posts on Facebook as possibilities for interaction, but some see it as obligations for interaction.

> I feel obliged to like all the pictures and posts of my best friend, or at least the pictures, not necessarily the posts, because maybe I won't look at the videos or other things she posts all the time, but the pictures, I like them all, because if I, her closest friend, didn't appreciate her, who else should? And she does the same for me. It sounds very very stupid... But if I go somewhere and I have just posted a picture, if not even your mom and your best friend like it, it sucks! (**SB7**—translated from Romanian)

Here, the subject explains she views giving feedback to her closest friends as a behavior that shows her support and proves her commitment. It is something a friend "should do". As discussed before, different tie strengths are constructed, negotiated, and synchronized in social interaction. Various behaviors are enacted by one person and read by the other participant to the interaction as indicators of different strengths of ties and different types of ties. After the tie gains stability and it is assumed to be mutually shared (i.e. we are friends), that meaning construction which is to an important extent based on one's own past experience (like other ties regarded as friendships) brings with it a set of expectations about how future interactions should unfold. This solidification of the tie can also be seen as a process of institutionalization of social interaction (Berger and Luckman 1966). Yet, irrespective of how we theorize it, it results in a clear association between certain tie strengths and certain interactions. While many of these associations are applied from face-to-face interactions on Facebook (i.e. if you are a good friend, you will not try to embarrass me in public), others are specific institutionalizations developed with the options available on Facebook. In the case of SB7, the habit of liking everything that her best friend posts publicly has become institutionalized. At the same time, that institutionalization arises from and is incorporated into the previous understanding of a set of other institutionalized habits that are framed by friendship.

Another example of institutionalization of Facebook public interactions is the hierarchy of feedbacks in relation to the strength of the tie. This is another issue on which almost all interviewees agreed.

> With the like I am more flexible. It still has to be someone who is a little bit closer. If it's just an acquaintance, even if they post something that is really interesting, I might be feeling uncomfortable. But if it's a bit closer, I might like it and if it's even closer, I might comment. (**SB15**)
>
> If it's people that are not part of my daily life, but they post something that I enjoy and let's say I want to, not give my approval, because they don't need my approval for anything, but send a positive vibe, well maybe a like is enough, because otherwise you might be participating in conversations that are not yours. (**SB11**)

These two fragments come to support the argument above about the institutionalization of certain habits. Just as SB7 saw it as a rule that you like everything your best friend does, SB11 and SB15 see it as a rule that you may like posts from weak ties, but you should only comment on posts from stronger ties. I believe one important reason for the development of this hierarchy of feedbacks is their different nature. On the one hand, "a like" is a trigger for an interaction because it addresses to the other certain information (however limited): I have seen what you shared and I enjoy it/agree with it/encourage it. It also says: I feel the strength of our underlying tie entitles me to communicate that to you. However, due to the standardization of this action (the content of the feedback is that and none other), it is too little to construct a full-blown shared lived experience unfolding in a common here and now. A comment, on the other hand, does not convey a predetermined message and thus implies a bit more access to the experience of the commenter by the author of the original post. The more elaborated the comment, the more it becomes part of a lived episode of interaction, because the interactors are experiencing each other through their words. That is why, in the examples above, in order for the commenter to feel comfortable with generating a common here and now in which him/her and the other would have a shared experience, they have to be strongly bonded. Yet, this is not always the case.

The Issue of Contents

Some of the interviewees have not linked commenting with tie strength or with any particular frame of interpretation in terms of the underlying tie, but focused mainly on the interaction as shared experience:

> I don't actually care if someone likes my comments, likes my posts or shares the things that I post. I only care if they comment, because than there is a conversation going on and of course I am paying attention to what they say. (**SB6**)

Here, the respondent points out that what he values most is if his posts are commented upon and that debates are born on the basis of the content he shared. Nonetheless, I believe his different approach from the ones of the other respondents who emphasized the importance of the bond they had with the commenter lies also in the type of content generating the interaction. If the content is not read as having been shared with ties of certain strength, the issue of entitlement loses its weight. For instance, in the case of the SB19, who was talking about her work colleague who tells her she saw what she did over the weekend, sharing that information and admitting to having acquired it are behaviors associated to certain tie strength. Contrastingly, publishing an article about the mistakes of the government is not an action indicating a particular level of bond, so even those who are not close to the author of the post might feel invited to intervene. SB1 explains this through her own experience:

> No, I am bothered only if a post is addressed let's say not to one single person but let's say to five persons. Then, if the person is not one of those five, than yes (laughs). But if it's general, like the Marx insulter (note: she

had had a recent post with a link that generated Marxist insults), that is not personal, so everybody can like it but I do expect that only persons who like Marx will like it. (**SB1**)

So, although she has a projection about the future feedback based on her previous stock of knowledge about her contacts, SB1 brackets the strength of the tie when she does not interpret the content she posted as personal.

In other words, the institutionalization of feedback stems from the institutionalization of particular behaviors in relation to the normativity of informal bonds. Thus, certain types of ties and certain levels of closeness will allow for certain sets of behaviors to be considered acceptable. What users have talked about with respect to Facebook public feedback has pointed out the same institutionalization of particular behaviors in relation to particular ties expands to the online environment. Thus, as there is a social convention of talking about the weather with weak ties, there is a social convention of liking, but refraining from commenting on their posts. Of course, the more personal the content being shared, the more important bond normativity becomes in moderating the behavior.

Understandings and Uses of the Publicness of the Interaction

On a related note, another respondent affirms:

> I think I like if people also like the post. I think it's a normal reaction, I don't think there is a difference between the online and the offline. It's the same thing. If you say something and people are interested and that creates a debate, it's always a good social reward to you. (**SB13**)

This person is also interested in creating conversation, but from a different point of view than the respondent above. If SB6 saw it as an opportunity for interaction to be experienced, SB13 sees it as an opportunity to validate himself socially, because we must keep in mind that all these interactions are public. They are accessible to others in the network and despite there being situations where the interactions spontaneously emerge in a public setting, there are also cases where there is a rationale behind them unfolding there. For instance, even in the above-discussed idea of entitlement, which seems to only refer to the existing tie between the one who posts a comment and the one who is addressed by it, the dimension of publicness has an impact:

> If I trust the person, I will wish them happy birthday publicly. If I don't, I'll send them a private message. I do this when we have less friends in common, because the public posts I believe are more for their circle and it would just seem like an unknown person appeared. Also on my own wall, it is forbidden for people to post. I only lift the restriction on the 3rd of November and on the 4th I close it again. (**SB33**—translated from Spanish)

Here, the subject is not only worried about how his action will be read by the person to whom it is addressed but also about how it would look for others who have access to it, namely, the friends of the addressee. He assumes the receiver has a group of close friends who will notice his presence there through birthday wishes and expects them to interpret it as a lack of understanding of the norms on his part. I find this fragment particularly interesting because it refers to an interaction that in most social contexts is not limited to strong ties. If one's birthday is today, any person who interacts with them and is aware of it might say "happy birthday!", irrespective of our tie or who else witnesses it. Nevertheless, as previously discussed, Facebook is a space constructed by the users through the contents they share and the interactions in which they engage (on the foundation of certain available possibilities). In this case, the respondent highlights the fact that he interprets public profiles of other users as a space of interaction for the owner's close ties. Thus, it does not matter the reason for posting, he still feels he is intruding and he is not entitled to be there.

The reverse side of this increased awareness of the public character of interactions occurring on one's wall is using them to publicly convey certain messages. Like SB13 above who interpreted feedback on his posts as a social reward, other respondents also read public social interactions in terms of constructing or reaffirming themselves socially. Some of the subjects affirm:

My friends tell me "oh, you didn't even like my picture. Come on!" and then I go and like their picture (laughs). Yeah, that is concrete pressure. But that is only with very close friends. Otherwise, no, I don't think I do (note: feel pressure). (**SB3**) Look, the last like I gave was for someone from my village, because they gave me 4 messages give me a like, give me a like, so I liked it. (**SB33**—translated from Spanish)

This quotation shows public feedback from close ties as a way of granting face to one's friend. The concept of face is defined by Goffman (1967) as it follows: "The term face may be defined as the positive social value a person effectively claims for himself by the line others assume he has taken during a particular contact. Face is an image of self-delineated in terms of approved social attributes-albeit an image that others may share, as when a person makes a good showing for his profession or religion by making a good showing for himself". According to the *Oxford Dictionary*, in English, the word "face" was initially employed among the English-speaking community in China, and it referred to the ways in which Chinese people behaved to avoid shame or disgrace. Moreover, it is still an important element in Chinese society. Going further, Goffman (1967) examines the theme of face work, which he believes to be a ritualized process, often referred to as tact, savoir-faire, diplomacy, or social skill. He states: "By face-work I mean to designate the actions taken by a person to make whatever he is doing consistent with face. Face-work serves to counteract 'incidents'—that is, events whose effective symbolic implications threaten face" (Goffman 1967, p. 12).

The events SB33 is describing in relation to his close ties corresponds to this conceptualization, with the amendment that in the interaction the interviewee is referring to, the author and the beneficiary of face work are not the same person. For this reason, rather than using face work, I prefer the expression "granting face". This practice could also explain the resorts behind the institutionalization of the habit of liking all the posts of one's best friend that SB7 was talking about above. In both these cases, the public interaction does not lead to any flow of experience because the participants are not even oriented towards each other, but, like in a play, constantly have in mind the audience. Unless the meanings others attribute to a post or an interaction were at stake, SB33's friend would have no other reason to ask him to give feedback to her public posts. The meaning the spectators construct for such interactions in which they are never immersed can only be an approximation based on an ideal type.

In this sense, just as public posts can be analyzed as attempts of constructing an imaginary about the separate world outside of reach of those who are at a distance, so that they can be read according to it afterwards, public interactions can also be interpreted as concerted attempts by the author of a post and his/her close ties to construct a similar imaginary. In public interactions, there are added elements of context for weak ties to typify (because strong ties might know the background plot or, even if they do not, they will already have an impression about the author). And these interactions function as a coordinated effort of face building for one or several of those who participate in them. Furthermore, they are indeed used in the construction of meaning by some of the interviewees:

> For instance, when you look at the pictures, you also notice the friends the person has, how many likes they got, because if they have many, it's like what they are saying is important and they have this popularity and I like this more than someone who posts something and nobody says anything about it. Of course, if a person adds more friends, more people will see what they do and they'll get more feedback, but I also think it has something to do with their popularity in their social life. (**SB19**—translated from Spanish)

This is an example of a weak tie overviewing and typifying the others according to the information she acquires from public posts and the feedback received for them. At the same time, as the interview fragments above show, typifications coming from the category of weak ties were the actual aim of many of these interactions, so as marginal as she may appear as a profile overviewer, SB19 might actually play an important part in the interaction as an observer with typifying power.

Previous Shared Experiences and the Unfolding of New Interactions

There are, however, instances where the subjects depict public interactions with strong ties within a different logic. One example in this sense is the use of inside jokes or specific references to past common experiences. An interviewee says: "I am a sportsman, so I might post things related to my sport, or something addressed only to those who are in the same team as me, some inside jokes. For instance, there was an inside joke about a song, and I posted a comment exactly with that joke" (**SB32**—translated from Romanian). Later on he talks about a different type of complicity, but from the perspective of the observer: "Sometimes you see two people who broke up and you have both of them in your list. You see them sending subliminal messages, usually songs. I think they Google it: I wonder if there's a song saying what I want to say now (laughs). It happens often, you can't miss it, really" (**SB32**—translated from Romanian).

These are cases of public interactions between strong ties, in which the participants to the interaction are not formally addressing each other, but which are paradoxically to a greater extent aimed at communicating with each other than most of the open interactions analyzed above.

In the first quotation, the subject talks about the issue of inside jokes, in which other respondents also admitted to have gotten involved. Since most of these instances (starting with the one quoted here) happen in public interactions, I believe besides the emphasis on the strength of the tie, these episodes also have an expositional component. Namely, inside jokes function as a mechanism creating a delimitation between the insiders and the outsiders. Those who are part of the subject's sports team, with whom he shared an amusing first-hand experience are told that that shared experience represents a ground on which he relates to them, thus emphasizing the strength of the tie. Furthermore, the lack of access of others to the initial experience or to the commonly shared meaning makes the ones who do understand it a privileged few and shows those who do not understand it parts of his experience while he was not in the same here and now as them.

In the second fragment, the one about the couple who broke up, the dynamics of the interaction are different. In contrast to the case of inside jokes where the aim was for those addressed to interpret the content as it was intended, in the interaction of the couple, the intention in relation to the other's interpretation is ambivalent. On the one hand, each of the interactants has a message to send and hopes the other will understand it as it was meant originally. On the other hand, they had rather communicate it in an ambiguous form (a song), so that they can avoid acknowledging the interaction. Here, the same uncertain directionality is purposefully employed to actually cultivate ambivalence. Another interviewee says:

> It so happens that we are fighting right now. I mean we had a fight and I got mad and I want to ignore him and now he keeps posting stuff on Facebook (…) I feel they are for me, I know it. Even yesterday he checked in a bar, which he never does. I sent him a message saying "Don't wait, because I am not coming". And he answered "Yeah, I was kind of thinking about that". So I was right! (**SB7**—translated from Romanian)

Also, unlike in the case of inside jokes where the addressee should know the message is aimed at him/her and the publicness is used only for creating the distinction between the inside and the outside, here the publicness is masking the direction. If we are to imagine in the inside joke besides the content, the author also writes the name of the friend he/she is addressing, that makes the intention more explicit, but does not change much in the nature of the interaction. Yet, in these examples of romantic tensions, tagging the one who is addressed would undermine the purpose of the entire post. So, the public character is here a camouflage, with no emphasis being paid to the construction of meaning by those who are witnessing the exchange. In other words, the publicness is used as a mask for what is a very targeted and private message, while in the case of the shared jokes, the public character was a means for delimiting the insider and outsider status.

What is unifying these cases is the accessibility of contents to large groups of people, and the existence of clear reciprocal directedness, and, inherently, social interaction. In this subchapter, I have discussed interactions by touching upon entitlement based on tie strength, institutionalization of certain habits, granting face for strong ties, and implicit, allusive messages based on previous experience. All of them are, in one way or another, filtered through reflection. None of the users mention getting carried away, engaging in a spontaneous interaction, and sharing an experience with people with whom they otherwise feel strongly connected. There is no immersion in a flow of a common here and now.

Weak Ties and Public Interactions

As some of the interview excerpts in the section on public interactions between strong ties show, the same type of interactions rarely appears between weaker ties. Most of the users stated they are reluctant in establishing public interactions with users with whom they do not feel strongly bonded. Above, I have explored the issues of entitlement, previous shared experience on which new interactions develop, and collaborative effort of strong ties to construct an imaginary for weaker ties. The lack of all these mechanisms means direct interactions with weak ties on Facebook public posts are rather improbable. There are, however, exceptions. One of them is the action of liking posts even for weak ties. Although most interviewees mentioned the strength of the tie as a central factor in initiating an interaction, and they associated different tie strengths with different feedbacks, the threshold on which they give themselves a green light to interact one way or another is different. And as they have affirmed, a comment is typically regarded as an appropriate interaction for a strong tie, whereas a like is the perceived lowest form of interacting. So, in this subchapter, the focus will fall mostly on meanings of likes, but other public interactions between weak ties will be analyzed to the extent to which respondents talk about them.

One of the main aspects that need to be acknowledged in relation to exchanges between weak ties is the institutionalization of interaction habits, which is perhaps more frequent and pronounced than in public interactions with strong ties.

> Sometimes I like things just to be polite. I always like it when someone posts a picture or an album of their kid or from their graduation, their wedding or something that I think is important for them, even if I am not impressed necessarily. Now if they keep posting things about it, I won't like if every time, but still… Then, I sometimes wait for something nice enough to like in the posts of others, just because they always like my things or because I want to maintain a relationship with them. (**SB26**)

In this example, the subject talks about the meaning she attributes to her likes for public posts by weak ties and what she intends to communicate by the action of liking. On the one hand, there is the issue to which she refers as politeness and which is a form of institutionalization (Berger and Luckman 1966, pp. 74–75). In the interaction posting/liking posts related to important life events irrespective of tie strength with the author, the part each participant plays has become habitualized and has begun being reciprocally typified, just as the participants themselves are reciprocally typified as well. Moreover, it is interesting to notice the level of generality and the pervasiveness of this institutionalized habit, since observation of Facebook pages has shown that posts with this type of content are constantly the ones receiving most feedback.

Another topic the interviewee above touches upon is the use of feedback for maintaining certain ties at certain levels of strength. This shows that the connection between tie strength and its indicators in interaction is not unidirectional. While the strength of the tie has an important impact on decisions related to interactions (online as much as offline), the users are also aware of the fact that the other will calibrate his/her understanding of tie strength according to indicators taken from the interaction. Thus, from this perspective, interactions become a tool in the negotiation of the strength of the tie. In support of this idea, another respondent tells the following story:

> It's related to girlfriends (laughs) with whom I had a good relationship and then sometimes I think maybe once in 3 months, I remember her and I go to her wall and take a look, I like some of their pictures or whatever. They do the same. It's interesting because it's kind of a let's say, online Facebook relationship. These people, or some of them, are now living abroad and it's a way of still getting in touch with them without having the necessity of sending them a message or to get into their lives again. (**SB13**)

In this case, the respondent decided on a very precise level of closeness with the other: he wants to communicate that he still feels bonded to her, despite their breakup and despite the geographical distance. At the same time, he feels sending them a message and initiating a full-blown interaction would be a way of entering their lives again, or, in other words, it would indicate a level of closeness or desired closeness on his side that he does not want to convey. So, the action of giving a like in itself, no matter for what content, is invested with the whole meaning related to the strength of the current tie from the perspective of the interviewee. In a similar vein, another user states:

> INT: But when you have a romantic interest in someone, do you check their profiles more?/ SB19: Yes! Absolutely! You go on his profile more often; you are more attentive to what he posts and maybe give them more likes. (**SB19**—translated from Spanish)

Here, the dimension of negotiation of tie strength through the action of giving feedback is also present. However, the tie SB19 has with her romantic interest might be weak in the moment when the interaction is initiated, but it is projected to become strong. So, she interprets giving more likes as a way of indicating her intended narrative about that tie. As standardized or simplifying as this explanation might sound, the actual negotiation of tie strength, as well as the level of disclosure of one's hopes, desires, projections, is very carefully nuanced, especially when an important tie is at stake.

> Well, there is a friend of mine who met a guy on Facebook and they lived in different countries and she somehow believed that he was the love of her life and that she had to meet him. I don't even know how they ended up being friends, but she started commenting on his photos and he didn't say anything for a while and she started regretting it and saying she made a fool of herself, that she shouldn't have done that, yeah. (…) He commented something back at some point and she got really excited about it and commented again more than she later thought she shouldn't have. It was like a circle. (**SB3**)

The girl from the story commented on the pictures posted by someone for whom she had a romantic interest, in order to signal her intention of strengthening the tie. She is acting mainly according to her own desired closeness, but also on the evaluation of the actual closeness, which is very strongly based on the imaginary about the other's view. When the man with whom she had been trying to strengthen the connection does not answer, she reads that as an ideal weak tie on his part and a misevaluation on hers. Moreover, she is feeling exposed and embarrassed by this asymmetry in desires between herself and the other.

General Public Debates

General debates are a theme I have briefly approached when talking about public interactions between strong ties. Then I have emphasized that the publication of certain contents, particularly less personally charged ones, minimizes the role of tie strength in the decision of engaging in a debate. When the information posted is, for instance, a newspaper article, which already had public status and was accessible to anyone, the other users do not feel like they learned about a content that was not meant for them and they would have never known about it if it were not for that context. So, in this section, I will focus on users' depictions of public interactions in situations where the strength of the tie was not mentioned as an element in the construction of meaning. Although this is not a very frequent occurrence, the interviewees who did approach the theme of public debates had a very well-defined attitude in relation to them:

> Once, I posted something that I knew would be controversial. I come from a Muslim family, but I am not religious and once I posted an article that I liked. It was something like 10 reasons why you shouldn't be religious. I knew my sister, who is very, very religious, would be offended by it and have a reaction. And she did. But we started talking and in the end we had a great conversation about it. It took me around 20 minutes only to write one reply and we had many, I think put together it would have been a conversation for 3 or 4 hours, but on Facebook we wrote every day and it lasted about a week. It was public, under my original post. But I think we could have never had that conversation face to face. Because on Facebook you had the time to read everything she wrote, think of every argument, say I agree with this, I don't agree with that, think about what you want to say. Face to face we probably would have said a few sentences, disagreed, gotten angry and that would have been it. (**SB2**)

In this quotation, the interviewee mentions that his debate was with his sister, but he does not refer to the strength of their tie in particular. Instead, his focus is on the unfolding of the actual debate. One of the interesting affirmations to keep in mind from this fragment is *It took me around 20 minutes only to write one reply*. The reason why this sentence is important is its relation to the subject's lived experience and his here and now. If we are to imagine for a moment a person involved in a heated debate, it seems very improbable that they would later describe it in terms of conventionally measured temporality. Using again Bergson's (1910) distinction between time-space world and durée, this sentence displays an anchoring in time-space world, whereas immersion in the experience of debating with someone face to face could unfold only in durée. At the same time, one could say, following Schütz (1976), that while the experience could have been lived in durée, the subsequent typifications and filtering through reflexivity are the reasons why this representation of the story is made from the standpoint of a time-space world. Yet, the latter explanation about the ways in which the experience in itself had been different from a face-to-face debate leaves less room for alternative interpretations. The subject explains the reflection on the other's words that went into his every reply and that would have not been employed face to face. The fact that they would have gotten angry would be precisely that common experience of the other and with the other in the same world within reach, an experience in which the reflective processes would be latent and the living of togetherness in durée would remain the main focus of the interactant. In elaborating on this issue, the respondent adds:

> Like in a conversation you might end up saying contradictory things, maybe someone convinces you of part of what they are saying, but if you do that on Facebook, people point out to you that you re contradicting yourself. (…) Like when you are talking to someone and you say something is true and they say the opposite and they just take out they phone and start to look it up on the Internet to see who is right. That really annoys me. I don't care who is right. We were having a conversation here. (**SB2**)

This quotation emphasizes the previous point about lack of flow, on the one hand, and increased reflectivity, on the other, that the subject has noticed in Facebook public debates. For instance, the problem of contradicting oneself in the course of a conversation is typical of the now where, as Schütz (1970) was saying, the subject cannot experience him/herself. That can only happen in *modo preterito*, when stepping out of the now and turning one's attention towards just now. Then, the example about someone taking out their phone and searching for certain information might seem out of context, but it refers to the same type of break in the flow of experience of the interaction.

One of the main factors influencing this issue is, of course, spatial, but particularly temporal distance. As the interviewee points out, the conversation did not take place at the same pace as a face-to-face debate, but spread over a week, which means the interaction was asynchronous. As a result, in order to post each reply, the user has to construct an imaginary of the copresence with the other and write what they would say. However, in doing so, he also gets the opportunity to break himself out of that imagined flow and reflect on how it would look, how the other would interpret it, would one word be too strong. For this reason, I argue that not even in the moment of maximum immersion in the interaction, when writing his contribution to the conversation, the user is still not experiencing an undisrupted flow. What remains is an addressed exchange of information which is reflected upon and which can lead to particular evaluations and reflections, be they of the other subject or of exterior attributes and situations.

Another respondent talks about public debates from a different perspective:

> I think the debates on Facebook can get too intense, because people can just go and say a lot of shit because they wouldn't meet each other, it's not the same as being face to face. You can just say whatever you want and it wouldn't have any consequence, or it would but I discovered that some people are limitless on Facebook. They would just go and write anything. I remember this story about a man who was leaving from a Latin American country and wanted to go and find a better life. He fell from a boat and died. It was a horrible story and I remember a woman commenting something like "Yes, one less of these emigrants." It was really heartless and it's the sort of thing I am not sure she could have said it in a public space, face to face with other people. (…) I would be interested in meeting this person, but I would go with a lot of prejudice about her from the start. (**SB34**)

Although the main topic here is not the strength of the tie, the fact that in this case, unlike in the one above, the respondent is referring to public debates between users who are not bonded in any way whatsoever remains relevant. Namely, this lack of a tie means that any typification the other would have based on an interaction would not contribute to a particular existent impression about them. In colloquial terms, there are no concerns about the other changing his/her opinion or how that would affect their relationship, because there is no opinion to change and no relationship to be affected. Moreover, the author of the comments is not confronted with many of the consequences of the new impressions that emerge from interactions in other contexts (not even the discomfort of being looked upon with disapproval). Indeed, this configuration of social interactions, where the impressions constructed by others have no impact on an individual who is part of an interaction, encourages certain liberties. At the same time, the respondent quoted above does not take into account the access of that person's contacts to her comments in public debates. This can result in a reshaping of the existing/potential tie by the overviewers who are part of her life, without her awareness. Thus, the evaluative dimension may be present even in the most tieless public debates, as what one writes publicly is available for those with whom that person is connected.

At the same time, when analyzing this quotation, I have insisted upon evaluations, whereas in the previous, I focused mainly on the discrepancy between lived and reflected-upon experience. The reason for this shift is the respondent's perspective regarding the debate. If the former subject was referring to a public interaction to which he had participated with his sister and representing to me his experience of that episode, the latter talks about an interaction she witnessed as an observer and thus had no access to the lived experience of the interactors. However, she had a reflective stance and made sense of the others based on it, which is just as important, given the publicness of the interaction.

Private Interactions

Up to now, I have examined meaning construction within ties on the basis of public contents in (1) non-interactional exchanges and (2) social interactions, respectively, but we must not forget that (3) interactions also occur in private settings. By this, I am referring to Facebook chatting, the option of selecting one or more people from one's contact list and sending them messages to which others do not have access. As discussed in the beginning of Chap. 3, these interactions are visually organized in a way that does not establish a different status for the initiator than the other participants and, thus, do not have a host. They are constructed, from this point of view, as a common space for the interactors. Nevertheless, the ways in which it is experienced by the users are not unproblematically derived from that architecture:

> I don't know. I just don't like Facebook chat. I just go on Facebook if I want to see something, have some news about my friends or related to the events or groups that I've created, so see where I am supposed to go, but personally I don't like to speak through this chat and to get in touch with my friends using this chat. (**SB13**)
>
> Chat, the private chat, the little window, I was using that, but not anymore. I don't know why. Maybe I don't have the time, because scrolling down is just a couple of minutes, maybe 5 minutes, but keeping up a conversation with some friend, you need some time to do that. The thing is that when I get home, I am too tired and I don't want to open the computer again. Now I check my Facebook page a couple of minutes on the iPad, but I don't chat. (**SB10**)

The quotation from SB13 is consistent with the above-discussed words of SB2, who was noticing the lack of flow in Facebook public debates. Although this subject does not explicitly refer to this problem, he mentions the most common ways in which he uses Facebook and none of them include an experience of lived durée with and of the others. He goes there to know of his friends, but not to experience something with them. And it is this understanding of Facebook that is incompatible with chatting, where the aim is constructing a moment of togetherness.

The second fragment, coming from SB10, underlines another dimension of the experience of interacting privately on Facebook. Namely, the previous commitment it requires. The subject explains she used to chat, so, unlike SB13 above, she does not perceive an incompatibility between these conditions and experiencing an interaction with the other in lived durée. However, she refers to the interaction in terms of objective time, because of the previous reflection it requires. In interactions occurring in the same here and now, the unfolding of different situations in different contexts often leads to interactions without the thought of interaction having been contemplated in advance. In order to initiate a Facebook private interaction, the subject has to reflect upon the idea of spending a given amount of time interacting with the other and he/she has to decide for doing that. It is an interaction into which subjects cannot get carried away. Once it has been initiated, the interactors may become immersed in a common here and now, but it is a here and now in which they must engage willingly and deliberately. Having said this, I will now move into the particularities of private interactions, taking into account the strength of the underlying tie between the interactors.

Strong Ties and Private Interactions

As the theory of the niche (Dimmick 2003) highlights, different interpersonal media compete to become the preferred means of communicating. Furthermore, as Dimmick et al. (2011) would point out, these niches are associated with particular tie strengths (e.g. close bonds—cell phone use, e-mails—all types of bonds except significant others, etc.). In this case, the niche effect is not only noticeable on different social networking platforms but in different functions of the same network. Namely, the chatting option constitutes a niche, typically correlated with particular bonds.

Not many of the respondents declared they used Facebook in engaging in private interactions. Nevertheless, those who did mentioned, just like in the case of public interactions, that the strength of the tie they have with the other is one of the main factors influencing their chatting habits. To illustrate, let us look at an example:

> I would probably chat with the people I am interested in getting in contact with. It would mostly be people around me. Like when I am in city A., I would mostly chat with the people that I am going to meet or just met, but, yeah, right now I realize that the people I chat with on Facebook are my real friends and my close friends, so… Also, if you don't know the person that well, it's weird to go and say "hey, what's up?". People I know well, I could chat with them for half an hour and just have fun. (**SB34**)

The interviewee points out that she is more likely to chat with the people she meets often. I believe that has two explanations. On the one hand, the constant interaction favors a strengthening of the tie, which, in turn, results in a similar entitlement as in public interactions. On the other hand, the frequent interactions mean the construction of some common experiences, common plots, and common plans and projections for future. Not all of these will be closed when the face-to-face interaction ends. Then, the triggers necessary for the initiation of a private interaction on Facebook chat are more likely to appear. A practical issue about the meeting planned for the next day, curiosity about what happened the night before, after one left the party, some information one knows the other was looking for, and so on can provide incentives for interaction. This solves to a great extent the issue approached above, about the necessity of a previous decision to interact, rather than being in a course of that leads to interaction.

The other aspect the respondent focuses on is the interaction with very close ties, her *real and close friends*. By saying she could *chat with them for half an hour and have fun*, the user confirms that the necessary element for the enjoyment of chatting is immersion in the interaction irrespective of its conditions. This is visible in the mention about the extensive character of the chat and in the representation of that chat as an experience, as "having fun". Last but not least, SB34 refers to the importance of a strong tie for this experience to be initiated. Since these interactions have to be decided upon, starting one without having a previously close tie involves the risk of having the other interpret that as an indicator of a desired strengthening of the current tie. Moreover, because of the scarcity of indicators that are otherwise used in interaction, launching a conversation on Facebook chat with a weak tie can be, in some respects, difficult to handle. In a close tie, even with a lack of other indicators, the other has already made an impression on the subject and new experiences will be lived in light of that impressions: "I am sure he is joking, although I cannot see the expression on his/her face, because this is something he/she always jokes about". Without the familiarity of a close tie, one might get lost in a Facebook conversation, or he/she might get so tangled in the interpretative process that a reflective stance takes over from the lived experience in durée.

Another interviewee also approaches this topic:

I am a heavy chatter. A few years ago I burnt a soup (yes, you can burn a soup) by forgetting about it for 5 hours because of chatting. There are 3 people I chat with constantly, 2 of them daily even. Sometimes it's easier with voice calls, but other times you start it by writing and you just keep going that way. I didn't use Facebook chat because I felt it was too out in the open, like someone could read it, although I knew nobody could. It felt unsafe, but a friend insisted and she was always on Facebook and never on my old chat, so I also moved. Now I got used to it. (**SB26**)

In the same vein as the interviewee above, SB26 also only chats with very close ties. To a greater extent than the quotation above, her words show the immersion in the here and now of the interaction, with all the consequences that have on the here and now of her physical world within reach. Yet, I have chosen to include this fragment especially for the way in which the user depicts her experience with Facebook chatting in particular. In my interpretation, an explanation for the user's concern with unwanted disclosure comes from her understanding of Facebook as a whole. Since it is a social space constructed through the actualization of certain possibilities by what users do, those users cannot be taken out of the conceptualization of that space. The presence of those users, testified by the contents they share, the interactions they engage in, the feedback they give occasionally, cannot be subtracted, because they are Facebook. That is what that space is made of. In this context, the separation, within this space, of private interactions, needed to be rationalized by the interviewee in order to be accepted.

Weak Ties and Private Interactions

In this final section of the chapter on social interactions unfolding on Facebook, I will explore private interactions occurring between users who are weakly tied. Despite most of the interviewees having stated that, if they chat, they do it with those with whom they are closely bonded, there have been a number of exceptions. One of them in particular I think is interesting to analyze:

If she thought that I was stalking her Facebook (laughs)… Usually I try to find a reason to talk to them. I think saying to someone "Hi! I was browsing through your pictures", I think that is stalking. If I have a pretext, like for example a friend of mine, also from the exchange period, she was now living in another city and she was studying a master in logistics, and I sent her a message, like "how's it going?", but only because she posted a message that was meant more for everyone. INT: So you feel sometimes like you're not the target audience? SB15: Yeah, I do that, for example with the likes. I would like a picture if I think that person would be comfortable with me looking at it. If not, I wouldn't click like because I would worry that person will think I was stalking because that was not meant for me. (**SB15**)

This is a fragment from an interview where a user talks about his reserves in initiating a private interaction with an old acquaintance about whom he is curious to know more. Despite that, he looks for a reason to talk to her, and place her, through his discourse in a category with others with whom he has a tie of a similar strength (he needs a reason to talk to them). At the foundation of this line of thinking lies his assumption about how initiating a private interaction with the other would be read by her as an indicator of him heading in the direction of a stronger tie. The interviewee feels the other perceives the tie as not very strong, but he also estimates she evaluates that lack of closeness positively, thus not expecting him to look at the pictures she posts or the information she shares. Then, in order to mask the decision of initiating a conversation (that he feels would be interpreted in a way with which he is not comfortable), he constructs it as a reply. In order to do that, the subject needs a hook, a content that he can construct as being addressed to him, even if it is addressed to him among others and not to him personally. In this example, the hook is a piece of information she shares publicly about her studies.

In all this unfolding of the interaction and in the projections that precede it in the mind of the initiator, it is interesting to notice that the subject is not trying to communicate a distorted message about his account of the strength of the tie. He is trying to send a message that would convey his actual intentions about the tie, but he is concerned his spontaneous way of engaging in the interaction would come across wrongly. Thus, he is willing to censor his behavior, in order to respect what he regards as the already solidified associations between certain behaviors and certain tie strengths.

To summarize, I will briefly go through the main points of the argumentation in this chapter. The main topic discussed here has been meaning construction in social interactions unfolding on Facebook. I have divided social interactions into two categories: public social interactions (taking place on users' walls, in feedbacks, in debates, etc.) and private social interactions (the chatting option). In each of those, I refer separately to the meaning construction when those interacting are in a strong or weak tie. Although I have mentioned this before, I feel it is important to emphasize that I do not understand weak ties and strong ties as a dichotomy, but as a continuum. Thus, the clear-cut distinction is only done for analytical purposes. I am not claiming that meaning is constructed in one way for those who are strongly tied and in another way within weak bonds, but that the stronger the tie, the more certain elements will prevail in the meaning construction, whereas in weaker ties other factors will have more weight in the meaning construction. Having said this, I will go back to the outline of the argument. Public social interactions are more likely to occur between strong ties as a consequence of a few patterns in the interpretative process. Namely, the most often discussed and the most insisted upon in the interviews is entitlement. By this term, I am referring to the underlying assumption of contacts overviewing public contents about the inexplicit addressability of those contents and the evaluation about whether they were among the ones addressed, based on the strength of the tie. Besides entitlement, another element influencing public social interaction is institutionalization of Facebook actions and behaviors in relation with tie strength. Certain interaction practices have become habitualized and they have been associated with interactants who read each other according to how close their bond is ("I always like what my best friend posts"). Furthermore, public interactions are also shaped by the contents themselves, because certain information is likely to be interpreted as having been shared with only close friends (although publically), while other contents are general enough to allow contributions from weak ties. Another aspect of public interactions between strong ties is the use of the close tie in a collective effort (of the subject and his/her close ones) to construct an imaginary about their common world within reach or the world within reach of one of them for the weaker ties who are overviewing the interaction on Facebook. Last but not least, behind public interaction between strong ties, there are a previously existing togetherness, complicity, and shared past experience. On that basis, interviewees talk about the occurrence of interactions that come as a continuation of that past experience.

In the following section of this chapter, I talk about public interactions occurring between weak ties. In relation to this topic, two issues have been approached. One of them is the institutionalization of the interaction, which describes a process similar to the one occurring between strong ties, but which is used more carefully in this instance, as the threshold of what is acceptable is lower in weaker ties. The other is the negotiation of a future strengthening of the tie on the basis of public interactions with users with whom the subject is currently loosely bonded. In the last part of the argument about public interactions, I have referred to the interactions in the representation of which the interviewees have not talked about tie strength. These were public debates. In relation to this theme, I have insisted upon (a) the experience of lived durée and the involvement of a posteriori reflectivity, on the one hand, and (b) upon the typifications generated by the overviewers, on the other.

In the second half of the chapter, the focus shifted to private interactions. Not surprisingly, the statements of the users support the conclusion that private interactions are also more likely to occur when the underlying tie is stronger. Some of the main ideas discussed in this section have been the deliberation about engaging in an interaction and the ways in which strong ties are more probable to encourage the decision of initiating an interaction. The immersion in a common here and now of the interaction has also been tackled, especially in connection with strong ties. On what private interactions between weak ties are concerned, the emphasis fell on the ways in which the initiator of the interaction manages the assumed interpretations of the other about the meaning of that private conversation.

References

Berger, Peter, and Thomas Luckman. 1966. *The Social Construction of Reality*. Harmondsworth: Penguin Books.

Bergson, Henri. 1910. *Time and Free Will. An Essay on the Immediate Data of Consciousness*. Trans. F.L. Pogson. London: George Allen & Unwin.

Dimmick, John. 2003. *Media Competition and Coexistence: The Theory of the Niche*. Mahwah, NJ: Lawrence Erlbaum Associates.

Dimmick, John, John Christian Feaster, and Artemio Ramirez. 2011. The Niches of Interpersonal Media: Relationships in Time and Space. *New Media & Society* 13 (8): 1265–1282.

Goffman, Erving. 1967. *Interaction Ritual: Essays On Face-to-Face behavior*. New York: Anchor Books.

Schütz, Alfred. 1970. In *Alfred Schütz on Phenomenology and Social Relations*, ed. Helmut R. Wagner. Chicago: University of Chicago Press.

———. 1976. *Collected Papers II: Studies in Social Theory*. The Hague: Martinus Nijhoff.

6

Social Networking and Emotions

Emotions are part of the ways in which we relate to the world in a meaningful way (Scheff 1990; Ahmed 2001; Barbalet 2002; Collins 2004), and
they are consequently a key element in carrying out a relational analysis of
any social phenomenon. On the one hand, utter emotionlessness in social
relations is unattainable—emotions exist and shape thoughts, behaviors,
and interactions. On the other hand, structural characteristics of social
actors and their relations favor the rise of certain emotions. Furthermore,
the concrete unfolding of social encounters, with inherent norms and
expectations, is deeply connected with particular emotions in various
contexts. Thus, there is no theoretical reason for choosing to discuss emotions separately from any other aspects of the link between Facebook and
the underlying social bonds. Yet, for the sake of clarity and systematiza-
tion, the current chapter is dedicated mainly to accounts of emotions
Facebook users shared with me. As emotions are not always in the foreground of one's conscious reflection upon their experience, I have chosen
to ask interviewees openly about situations when Facebooking made them
joyful, sad, angry, proud, or ashamed. And if emotions had not always
been spontaneously part of their narratives, open questions revealed the
emotional component to be not only present, but also fairly strong.

© The Author(s) 2018   **141**
G.-I. Ivana, *Social Ties in Online Networking*, Palgrave Studies in
Relational Sociology, https://doi.org/10.1007/978-3-319-71595-7_6

Pride and Shame

Scheff (2014) argues that a pride/shame system functions in most social interactions. He traces this idea back to two main sources: Goffman with his "esprit de finesse" (intuition, richness of details, etc.) and Cooley with his "esprit de geométrie" (analytic and synthetic power). The insights about pride and shame and their social roots and ramifications which lay at the intersection between the two interactionist scholars are what Scheff calls the Goffman-Cooley conjecture. In this context, of particular relevance is the relational rather than individual character of both pride and shame. The risk of shame which Goffman (1959) identified in all cases of interaction is not simply derived from one's own lack of confidence or anxiety, but from what Cooley (1964) named the looking glass self, a constant estimation of the other interactant's perspective. As Scheff also remarks, Mead (2015) opened the way to these ideas through his elaboration on role taking as the staggeringly fast process of imagining oneself in the other's position and returning to one's own to come up with responses in face-to-face communication. Role taking (in the sense Mead uses it) is at the core of both pride and shame, and more widely self-administered social control. Given the social implications of these two emotions, as well as their pervasiveness, I begin this discussion by referring to pride and shame. Furthermore, it is not accidental that these are also some of the emotions Facebook users mention most often. However, the fast role taking to which Mead was referring belonged to the realm of face-to-face interaction. It also makes sense to expand it to synchronous online interactions. Yet the different pace of non-synchronous interactions and interactionless (or unaddressed) Facebook posts throws Mead's role taking and Cooley/Goffman's views on emotions like pride and shame into a different dynamic. And it is important to note users' mentions of shame and particularly pride were typically made in contexts where direct interactions were missing. Namely, pride appeared in discussions about posts on one's wall, mainly as a result of their public character. When asked about her most recent public posts, an interviewee mentioned she posted a song by a band called Tricky. After my inquiries about the reasons behind her action, the girl states:

Tricky of which I just found out will come to Optimus, the festival I'm also going to in July, yay, and yes, everybody must know it (laughs). No, I am joking right now, but you know, it is a reason of pride to go to a festival where I'll see a band I want to see so much. (**SB1**)

Here, it is made explicit that pride relates to everybody acknowledging an accomplishment and this necessarily relies on a general understanding of what constitutes an accomplishment. Thus, the interviewee must have taken the role of the other, or must have seen her own post through what she presumed to be the eyes of the other, and expected it to gain admiration. Yet, if in a face-to-face conversation the other is well established, in the case of public posts it is not. Hence, instead of the role taking which takes place in a traditional interactional act of communication, here there is a generalized other, to use another of Mead's terms or, as the interviewee says, "everybody". Also, it must be added that, as Scheff (2005) points out, Cooley's view on pride (since Goffman is more focused on shame) is very much in line with Mead's work, but at the same time valuable in its own right, especially for the inclusion of emotion. And this intertwined cognition about the generalized other and emotion about how they might read the user is exactly what pride seems to describe in Facebook public posts. At the same time, I would add, the generalized other which lays at the foundation of pride is also inextricably connected with the normativity and social control that Goffman was exploring with respect to shame. It is a crystallization, in one's own understanding of wider trends, societal values, and largely embraced norms, from her contact with particular others. It is in this form of the imaginary of the generalized other that the user calibrates her compass about what is worthy of pride and, one might add, what is worthy of being enjoyed as good music in the first place.

However, the generalized other to whom this interviewee is referring cannot be "everyone". It is not the averaging of opinions and evaluations from people with whom she came in contact that guides her. Rather, it is a narrower other, a generically relevant other whose role she briefly takes and who gives her the feeling of pride. It is the person she believes listens to this sort of music or would be interested in going to said festival that matters. To put it differently, her doing something which is in accordance to the expectations of the subculture to which she hopes to belong is part of the feeling of pride. Moreover, what is special on Facebook is the apparent plunge into a nebula when posting something publicly. If in face-to-face conversation pride may come from sharing something note-worthy and receiving positive feedback for it, when posting, that is not an option. Thus, what is actually highlighted is the fact that the very expectation of a positive feedback from the other can be enough for pride to develop, even before any act of communication is initiated. The inherently and purely social character of how one decides what is deserving of pride points once again to a social construction of values and norms which long predates Facebook. Having said this, besides familiarity with the social expectations of a particular group, which can make one feel proud even before she shares her achievement with anyone, actual social actors still matter. In the story above, it is not the same for the interviewee whether she receives enthusiastic feedback or no feedback at all. Despite their reactions coming after her pride has already taken shape, they have the potential to confirm it or to deny it. At the same time, the abovementioned notion of a non-individualized other, but one who is nonetheless defined by particular characteristics, what I called the generically relevant other (simultaneously different from the generalized other and from the particular other) connects this user's pride with emotion informed theories of identity (Stryker 2004). This is something to which I will come back when analyzing feelings of belonging.

Another person mentions pride when trying to explain why she thinks the social networking platform is so popular:

> Anyway, I am under the impression that there is kind of a constant need of showing those you know… or maybe it's just me, of showing them not necessarily what you've got, but that you take pride in what you do. This is how I would explain the food photos or the check-ins which really have no other purpose. They bring you no gain whatsoever; you simply want to show where you are and what you do and who you do it with. I think in a way you take pride in that, because you wouldn't hit "check in" in an ugly place, but knowing you're in a better restaurant or in a fancy club, then you want to do it. That's what I say (laughs). Oh, how stupid it sounds! It sounds stupid, but that's it in fact, the wish of showing those you know how far you've gotten. (**SB7**)

In this quotation, there is, again, confirmation of the sociological perspective on pride. The importance of the others, of how one imagines they are perceived from the outside, is fully revealed as this user talks about what she finds is the very rationale of Facebooking. There is a strongly relational thread here, as other people are in the foreground of sharing information about what makes us proud. However, this person, similarly to the one above, talks about "people you know", rather than friends or other close ties. In both examples, and in others, the external entity to whom such information seems to be addressed is almost entirely depersonified. Whether we speak of a generalized other, or a more specific relevant other, they still lack a face and a strong bond with the user. The dummy of the other stands for criteria and narratives of success, for tastes and lifestyles of certain social groups, and for the exigence required in order to generate evaluations. If receiving information from ties of various types and strengths was typically read with respect to the person who posted it, the analysis of pride, which brings us mostly into what users themselves share, highlights a different angle to the experience of Facebooking. In the previous chapters, I had referred to the fact that with weak ties reductions to ideal types are more likely than attempts at reconstituting the life flow of the absent other. When posting content available to weak ties, users subject themselves to the same reductionist practice, awaiting and embracing the typifications they are likely to receive. Yet, beyond the cognitive elements, being matched up against an ideal type is a reason for pride, if one believes they would be matched up against the right ideal type. Thus, the often impersonal, non-interactional character of public Facebook information sharing allows the gaze of another who is farther away than in most other contexts, and who is likely to look at the bigger picture of ideal types of individuals and their life trajectories. Particularly in this quotation, the reference to pride about how far one has come in life indicates the expected level of generality of the other and of their evaluations. In this case, isolated events or achievements from which one might ordinarily take pride are imagined to be put by the other into a wider narrative. Then, being in what one might consider a good restaurant might be a slight reason of pride in itself, but a more definite one in light of what it suggests about the user's life.

Another aspect related to pride which was not common, but nevertheless appeared in a few conversations with users, is the division of platforms according to content. More clearly, not everything that is worthy of pride belongs on Facebook, as this platform is seen as (1) informal (made mostly of friends, family, friendly acquaintances, or colleagues) and (2) non-specialized (the people on Facebook are typically not a niche audience). This specific flavor of the network has made one interviewee define it as the place on the internet where grandmothers also fit in. In the context of pride, another respondent who is a professional photographer states:

> All kinds of communication I am very positive about, and sometimes I post pictures just for fun, some funny stuff, with some sort of goal of communication or receiving feedback, but not "look what a great picture I made". I use Flickr for that. (**SB12**)

Thus, when he derives his pride from a professional achievement, he prefers using Flickr, precisely for its specialized character. In the same vein, I argue, contents from platforms of academic research, like ResearchGate or Academia, rarely overlap with what is shared on Facebook, despite pride being a factor in decisions about public sharing.

When asked about shameful Facebook-related situations, most users did not have anything in particular to share. They did not negate the risk of shame, and they mentioned they could see, for instance, how one being tagged in an image where they are obviously drunk would be embarrassing. Several interviewees also mentioned the issue of publishing sexual images while having one's parents' in the list of contacts as embarrassing. Here, we must observe, strong ties come back into the picture. Pride was somewhat flexible with its audience; shame is not. One may be proud of a particular achievement according to what they have grown to consider desirable in general and in this case their pride may remain unshaken irrespective of those with whom they share it. Embarrassment, on the other hand, depends more often than not on the link with the particular other towards whom one is embarrassed. While we can think of actions which are embarrassing in any context, they are rare. Being drunk with friends or being sexual with a romantic partner is deemed socially acceptable. Thus, in the case of shame, more than pride, the normativity within a given type of bond is central. An argument has been made that the importance of individual others, like parents or acquaintances, in the development of shame is culturally dependent (Cohen and Nisbett 1994; Cross et al. 2014; Gunsoy et al. 2015), with so-called cultures of honor valuing external input more. While there is definite substance to this argument, it must be pointed out that beyond differences in magnitude and in the specifics of what is shameful, the social mechanisms which provoke shame and the role of the others in reinforcing those mechanisms remain common threads in different cultural settings.

The importance of particular ties in defining what is shameful to do on Facebook brings us close to an aspect which was obscured (but not absent) in the above mentions of a generic relevant other: social structure. Structure manifests itself in the shape taken by the imaginary of the evaluation from the other, according to who that person is and the type of bond the user has with them. As I have already mentioned throughout the previous chapters, bonds do not only refer to varying distances between social actors but also to different types of relations between them. These differences in type of bonds are dependent, among other things, on disparities of status or power. Kemper explains it in the following words: "The fundamental theorem of the power-status approach to emotions is that a very large class of human emotions results from real, anticipated, imagined, or recollected outcomes of social relations" (Kemper 1978, 1991). With respect to shame, what is significant is not the power (understood of one's ability of forcing their way upon others), as much as the status (one's ability to become respected, convincing, valued enough for others to willingly obey) of the evaluator in the eyes of the evaluated. The appraisal of one with a high perceived status has more weight for the receiver. It is also more likely to be negative, given the other's lack of social constraints and even the legitimacy of critical judgment conferred by status. Bearing this in mind, the mention of parents, or more rarely, teachers as being in one's Facebook circle, highlights the hierarchy existing within certain bonds and the emotional component which is intertwined with the meaning of that hierarchy. In this sense, the somewhat rare appearance of narratives of shame as compared to narratives of pride from Facebook users is due to the horizontality of the networks of ties within the platform. Going back to the brief interview excerpts about pride from above, they can also be read in terms of status. Namely, information is shared by Facebook users (be it about cultural events attended, check-ins, family pictures, etc.) in an attempt to increase their own status, and it is precisely the assumption of a better status which generates pride. Thus, we can speak of a more or less general other who stands for social norms and expectations, and directs the subject with respect to what they may be proud or ashamed about. We can also speak of the specific other with whom one engages in interaction regularly, who has certain structural features, like power and status, and who brings nuance and variation to the emotional scenery of different concrete contexts and bonds. My own discussions with Facebook users indicate they relate pride more to the generally relevant other and shame to the specific other. However, this is a tendency, rather than a clear-cut separation.

Another way in which shame narratives seem to differ from pride narratives is the treatment of the body. If pride is sometimes drawn from body image or scrupulous body management (workouts or diets), it also relies on various other grounds. Shame, on the other hand, is overwhelmingly directed towards the body, in the shape of aesthetics, intoxication, but most of all sexuality. With respect to this, it has been documented that self-surveillance increases the likelihood of shame (Grabe et al. 2007; Quinn et al. 2006; Manago et al. 2015). A sociological perspective on such social psychological findings would highlight it is the underlying constant concern for social evaluations and the desire to avoid shame that leads to self-surveillance from the beginning. However, this is a vicious circle, since the more one worries about the possibility of being shamed, the more self-conscious and ultimately ashamed they are likely to be. Regarding social networking, Manago et al. (2015) indicate that usage correlates with increases in feelings of shame for everyone, but particularly for girls. This is not something I have encountered explicitly in my fieldwork. However, two interviewees, both girls, have mentioned choosing their outfits for social occasions on the basis of how they would look in Facebook pictures and whether they already have public pictures dressed the same way. While neither of them linked this practice with feelings of shame, the increase in self-surveillance is clear. It is also understandable, since it comes from the awareness of increased surveillance from the outside, given the public, static, ever accessible character of Facebook posts. Others (at least a predetermined group of others) may always take a look, they may even come back to old contents while browsing randomly, and they may take their time noticing details in ways which are not acceptable in direct interaction. Facebook favors lateral surveillance (Andrejevic 2006; Ivana 2013). Knowing it and wishing to control the outcomes inevitably leads to increased self-surveillance.

In my discussions with users as well, the aspect emphasized regarding shame was control, being vigilant, and making sure the potential for circumstances of shame is reduced to a minimum. One way of doing so has reportedly been the Facebook option of checking tags posted by others before allowing them to be public on their walls. This interest in avoiding shameful situations is perfectly in line with Goffman's argument about the pervasiveness of shame and the constant risk which haunts social interactions (and here even non-interactional information sharing). Shame as the emotion most characteristic to social rejection is also linked to bullying. In such cases, ways of bypassing the control mechanisms devised by Facebook can be found (e.g. not tagging the bullied person, as all common friends of the bully and the bullied have access to the information anyway). With respect to this matter, one interviewee, who is also a parent, says:

> I have seen it happening in other people's profiles, for instance, when someone posts a photo of you. That is really tricky, because you don't have to agree necessarily that this picture is on the internet, or on a public profile and this is an area of… informal negotiation, or whatever you call it, that worries me a little bit. But I am more worried about my daughter than about myself (…) She is just 2, but in the future I am more worried about her, because I need to educate her and to teach her how to use it. (**SB11**)

Here, the emotional spectrum is more complex. Besides the possible shame one risks, there is also the concern for those around. The state of being worried strongly resembles pure anxiety, which can be defined in the following terms: "When there is an imbalance in the power relationship between actors, the one with relatively less power is vulnerable to the encroachments of the other, and the anticipation that other will use power is the core of anxiety. Whether or not the anxiety is of pathological intensity and related to repressed experiences, the relational context is one of power relations" (Kemper 1978). The lack of control over what would happen in his daughter's social circle is transparent from the words of the interviewee. In this case, Facebook simply fulfills the role of any other social arena, and its importance is enhanced by its publicness and visibility, that is to say by the "presence" of others. What is interesting in this fragment, I argue, is the fact that he does not speak of typical anxiety, but of concern for another. This emotion captures the strength of his bond with his daughter, his wish to protect her, on the one hand, and his anxiety about the potential unfolding of her interactions with others, on the other hand. Furthermore, the anxiety he experiences when projecting such scenarios does not need to be mediated by him empathically putting himself in the role of his daughter; it affects him directly by virtue of the bond he already has with his daughter. Here, again, that which may happen online is relevant for one's emotional experience by virtue of stable bonds with brief online manifestations.

Another aspect which must be pointed out in the analysis of pride and shame is that online pride is associated with that which happens in one's offline world and the action of sharing/displaying it on Facebook is conditioned by the pride one feels regarding a certain achievement. Shame, on the other hand, is the consequence of posting. That is not to say that pride and shame are moved by different mechanisms, but that when shame appears (as pride would) from projections made prior to posting, it results in inhibiting the post. This explains why narratives of shame are not as frequent: they function as quiet barriers which suppress one's intentions of becoming visible in the online social environment. Put simply, those who are ashamed to post something will not do it; those who were not ashamed to post it will probably not be ashamed after having done it either. Thus, the only situations when shame is really likely to be present are misjudged actions of Facebook display, or users sharing contents without calculating the shaming risks of doing so. Alternatively, when shame is caused by another, it may also be regarded as malevolent rather than misjudged. To conclude, the emotions of pride and shame can be found behind some of the central mechanisms for the public dimension of Facebooking. More precisely, pride lies at the core of most positive incentives to manifest oneself publicly, while shame is tacitly and discretely one of the negative regulators, which filters out what one should not share, in light of their bonds with the other users.

Facebook Sharing of Emotions

There is a distinction between (a) emotions experienced as a result of online occurrences (like being ashamed about something posted about you) and (b) emotions producing online occurrences (like posting an achievement because you feel proud of it) despite having been generated offline. For instance, most interviewees agreed the content they publish on the platform is strongly dependent on the emotions they are experiencing at the time. The typical examples include posting sad music, changing profile pictures so that the expression on the face in the picture mirrors their happy/melancholic/careless mood, or explicitly posting about certain everyday life events and the emotional impact they have had on the user. Psychology has already discussed at length the emotional self-regulating role of listening to music and about strategies of mood control (DeNora 1999; Thayer et al. 1994; Saarikallio 2011), but I argue actions of sharing are different from pure self-regulation. It must be said direct versus allusive posts regarding feelings are becoming more and more preferred by the interviewees, as suggestions are often deemed immature, transparent, or laughable. The following excerpt comes from a user who, when asked about his views on factual versus openly emotional posts, remembers having tried the latter:

> INT: What about people who share emotional things, how they are feeling or how their day was like or if they are depressed?
> SB6: Oh, that's ok. I don't think it's too much as long as it's an honest post, it's ok, it's who they are. Like for example I remember that once I posted something like "I am sick and tired of NGO's" because I was working on a project related to NGO's and I had some difficulties interacting with NGO's. And I was actually sick and tired. So I said that on my wall, and it was actually quite interesting, because some people started talking to me, e-mailing me, messaging me, saying: "Hey! Are you ok? What I the problem? Can I help you with something?"

INT: And had you expected that?

SB6: No, not really. That is what made it interesting.

INT: But generally, did they contact you in private, or did they post it on your wall?

SB6: Some of them commented on my post, some of them messaged me, some of them even called me (laughs)... the ones who work with NGO's or who are in the NGO sector. (**SB6**)

This fragment reveals both the emotional tableau which generates posts and the emotions following the post, as in this case, they differ. The initial emotion originated in a context entirely unrelated to Facebook. The user felt "sick and tired", which can be read as frustration coupled with low emotional energy (Mazur and Lamb 1980; Kemper 1990). In this circumstance, the social network represents only an outlet for the emotion. Through the temporal and causal sequence of emotion—Facebook action—this case is similar to the example above where pride was the motor behind the girl posting about her festival attendance. However, pride still needs confirmation or denial from those who receive the post in order to be fully valid. This man's emotions, on the other hand, do not. Feeling sick and tired of a work-related situation is not dependent on estimating evaluations from others. Rather, it is clear that there is an underlying structural ground in which his emotion is anchored. The lack of a power/high status position which would have allowed the interviewee to impose his perspective in the interaction with the people working in the NGO sector is at the basis of his emotions, which, in turn, fueled his decision to write publicly about the situation. Yet, what is interesting is that the emotional color of his narrative changed nevertheless as a result of the interventions of the other Facebook users who had unexpected, but comforting reactions. While the interviewee is not naming the emotions he felt after others contacted him and tried to help, the tone of the narrative suggests an unmistakable shift. This highlights the fact that even with emotions which are temporary, limited to certain settings and people, or which seem less clearly regulated by wider social expectations, validation and support from others are still of paramount importance. Feeling understood, having the legitimacy of one's emotion reinforced is what changed the tone of the narrative. The user's mention that it was people within the NGO sector or working with the sector who reached out to him points out precisely this dimension of legitimacy. While on the surface this confirmation of legitimacy may seem to augment the initial emotion, if anything, the paradoxical result is that it diminishes it. One way of explaining this is, structurally, that it reassures the subject that he has the wider social legitimacy on his side, which may increase his status enough to overturn the interaction, or to be unaffected by its course. Thus, I argue it is this infusion of legitimacy which is one of the main reasons why sharing feels good, and receiving supportive feedback feels even better.

Having said this, not all sharing of emotional aspects is linked to momentary emotions. In order to illustrate this idea, I have chosen a fragment which reveals a distinct facet of sharing as compared to the one above:

> SB15: I hate all trends, like planking, Harlem shake, I think they are cool when they are a bit obscure, but when everyone does it, it's awful. But there was one I liked: everyone was changing their profile picture to a cartoon of their childhood.
>
> INT: Oh, I remember that one.
>
> SB15: Well, that one really hit (gestures to the heart). Maybe I am a grown up child, I don't know, but I thought that was really cute. So I changed my profile picture to Kenny from South Park, which is kind of my childhood. I picked this picture because it was a cartoon, but Kenny was also a bit twisted and I like having this twisted persona, and being interesting and making things that are different. I have to admit it. So I picked Kenny because he was a childhood character, but not quite.

Through his choice of a cartoon character, this man expresses publicly parts of what he considers to be his self, and especially his emotional self (Farnsworth and Sewell 2012). In this case, the thrill of not being understood is central, as is the presence of a generalized other. His words about being twisted and making things that are different imply a dimension of normativity and the emotions derived from not always obeying it. The enjoyable, implicit, yet almost proud lack of conformity to social expectations as a defining characteristic of the self lies in what the interviewee is communicating. The desirability of unicity and authenticity, which is included in most socially accepted discourses about the self (Sennett 1992; Vannini and Franzese 2008), overrides in this case the wish to be evaluated positively by another. Yet, even this rebellion is mild, as the user gets the satisfaction of uniqueness not by being offensive, or disruptive, but only twisted and difficult to understand. Thus, the projection of the dialogue with the generalized other is similar to shame and pride, but the imagined outcome is the other being confused, rather than appalled (as with shame) or admiring (as with pride). Another definite emotion present in this quotation is melancholy, and if this wider emotional self-disclosure is quite rare on Facebook, melancholy is common.

Memories, Nostalgia, and Reminiscing

The relation of memories and the digital environment is a topic which has received great scholarly interest (Foot et al. 2005; Hess 2007; Garde-Hansen et al. 2009; Pentzold 2009). Most such works discuss memory in relation with hegemonic discourses and common cultural patterns. As a result of engaging with macro-social themes like the production of collective memories, one aspect that gets easily understated is emotion. An exception is Lohmeier and Pentzold's (2014) recent study on what they call "mediated memory work", which consists of practices of remembering; these practices are always space-bound. At the same time, they argue for "the cardinal role that the corporeal and dispositional embodiment of memories plays in mnemonic techniques and in recalling motor sequences, tastes and emotions" (Lohmeier and Pentzold 2014, p. 779). The other characteristics of mediated memory work are, according to the same authors, the connection to the sense of self and individuality, the embeddedness in culture and normativity, and the archival accessibility which is enabled by the media. While these are all aspects which appear in the stories of Facebook users, the focus in the current section will be on the emotional aspects of mediated memory work.

One emotion which is intertwined with memory and which is often cited by Facebook users is melancholy. As Radden (2000) points out, the terms "melancholia" and "melancholy" have been used in a wide variety of contexts, in writings starting from ancient Greek philosophers to today's psychologists. The significance of the concepts ranges from sorrow, to fear or idleness, from momentary to recurrent states, and from "normality" to pathology. Current works typically link melancholia with clinical conditions (mostly depression) and melancholy with a situational experience of sadness or grief; melancholy can transform itself in melancholia, but it does not necessarily have to go in that direction. Having said this, the use of melancholy in interviewees' narratives seems to highlight the affective component of memory sharing, namely, the current emotional involvement with past events and with how they touched the subject when they were lived first hand (e.g. present melancholy over past joy, over naïve romantic enthusiasm, or simply melancholy over lost lightness of heart). From this point of view, in order to capture this form of reminiscing, which does not have the element of despair or the depth of sorrow often associated with melancholy in scholarly analyses, a fitting concept is that of nostalgia (Boym 2001; Holdsworth 2011; Pickering and Keightley 2006). Schiermer and Carlsen (2016) distinguish between three types of nostalgia: restorative (which has a clear end point and sees itself more as conservativism or traditionalism), reflected (where the subject is aware of her nostalgia), or ironic (mimicking the restorative one). The quotation above, where an interviewee was talking about the trend of posting a cartoon character as a profile picture, is an example of reflected nostalgia. In a similar vein, when asked about why she posted information about a documentary, one user says the following:

> And oh, the documentary, because well it is more personal, I mean it's the melancholy of old times when I used to study klezmer and now somebody made a documentary about klezmer that will be launched in a week and I want to watch it. (**SB1**)

In their theorization of mediated memory work, Lohmeier and Pentzold (2014) revealed the importance of the sense of individuality and the self, upon which this fragment touches. The subject remembers a particular stage of her life, her formative years of study, which were connected to klezmer music. She feels this aspect is part of her construction as a subject and it is for this reason that her memory has an emotional charge of which she is fully aware. Furthermore, it is important to observe that, like the user talking about childhood cartoons, this person is also nostalgic about a period of time, rather than about specific occurrences. While that period is undoubtedly associated with particular events, which are space-bound and which have an unequivocal temporal unfolding, the events are deeply meaningful for the total they constitute, rather than separately. Whether or not this nostalgia is based on idealizations (Jameson 1991; Higonnet 1998; Kincaid 1992), it remains relevant for Facebook users both in their own constructions of significance, and in their posting behavior.

At the same time, by posting on Facebook contents related to one's nostalgia, the events about which one had reminisced and the nostalgia itself are likely to gain a particular status in that user's online presence. This is facilitated by Facebook displaying to users themselves their own posts from several years before under the title "Share a memory". To be sure, the klezmer documentary and Kenny will come back to gently haunt these respondents' News Feeds bring back old posts together with the emotions in which the initial posts had originated. The "time line" type of organization of one's past activity, with the chronological reconstitution of life events, serves the same infusion of nostalgia.

While the sense of self and one's own past are a fundamental part of nostalgia, another thread which must not be overlooked refers to social bonds. This is particularly emphasized by one informant who recalls the time when she first started using Facebook. She states:

> Almost all my Facebook photos at the start were of my friends, me with my friends and my dancing. I dance flamenco so I had photos of me dancing flamenco (…) it was only for me like having a memory of the things I did. One of the most important things when I started using Facebook was having contact with my friends and writing to each other and leaving like messages. And I think that even nowadays that is still the most important things I have on Facebook. (**SB5**)

This person makes it very clear that her posting of a memory of something she did is very strongly linked to her relation with others. She wants to share that memory with her friends. Moreover, her friends were included in the pictures and, implicitly, in the memory. Thus, it can be argued that from this perspective posting a picture where one appears with one's friends is a form of sharing the nostalgia over the time when the picture was taken. This is an emphasis on the interconnectedness which constituted the bond, which means it is also a ground for maintaining or developing the strength of the bond.

Tastes, Identity, and Belonging

Another emotional aspect which intersects the narratives about past experiences with others (usually close bonds), and nostalgia over those moments of togetherness, is belonging. For instance, when asked about what he choose as a cover photo and why he chose that, an interviewee described an image of him together with six friends, in a train station, all laughing and jumping up. He also mentions he is not likely to change it any time soon, and that it means very much to him, because they were childhood friends and who now live apart. They still met on a regular basis, but only in groups of three or four. So, this was their most recent picture together on a very rare encounter to which everyone was present. They were in a train station as they were traveling to different destinations and somehow managed to synchronize their trips so that they met for a relatively brief time. He explains the moment when they all jump and laugh (which is captured in the photo) as very lively, joyful, and special. As May (2017, p. 401) points out in her paper on nostalgia, "past sources of belonging can endure in a virtual sense through the act of nurturing the connection in memories and can be used to 'warm up' and give vitality to the present". The sharing of nostalgia which is encouraged by bringing up a memory of togetherness is, thus, at the same time a way of reinventing weakening ties, as well as the emotional re-living of the interconnectedness which lies at the foundation of the bond. This interconnectedness, the moments lived with others, and the experiences which cannot be broken down to aggregations of individual subjectivities are what gets sedimented into strong bonds. As these first-hand experiences are temporary, what are left after they finish are the bond and the settled emotion of belonging, which is what the interviewee feels. Furthermore, the size of the group is important. Larger rather than dyadic groups function as a social microcosm. Drawing on insights from Simmel (2009), the affect theory of social exchange (Lawler 2001; Lawler et al. 2008, 2009) explains that triads generate more cohesion than dyads. The opposite claim has also been made by several scholars (Emerson 1972; Homans 1950, 1961; Molm 1994). Having said this, through their empirical work Yoon et al. (2013) convincingly show there is typically a structural dynamic, the cohesion is stronger, the roles are diversified, the internal norms are reinforced, and sanctions are available as a result of a higher number of members within a group.

What at group level represents social cohesion is reflected at the level of social actors in belonging, and Facebook users also confirm the Simmelian hypotheses. Namely, like in the example above, belonging, or in other words, emotional commitment derived from an insider status, is present predominantly in narratives about larger groups. This is not to say dyadic bonds are not as strong, but it is to say that dyads are typically framed differently than through membership; consequently, other emotions are more prominent than belonging. Yet, the question remains, what is the link between the emotions originating in group membership and Facebook? The interviewee talking about his childhood friends uses Facebook both as a way of expressing his feelings of belonging and as a way of reaffirming them. As the insider status is the structural (network structural, not macro-structural) basis for belonging, preserving and asserting that status becomes a great emotional stake. Additionally, as this particular group has changed when its members grew up and moved out of town, the threat to this user's insider status increased not because of an internal mechanism excluding him, but because the group itself has lost its cohesion. Thus, the recent moment of togetherness becomes a resource for maintaining unity and sharing it on Facebook is both fueled by and fueling of feelings of belonging.

Besides the network-based belonging this Facebook user refers to, it is no coincidence that most works on belonging focus on identity; macro-structural attributes of race, religion, and so on; and the relation of social actors with wider communities more than on dyads (Yuval-Davis 2006, 2007; Innes et al. 2013; Yngvesson 2010). If the person above mentioned belonging to his group with specific members, others talk about the experience of belonging based on given characteristics or tastes. One interviewee puts it in the following words:

> I think this is the coolest thing about Facebook. To have this kind of connection with someone who was your friend and might still be your friend if you were to meet in other circumstances, but some reasons it's not. It makes me feel like we're still sharing a bond. For example, I have an anecdote: you know Reddit? I browse Reddit a lot. I met one friend in Erasmus, he was also a Reddit-er and sometimes I post articles and stuff that I find on Reddit and people ask me where I find that stuff, except for those who browse Reddit and who know it. And this friend of mine commented on something that he noticed I posted from Reddit and he said: "Hey, man, I know we don't talk that much, but I noticed that you post plenty of stuff from Reddit and I'm glad we share this." We never really talked, but it was cool to have this connection. In the space of reconnecting with people with whom you were close before I think Facebook makes me feel really good. (**SB15**)

This fragment is interesting because on the one hand it appears to touch upon belonging through the lens of old personal bonds, but on the other hand it highlights the potential for the development of belonging through a sort of bondless imagined community (Anderson 1983). This person talks about his posts and about the positive feedback he received for them firstly in terms of "connecting with someone who was your friend". However, the example he uses to illustrate this idea is centered on a very weak bond. The other is someone whom he met several years before and with whom he confesses he never really talks, yet their connection is based on belonging to a community of "Reddit-ers". In this case, I read this particular other as the incarnation of a general relevant other with whom my informant is not personally bonded, but is nonetheless connected. In this case, belonging neighbors pride, as it also involves the satisfaction driven by the positive appraisal of another (be it in an imagined dialogue, or, as here, in an actual one). However, if pride often also involves a hierarchy where the evaluator may have a higher status and may represent social normativity, the emotional reward one gets from belonging to the same community as another is more horizontal. This Facebooker and his "friend" are in the same position. The hierarchical element only appears in relation to the outsiders, those who are not on Reddit and thus cannot trace the origin of the articles he posts.

The other aspect which is important to point out is the construction of an identity. Burke and Stets (2009) and Stets and Carter (2012) explain in a systematic manner the relation between identity and emotion. They write: "In the control systems approach of identity theory, when an identity is activated in a situation, a feedback loop is established (Burke and Stets 2009). This loop has six components: (1) the identity standard (the meanings of an identity), (2) output (behavior), (3) input (how people think others see them in a situation [i.e., reflected appraisals]), (4) a comparator (which compares the input with the identity standard), (5) emotion (that results from the comparison process), and (6) situation meanings (which vary in the degree of correspondence with identity standard meanings)." Going back to the example of the interviewee who follows Reddit, his narrative starts with the output, namely, the action of posting contents from Reddit to Facebook. This is followed by an input, which is not only assumed by the subject, as someone openly speaks their mind about it, and reveals the source of his posts. Moreover, the other already attached the appraisal to the identity of "being a Reddit-er". The interviewee compared this tag against his identity standard, that is, the way in which he generally sees himself, and was comfortable with the comparison. Hence, the emotion of belonging set in.

It must be said, while Reddit may be read as a virtual community, where people actually share contents with each other and communicate directly, belonging to communities of taste, loving the same genre of music, and going to the same events as others are topics users touch upon in various ways. Some talk about their own posts made in an effort to belong; others mention the pleasant feeling they get when unexpectedly seeing someone else post things they also enjoy.

Anger

Another emotion which is often present in people's stories about their Facebook activities and about the significance of these activities is anger. When asked about online practices they dislike and about negative emotions either brought on by Facebook exchanges or expressed in this environment, most respondents discussed anger or, its milder version, annoyance. The examples interviewees used typically described their own anger over various comments, debates, or independent posts made by others. One frequent topic for anger referred to intolerance towards diversity, denial of human rights, and conservative political stances. One user affirms she finds all types of frustrations annoying, from political to sexual, and from jokes made in poor taste, to open racism and homophobia. Debates over feminist causes, migration, and far-right movements are also often described as the online contexts which anger users.

Regarding these statements, I believe a helpful tool for analysis comes from Collins (1990) who distinguishes between different types of anger, one of which is righteous anger, also taken up by Gamson (1992), Collins (2004), Flam (2005) and Kemper (2011). "Another especially Durkheimian form of short term emotion is righteous anger. This is the emotional outburst shared by a group (…) against persons who violate its sacred symbols. It is group anger against a heretic or scapegoat" (Collins 1990, p. 44). Despite my interviewees talking about their solitary experiences of Facebooking behind a computer screen, I argue righteous anger, the emotional outburst shared by a group, is what they have been reporting. By sustaining a progressive discourse, which is likely predominant in their own circles (since most were aged less than 40 and had a higher education background), they were putting themselves "on the right side" of the debate. In other words, the social legitimacy of their own opinion was stronger than of the opposing one, which placed them in a position to experience righteous anger. Furthermore, with respect to questions of normativity and emotional management, it is important to keep in mind negative emotions are not always socially accepted. Thus, when asked openly about moments when such emotions occur, it is understandable that users would allow me to know precisely about righteous anger. Furthermore, it may also be the form of anger they allow themselves to freely experience, as this is the legitimate anger, the sort that a subject "ought" to feel. As many of the other emotions discussed in this chapter, righteous anger also originates in estimating the position of a relevant general other through role switching, on the basis of well-established social norms. Thus, whether progressive political views are prevalent or not in a given context, the subjective construction of legitimacy and the estimation that one's anger is indeed shared by many others make topics like feminism, human rights, or religious freedom great candidates for igniting righteous anger, even in situations (like these) where the others who might share that anger and who give it social legitimacy are not present.

Unlike in the cases above, where users themselves are angered by the contents to which they are exposed, another interviewee talks about anger which (1) comes from another subject than herself and (2) is directed towards a topic without political implications:

> Like some friend of mine posted some fun sentence about Real Madrid, making fun of them because they were losing, a couple of years ago, maybe less… a year ago. And then there's this option where other people can see what you and your friends are talking about in the initial page and a cousin of mine, who is my age (note: 26 years old), saw this comment and he likes Real Madrid. He got so angry and he became… I don't know… he started swearing against my friend and he knows she is my friend. That was hard, because I love him so much, he is my cousin, he is my age, I've been with him since forever, playing… And I said "Wow! It's just football, you know! Grow up, please!" (**SB10**)

This fragment has been selected as it sheds light on the other kind of anger, the one which is read as an overreaction, as having no social legitimacy and as being in need of suppression. Interestingly, when anger became an emotional violation of social expectations rather than a justified reaction towards unacceptable behavior, the protagonist of the narrative she chose was someone else. Following Collins' (1990) typology, what she described is disruptive anger, which is born out of frustration and powerlessness. In this case, it is given firstly by the informant's cousin's inability to change the outcome of Real Madrid's matches and secondly by his lack of control over someone else's ironic remarks. The role of Facebook, here as with righteous anger, is mainly to allow communication, as the same emotional developments can easily be imagined in a face-to-face context. Yet, what is less common offline is the level of publicness one's angry outburst reaches. For righteous anger, publicness is an additional incentive for expression, as one takes comfort in the assumption that as more people witness a debate, more will share that anger. With disruptive anger, the subject's structural position, which denies him the power to influence the undesirable situation, may be enough for his own anger, but it is not enough to socially legitimize it. Consequently, when such outbursts become public on Facebook, they will be interpreted as breaking feeling rules. The fact that SB10 says her cousin should grow up highlights precisely that she finds his expression of anger lacking the control of maturity or, in other words, lacking full socialization within the frame of emotional management. His emotions are not in line with social norms with which he is familiar, and which he is capable of following, according to his age. This is the respondent's view, and it is one which greatly reflects the societal sanctions which derive from expressing disruptive anger on Facebook. Most other emotions deemed too negative/dark/aggressive or too intimate for sharing on Facebook fall into the same mechanism.

Lastly, another important part of anger on Facebook is captured by an interviewee who confesses he gets annoyed when people share one-sentence quotations in an attempt to appear profound and insightful. At the same time, he says that despite being irritated and thinking they are stupid, he also takes joy in knowing he would never do that. On a similar note, in the subchapter about overviewing the activity of weak ties, several other interviewees were quoted saying they sometimes keep people in their circles of friends despite not having any bond with them. They were very critical of what those people posted, but enjoyed following it anyway and laughing at it. This is an interesting emotion and, unlike the ones above, it is specific to Facebook. As the environment allows seeing without being seen, a form of emotional exteriority becomes intertwined in the experience. So, if, for instance, the user who is annoyed by those posting quotations met them and they started giving him advice by using those quotations, it is expected his annoyance (if not anger) would increase. But on Facebook this experience of interacting can be avoided and when that happens, the shared stakes of the interaction also disappear. Thus, instead of negotiating structural positions (e.g. convincing the other they are not increasing their status in relation to him by the use of those quotations), the interviewee has the possibility to look at such actions from the outside. The result is feeling mild anger, but also mild satisfaction, which comes from the awareness of a higher social status, in this case based on more/better education.

Romance, Sexuality, and Their Display

Last but not least, users typically make explicit references to emotions in their narratives about romance. A common issue is the practice of publicly and repeatedly declaring one's love for their romantic partner. More precisely, when asked about exposure on Facebook and what too much exposure meant to them, several interviewees talked about couples who constantly posted photos together or who had small dialogues on their walls about how they felt about each other. All of those witnessing such actions found them unnecessary and inappropriate. A related practice which less users noticed, but which nevertheless came up in a few cases, refers to couples who create collective profiles (e.g. Jane and John Smith). Here, again, the theme of emotional management is central, as is the importance of the norm about how much emotion one may publicly express before it becomes uncomfortable for the bystanders. Hence, two aspects are particularly relevant with respect to this topic: (1) the structural patterns of norms and expectations and (2) the publicness of Facebook.

Norms and expectations play a role in all forms of emotion management, and they are especially visible with respect to negative emotions, like outbursts of anger. Yet, with romantic emotions as much as with anger, but in different ways, social normativity is nuanced and patterned. Nuanced, because some expressions of love are read as "endearing", "cute", or "lovely", while others are "obnoxious", "fake", and "out of context". Patterned, because the social sanctions and rewards for displays of romantic emotions vary significantly according to the structural making of the subject witnessing them. Thus, with respect to the actual content of the emotionally charged exchanges, the level of detail and the amount of posts dedicated to one's own romantic partnership are what marks the difference between acceptable and unacceptable. It is acceptable to present an overall image of one's romantic relationship as fulfilling and happy, but it is not acceptable to share photos from the cooking classes the partners take together; and it is even less acceptable to display fights or conflicts. As mentioned in the subchapter on shame, sexual displays are also typically regarded critically. For instance, one user said she considered the picture of a couple French kissing repulsive. Others were not as categorical, but still spoke of Facebook as an unsuitable context for manifestations of sexuality. While these trends of interpreting content are quite common, they are also strongly dependent of the interpreter. Thus, the patterns originate in the interpreter's ages, in their social status, and their education. Whether research with teenagers, for instance, would reveal a different facet of Facebook displays of romance and sexuality cannot be answered here. Nevertheless, the mechanisms through which social norms, bond expectations, and emotions are intertwined with Facebook activity, decisions to post, and users' mutual readings of each other remain as important across contexts.

The publicness of Facebook shifts the accent back on the bonds between the overviewer and the overviewed. Besides somewhat general ideas of appropriateness, users insist on the fact that on Facebook one is seen by many. The different relation the author of a post has with those in her circle of friends calls for different behaviors and different measuring sticks. As many Facebookers like to point out, the term "friend" does not always designate one's friends. In that sense, even profiles which are not public require one to act as if they were "in public" rather than "among friends". In addition to the issue of who has access to a given content, Facebook posting of overtly emotional contents also poses the question of publicness in a wide sense. One user described emotion in general as too personal to share and mentioned that by the simple fact that it appears on Facebook, even the most emotional message decreases in intensity and depth, and becomes less credible. Consequently, displays of romantic love are read with skepticism and dismissed as "a circus". The way in which the interpretation of the content is shaped by the very fact that it is publicly displayed on Facebook reveals the developing normativity which is specific to this environment and which overlaps with the other coordinates according to which an action becomes meaningful for oneself and for those around.

This being said, the relation between emotion and how one expects or imagines their actions might be interpreted by another (the topic on which authors like Mead, Goffman, Cooley, Collins insisted) is very important for the Facebook expressions of romantic bonds. One user remembers a telling story:

> At some point I had my relationship status as 'Single' and a friend of mine told me: 'Dude, you look desperate if you have single on Facebook.' I was like 'I don't care, I am not desperate and if someone thinks so, it's their problem, not mine.' Maybe now I wouldn't fill in that field, so that I wouldn't look desperate, but at that point, I didn't feel the need to change it. But I changed it when I was going out with this girl and we were at this point where you're not serious, but also not single, and I had my single status. Then I thought, maybe she gets offended if she sees it. She will think that even though I am hanging out with her, I am still looking for other people, but I also didn't want to say 'in a relationship' because that might scare her, and me as well (laughs), so I thought 'ok, I am just going to hide it from the public' and that is what I did. (**SB15**)

The issue raised by the interviewee's friend about "looking desperate" is a very typical illustration of the symbolic interactionist view about exchanging roles with hypothetical others. The prediction about how another might relate to this given situation is shaped by the same normativity of emotional management and, to an even larger extent, emotional display. There is less socially wrong about being single or feeling lonely than about openly presenting that on Facebook. Thus, in a certain sense, feeling rules do not translate perfectly into desirable Facebook activity. Statuses, dialogues, and pictures posted on the platform originate first and foremost in rules of emotional display, which may strangely disconnect the emotional front one must put up from their actual ability of emotional management. In this interview fragment this lack of connection between actual emotional management and its display is evident in the fact that how the user feels or even how he ought to feel about being single is not mentioned at all. In terms of social theory, Facebook fosters a sort of reversion towards an early Goffmanian dramaturgy in which a presented self and a "real self" can be distinguished.

Coming back to the interviewee's narrative, it was not the concern about "looking desperate" which made him change his relational status. Rather, it is being involved in a type of bond where the frame of expectations did not overlap with the Facebook tags available. He considered himself neither single nor committed, and a mislabeling was likely to have emotional consequences (e.g. his partner being disappointed or bothered, him being scared). In this respect, by being a vehicle for publicness, expression, or display, Facebook becomes a deep part of the bond and influences its emotional making and unfolding.

References

Ahmed, Sara. 2001. The Organisation of Hate. *Law and Critique* 12 (3): 345–365.

Anderson, Benedict. 1983. *Imagined Communities: Reflections on the Origin and Spread of Nationalism*. London and New York: Verso Books.

Andrejevic, Mark. 2006. The Discipline of Watching: Detection, Risk, and Lateral Surveillance. *Critical Studies in Media Communication* 23 (4): 391–407.

Barbalet, Jack. 2002. Why Emotions are Crucial. In *Emotions and Sociology*, ed. J. Barbalet, 1–9. Oxford: Blackwell Publishing.

Boym, Svetlana. 2001. *The Future of Nostalgia*. New York: Basic Books.

Burke, Peter J., and Jan E. Stets. 2009. *Identity Theory*. Oxford: Oxford University Press.

Cohen, Dov, and Richard Nisbett. 1994. Self-Protection and the Culture of Honor: Explaining Southern Violence. *Personality and Social Psychology Bulletin* 20 (5): 551–567.

Collins, Randall. 1990. Stratification, Emotional Energy, and the Transient Emotions. In *Research Agendas in the Sociology of Emotions*, ed. T.D. Kemper, 27–57. Albany: State University of New York Press.

———. 2004. *Interaction Ritual Chains*. Princeton, NJ: Princeton University Press.

Cooley, Charles. 1964. *Human Nature and the Social Order*. New York: Schocken Books.

Cross, S.E., A.K. Uskul, B. Gercek-Swing, Z. Sunbay, C. Alözkan, C. Günsoy, B. Ataca, and Z. Karakitapoğlu-Aygün. 2014. Cultural Prototypes and Dimensions of Honor. *Personality & Social Psychology Bulletin* 40: 232–249.

DeNora, Tia. 1999. Music as a Technology of the Self. *Poetics* 27 (1): 31–56.

Emerson, Richard M. 1972. Exchange Theory Part: 2 Exchange Relations and Networks. *Sociological Theories in Progress* 2: 58–87.

Farnsworth, Jacob, and Kenneth W. Sewell. 2012. Fearing the Emotional Self. *Journal of Constructivist Psychology* 25 (3): 251–268.

Flam, Helena. 2005. Emotions' Map: A Research Agenda. In *Emotions and Social Movements*, ed. H. Flam and D. King. London: Routledge.

Foot, K.A., B. Warnick, and S.M. Schneider. 2005. Web-based Memorializing after September 11. *Journal of Computer-Mediated Communication* 11 (1): 72–96.

Gamson, William A. 1992. The Social Psychology of Collective Action. In *Frontiers in Social Movement Theory*, ed. A.D. Morris and C. Mueller, 53–76. New Haven, CT: Yale University Press.

Garde-Hansen, J., A. Reading, and A. Hoskins, eds. 2009. *Save As… Digital Memories*. Basingstoke: Palgrave Macmillan.

Goffman, Erving. 1959. *The Presentation of Self in Everyday Life*. New York: Doubleday.

Grabe, Shelly, Janet Shibley Hyde, and Sarah M. Lindberg. 2007. Body Objectification and Depression in Adolescents: The Role of Gender, Shame, and Rumination. *Psychology of Women Quarterly* 31 (2): 164–175.

Günsoy, Ceren, Susan E. Cross, Adİl Sarıbay, Irmak Olcaysoy Ökten, and Meltem Kurutaş. 2015. Would You Post that Picture and Let Your Dad See It? Culture, Honor, and Facebook. *European Journal of Social Psychology* 45 (3): 323–335.

Hess, Andreas. 2007. Against Unspoilt Authenticity: A Re-appraisal of Helmuth Plessner's The Limits of Community (1924). *Irish Journal of Sociology* 16 (2): 11–26.

Higonnet, Anne. 1998. *The History and Crisis of Ideal Childhood*. London: Thames and Hudson.

Holdsworth, Amy. 2011. *Television, Memory and Nostalgia*. Basingstoke and New York: Palgrave Macmillan.

Homans, George Caspar. 1950. *The Human Group*. New York: Harcourt, Brace.
———. 1961. *Social Behavior: Its Elementary Forms*. London: Routledge & Kegan Paul.

Innes, Joanna, Steven King, and Anne Winter. 2013. Introduction: Settlement and Belonging in Europe, 1600–1950: Structures, Negotiations and Experiences. In *Migration, Settlement and Belonging in Europe, 1500–1930s: Comparative Perspectives*, ed. S. King and A. Winter, 1–28.

Ivana, Greti-Iulia. 2013. A Postmodern Panopticon: Lateral Surveillance on Facebook. *Global Media Journal: Mediterranean Edition* 8 (1): 1–14.

Jameson, Fredric. 1991. *Postmodernism or, The Cultural Logic of Late Capitalism.* Durham, NC: Duke University Press.

Kemper, Theodore D. 1978. *A Social Interactional Theory of Emotions.* New York: John Wiley.

———. 1990. *Research Agendas in the Sociology of Emotions.* New York: State University of New York Press.

———. 1991. An Introduction to the Sociology of Emotions. *International Review of Studies on Emotion* 1: 301–349.

———. 2011. *Status, Power and Ritual Interaction—A Relational Reading of Durkheim, Goffman and Collins.* Farnham: Ashgate.

Kincaid, James R. 1992. *Child-Loving: The Erotic Child and Victorian Culture.* New York and London: Routledge.

Lawler, Edward J. 2001. An Affect Theory of Social Exchange. *The American Journal of Sociology* 107 (2): 321–352.

———. 2009. The Power Process and Emotion. In *Power and Interdependence in Organizations,* ed. D. Tjosvold and B. van Knippenberg, 169–185. New York: Cambridge University Press.

Lawler, Edward J., Shane R. Thye, and Jeongkoo Yoon. 2008. Social Exchange and Micro Social Order. *American Sociological Review* 73 (4): 519–542.

Lohmeier, Christine, and Christian Pentzold. 2014. Making Mediated Memory Work. Cuban-Americans, Miami Media and the Doings of Diaspora Memories. *Media, Culture & Society* 36 (6): 776–789.

Manago, Adriana M., L. Monique Ward, Kristi M. Lemm, Lauren Reed, and Rita Seabrook. 2015. Facebook Involvement, Objectified Body Consciousness, Body Shame, and Sexual Assertiveness in College Women and Men. *Sex Roles* 72 (1–2): 1–14.

May, Vanessa. 2017. Belonging from Afar: Nostalgia, Time and Memory. *The Sociological Review* 65 (2): 401–415.

Mazur, Allen, and Theodore A. Lamb. 1980. Testosterone, Status, and Mood in Human Males. *Hormones and Behavior* 14 (3): 236–246.

Mead, George H. 2015. *Mind, Self, and Society. The definitive edition.* Chicago: University of Chicago Press.

Molm, Linda D. 1994. Is Punishment Effective? Coercive Strategies in Social Exchange. *Social Psychology Quarterly* 57 (2): 75–94.

Pentzold, Christian. 2009. Fixing the Floating Gap: The Online Encyclopaedia Wikipedia as a Global Memory Place. *Memory Studies* 2 (2): 255–272.

Pickering, Michael, and Emily Keightley. 2006. The Modalities of Nostalgia. *Current Sociology* 54 (6): 919–941.

Quinn, Diane M., Rachel W. Kallen, and Jean M. Twenge. 2006. The Disruptive Effect of Self-objectification on Performance. *Psychology of Women Quarterly* 30 (1): 59–64.

Radden, Jennifer. 2000. *The Nature of Melancholy: Readings on Melancholy, Melancholia and Depression from Aristotle to Kristeva*. Oxford: Oxford University Press.

Saarikallio, Suvi. 2011. Music as Emotional Self-regulation Throughout Adulthood. *Psychology of Music* 39 (3): 307–327.

Scheff, Thomas J. 1990. *Microsociology: Discourse, Emotion, and Social Structure*. Chicago: The University of Chicago Press.

———. 2005. Looking-Glass Self: Goffman as Symbolic Interactionist. *Symbolic Interaction* 28 (2): 147–166.

———. 2014. The Ubiquity of Hidden Shame in Modernity. *Cultural Sociology* 8 (2): 129–141.

Schiermer, Bjørn, and Hjalmar Bang Carlsen. 2016. Nostalgia, Irony and Collectivity in Late-modern Culture. *Acta Sociologica* 60 (2): 158–175.

Sennett, Richard. 1992. *The Fall of the Public Man*. New York: WW Norton Publishing.

Simmel, Georg. 2009. *Sociology: Inquiries into the Construction of Social Forms. Vol. I and Vol. II*. Eds. and Trans. Anthony J. Blasi, Anton K. Jacobs and Mathew Kanjirathinkal. Boston: Brill.

Stets, Jan E., and Michael J. Carter. 2012. A Theory of the Self for the Sociology of Morality. *American Sociological Review* 77 (1): 120–140.

Stryker, Sheldon. 2004. Integrating Emotion into Identity Theory. In *Theory and Research on Human Emotions*, ed. J.H. Turner, 1–23. Emerald Group Publishing Limited.

Thayer, Robert E., Robert J. Newman, and Tracey M. McClain. 1994. Self-regulation of Mood: Strategies for Changing a Bad Mood, Raising Energy, and Reducing Tension. *Journal of Personality and Social Psychology* 67 (5): 910–925.

Vannini, Phillip, and Alexis Franzese. 2008. The Authenticity of Self: Conceptualization, Personal Experience, and Practice. *Sociology Compass* 2 (5): 1621–1637.

Yngvesson, Barbara. 2010. *Belonging in an Adopted World: Race, Identity, and Transnational Adoption*. Chicago: University of Chicago Press.

Yoon, Jeongkoo, Shane Thye, and Edward J. Lawler. 2013. Exchange and Cohesion in Dyads and Triads: A Test of Simmel's Hypothesis. *Social Science Research* 42 (6): 1457–1466.

Yuval-Davis, Nira. 2006. Belonging and the Politics of Belonging. *Patterns of Prejudice* 40 (3): 196–213.

———. 2007. Intersectionality, Citizenship and Contemporary Politics of Belonging. *Contemporary Review of International Social and Political Philosophy* 10 (4): 561–574.

7

The Structural Underpinnings of Online Bonds

In the previous chapters, I have discussed at length the importance of analyzing social networking through the lens of existing social bonds. Posts, feedbacks, and interactions must be understood in the relational context to which they belong. Following distinctions made by users, I have emphasized the different logics in which actions of and interactions with ties of varying strengths unfold. Tie strength and type have been depicted as crystallizations of previous experiences of togetherness, projections about the future of that tie, shared memories, and emotional connections. Having said this, the friendships and romantic partnerships, the admiration of others, the wish to impress, and the stopping of a weak (but strengthening) tie in its tracks are all marked by particular patterns. Tastes, hierarchies of prestige, and indicators of social status make some ties more likely than others. One's life trajectory, the relational configuration of the physical space in which she typically moves, the gradual sedimentation of specific sets of values and beliefs she holds, and the variety of practical constraints of everyday life will shape intentions and projections about ties. These elements will limit the odds of her getting close to certain people; they will even limit the odds of her ever meeting certain people. Thus, this chapter is still dedicated to practices of Facebook users

© The Author(s) 2018
G.-I. Ivana, *Social Ties in Online Networking*, Palgrave Studies in
Relational Sociology, https://doi.org/10.1007/978-3-319-71595-7_7

and to the meanings with which those practices are endowed as a result of the relational framework in which they were generated. Yet, this time the accent falls on discussing the patterns of bonds between users, how these patterns fluctuate, and the role of online exchanges in the fluctuations.

Discussing the importance of one's socialization, the hierarchical character of social differences, and the external limitations to one's choices leads us towards theoretical debates about structure and agency. Combining insights from Bourdieu's habitus, Giddens' structuration, and Archer's reflexivity, numerous authors have argued, in different ways, for an understanding of social actors as simultaneously acting according to particular dispositions and critically engaging with those dispositions in reflection and decision making (Elder-Vass 2007; Adams 2006; King 2010; Rafieian and Davis 2016). While this mix of structural and agentic factors is also included in this exploration of social networking practices and their significance, I argue the analysis should not stop there. Namely, thinking of structure and agency in relational terms sees the subject fully immersed in a universe of more or less stable bonds with others. So, her decisions and intentions, her routine actions, and her evaluations of her surrounding world will be filtered through her active presence in that world and her connections to others who inhabit it. Having said this, I will proceed with the analysis of patterns within Facebook bonds and situate it in the theoretical conversation about how a relational approach would help avoid substantialist concepts of both structure and agency.

Homophily and Social Networking

An unequivocal and empirically sound entry point into the discussion of patterns when it comes to bonds is the concept of homophily, which captures structural dimensions such as race, gender, religion, and so on, the subject's critical relation with those dimensions within herself and others, and the patterns of similarity in the likelihood of bond formation. Lazarsfeld and Merton (1954), quoted by McPherson et al. (2001), identified two kinds of homophily: status and value. Status homophily is based on socially ascribed qualities, like socio-demographic variables, while value homophily is based on beliefs, attitudes, and values social actors hold. Countless sociological studies have illustrated the patterns of relational closeness are strongly dependent on race, ethnicity, gender, age, and education. Value homophily has also been explored at length, either in itself, or in correlation with status commonalities within networks. Some recent research has even focused particularly on homophily on Facebook (Barnett and Benefield 2017; Wimmer and Lewis 2010). Yet, it is important to note these works are part of a factual rather than interpretative frame. From this perspective, since Facebook contacts are mostly collections of one's ties from various points in their life, it constitutes a great resource for revealing levels of resemblance between one's contacts on a variety of socioeconomic indicators; in turn these configurations of users' social networks can be expected to have an influence on their opinions, beliefs, taste, and so on. Then, Facebook behaviors can be read as confirming similarities in order to reinforce belonging to a particular ethnic group, religious community, political activist movement, and so on. In other words, homophily helps with the question of who is likely to become bonded with whom. However, the question of why and how they become bonded remains open. On the one hand, in a Bourdieusian tradition, field theorists talk about structural positions which increase the odds of particular social actors developing a similar habitus, which in turn offers a good ground for bonding. On the other hand, in a Barry Wellman/Harrison White line of thought, network theorists answer the question of how bonding patterns appear through looking at the dynamics of concrete social exchanges, with their fast pace and lack of stability. It is argued that here lay the mechanisms which make certain people more likely to become connected than others. Yet, with Singh (2016), I argue these two standpoints are not mutually exclusive. The main incompatibility identified between the two has been Bourdieu's tendency to discuss the structure of the social field in terms of objective relations between positions, rather than as actual relation between social actors. In this respect, the move proposed by Bottero (2009) and Bottero and Crossley (2011) to de-formalize Bourdieu's social relations and think them within rather than above social exchanges offers some solutions for bridging field theory with network theory. Having said this, it is important to acknowledge that networks of relations function within the frame of a particular symbolic order (Singh 2016). With these considerations in mind, I will turn to Facebook and focus the analysis precisely on the symbolic order which runs through the bonds between users as well as through their online exchanges. Facebook users talk about how symbolic order structures their bonds in two main ways. Firstly, they discuss the others' resemblance to themselves in positive terms; secondly they discuss the practices and characteristics of others in relation to their own understandings of what is more generally socially desirable, acceptable, valued.

Thus, going back to homophily and to the mechanisms through which similar people are more likely to become bonded, they reveal both a process of interpersonal network formation and a particular system of meanings where some common treats are appreciated over others. Despite similarity not being very often brought up, I will look into the few mentions of homophily that did occur in the conversations with Facebook users. For instance, when asked whether they experience the problem of conflated audiences when they post, or whether they divide their contacts into circles, several interviewees said this is not an issue, because their friends are very similar to them, and even when their opinions diverge, it is generally not to the point where it becomes problematic. Other users pointed out that if others were to be offended or disagree with their posts, it means they were not that close anyway and their view does not matter. One person said: "Offend someone? Well, since they are my contacts, it means that I actually know them and if I know them, to a certain extent we are similar, therefore nothing that I would post would offend them because if it would offend them, it would also offend me. So it's a nonexistent issue for me" (**SB6**). Thus, value homophily in these cases is clearly identified as a unifying factor in users' networks. Furthermore, dissolving bonds with people who have proven themselves to be dissimilar is fully embraced. For some users, the destruction of such bonds is actually sought after. Political posts in particular have been signaled by a couple of users as the reasons for severing ties with the authors of those posts. This is something which not only came up in interviews, but the interviewees also wrote publicly in their profiles about their decision to unfriend all those with a certain political view. Then, value homophily goes beyond the formation and maintenance of ties with people who are fairly similar on several axes. It becomes publicly assumed as a legitimate principle of organizing insider and outsider status. Users take pride in "cleaning up" their circles, in closing up their own gate of access to the network, and, in doing so, encouraging other insiders to close theirs.

This being said, interviewees have approached status homophily with varying degrees of openness, depending on the criteria on which it was founded. Race and ethnicity are never explicitly mentioned. Age appears occasionally as a criterion of differentiation, especially in the context of older people having other Facebooking habits, other uses of images and emoticons, which is read with mild superior amusement by their younger counterparts. However, the bonds my informants have with people of different ages are typically linked to their families or to social contexts in which they happened to be, rather than their choices of networking. While dissimilarities between age cohorts exist, they do not lead to particular shifts within the bond, and they do not appear to create strong influences over practices (at least not in the direction of young adults, my category of interest). Instead they are taken for granted and regarded as marginal, which in itself is telling of how their bonds are organized. The relation with users younger than 18 years of age does not preoccupy the informants at all. With respect to gender, several female interviewees acknowledge the fact that most of the people in their Facebook network are women and, when asked about whether they have noticed any gendered practices, they affirm they do not have links to enough male profiles to tell. This reflects the same objective reality of homophily on gender criteria, with people of the same gender being more likely to bond. Facebook is, in this case, a mirror for social configurations, with little influence on reshaping them. It is interesting to note that, unlike value homophily which is overtly embraced, status homophily is presented mostly as a state of facts which the respondents find neither particularly desirable nor disconcerting in any way. Whether the intentional component is weak or it is simply more socially acceptable to say "I happen to have mostly female friends" than it would be to say "I have a clear preference of befriending only one gender" is difficult to establish within this context.

Consumer Culture

Yet, one area where Facebook users actively engage with the symbolic order which is interwoven within their bonds is consumer culture. Soon after its release, Bourdieu's theory of taste and class distinction (Bourdieu 1984, 1986) has been adapted to network literature (DiMaggio 1982; Bryson 1996; Peterson and Kern 1996; de Nooy 2003; Crossley 2008; Puetz 2015). These works discuss the patterns of social networks and point to the importance of social actors' taste in general, but specifically their use of consumer culture, as a central tool in shaping their links with others. Regarding the meanings of the goods which are consumed, Featherstone (1991) was arguing, following Saussure and Baudrillard, that consumption as we know it today is based on commodities becoming meaningful through their position in a self-referential system of signifiers (Featherstone 1991, p. 85).

Going further, one may ask about the actual mechanisms through which consumption practices are linked to personal networks. How does consumption practically contribute to bonds? As Puetz (2015) summarizes, the answers are divided into several categories (sociability, implicit cognition, group identity performance). For the purpose of this argument, I will collapse those categories even further and distinguish between two: the interactional and the expositional. The interactional mechanisms (Lizardo 2006; Vaisey and Lizardo 2010; Collins 2004; Tavory 2010) view consumption as fostering conversation, providing pretexts for shared experiences and generating more or less conscious contexts favorable to bonding. The expositional mechanisms rely on imagined communities (Anderson 1983; Straw 1991; Peterson and Bennett 2004). In this case, the performance of an identity is central. People gain membership to particular groups simply as a result of their tastes, which are enacted in consumption practices. Puetz (2015) views this latter approach as less network oriented, as the actual interactions between people are secondary to the criteria of inclusion. According to this categorization, there is a type of non-interactional exchanges on Facebook (e.g. vacation pictures, food consumption, check-ins at particular events) which appear as entirely expositional. However, I argue they are not. Rather, they are an unusual hybrid, which, despite not involving interactions, still involves bonds. In order to fully explain this, I will firstly analyze consumption-related posts and then turn towards those with a stronger interactional component (e.g. writing something controversial or posing a question linked to the consumption of a particular product). Last but not least, I will discuss the other aspects of social structure which are not openly linked with consumption.

Non-interactional Consumption Posts: Goods and Their Symbolic Meaning Within Bonds

When posting publicly, Facebook users often do not engage in any inter-action, if their posts are not also accompanied by a clearly directed question, or by a statement addressed to someone in particular. Many posts are a picture, an article, a song, or a few lines written by the user and addressed to everyone who might read them. When these messages contain a clear element of consumption, which inevitably intersects with social structure, the dynamic and the context are not always suitable for generating a conversation or encouraging interactions. Such posts are typically related to the (a) consumption of cultural products displayed through sharing music, movie trailers, and book ads, (b) food consumption and diet choices, or (c) location-bound consumption through check-ins. Some cases are a mixture of all the above, like vacation images. In these situations, feedback may be given and a minimal interaction may be established, through "a like" or a brief polite comment complimenting the author/their choice of food/their taste in music, but a lengthier or more significant interaction is unlikely to be born from there. In this respect, the action of publicly posting any of these contents seems purely fueled by a performative attempt to demonstrate one's belonging to a particular group identity. And this is definitely an element of it. However, understanding these practices with the help of imagined communities draws attention away from what users have time and time again empha-sized—namely, the importance of Facebook as a result of the people who are there, not only as the imagined whole but also because of who they are separately. The specifics of the connections between their bonds and their consumption practices (who in particular they wish to impress, whose tastes guide their own, etc.) are something most users are reluctant to discuss. However, interviewees do agree they expect certain people in their circle to appreciate specific posts and many say they do keep that in mind, even loosely, when choosing what to share, or more so when deciding against sharing something. One of the more open comments made in the direction of the link between taste, consumption, and social status came from a user who said:

> With the girlfriends that I've had, we always watched many movies and I cannot sit through dubbed movies. For me that is a no go. It's worse than with music. I don't know how you pick on these things, but if you do… But one thing goes through the other. If I see this, then I won't be attracted to her. (…) Also, I know I am a big, big, big music geek and I know I cannot expect people to be as fascinated about the same things I am fascinated about. That is unfair. I spend a lot of time with my hobby so I know it's unfair. But if someone just listens to what they play at the club and they are happy with what they are getting through mainstream radios or media, then I think… I don't think they are bad people. I just think they are not people I am interested in. (**SB15**)

Firstly, this highlights a form of symbolic order, which encapsulates a hierarchical organization of the social world and in which cultural consumption is an important indicator of one's status in that system. Secondly, it also highlights the critical and agentic stance where one intentionally adopts and displays certain consumption practices, also being aware of the symbolic weight those practices carry in themselves and in others. Thirdly, it highlights the ways in which the structural and agentic aspects become intertwined within social bonds. Outside of the bonds with others seen through the user's own eyes rather than from above, and outside of the potential of particular consumption practices to communicate certain symbolic messages *to others*, the entire conversation about consumption is meaningless. The music taste of the person whose profile my interviewee was browsing gave him the indicators he needed in order to establish the desired strength of this bond in the future. Were it not for the stake of the potential bond, her taste in music would not matter at all. Also, were it not for his own taste as reference point, her preferences would be, again, insignificant.

This example is mostly based on the typification of the other in light of particular information, rather than on constructing an imaginary about them in their ongoing experience. In the chapter on monitoring especially, I have argued such typifications are common for weak and/or new ties. And going further, it can be said with little doubt that consumption-related posts are indeed addressed to and of interest for weak ties who will likely use them in typifications.

Yet, let us go back to the mechanisms through which consumption practices are linked with creating and maintaining ties. If typifications are what is aimed or at least what is obtained through consumption displays in social networking, one may argue public posts focused on consumption are in fact clear cases of solitary identity performance. I claim these public Facebook posts are not interactional, but they are not expositional either. *The key idea here is that the typifications users make of each other and have come to expect from each other have a relational logic and often also a relational end.* The user in the example above did not engage in any interaction with the person in question on Facebook. Despite the lack of interaction, his interpretation was constantly linked with his own preferences and how they match up. This logic is also illustrated in a poignant phrase by another user: "for example someone sharing like… some music that I also like. I also get a positive feeling that my taste matches other people's" (SB12). At the same time, SB15 was assessing the potential of a bond and the typification was part of that assessment. The same sort of mechanism, in reverse, also occurs when someone shares consumption-related content. They are aware they will be typified, and view that typification (accurately I would say) as part of the negotiation of their status within their network of ties, especially weaker ones.

This being said, it is important to acknowledge that while consumption-related information may constitute the basis for typification, and while users themselves may know that well, that does not mean all consumption-related posts are subordinated to this expected meaning-making pathway. There is a variety of other rationales and contexts behind sharing consumption practices. There are also a variety of public posts where the consumption itself is collateral to what is being said. Nevertheless, since

the focus of this discussion is on the link between bonds and social structure, consumption is regarded mainly through the lens of the hierarchical
meaning it indicates. And in certain cases, the statement about social
difference is unmissable in consumption posts, as one interviewee puts it
when asked about check-ins:

> I know people who do that. I don't see a point to it though. For example
> saying "I have eaten in this restaurant", not mentioning whether you liked
> it or not… If you say that you like it, I see the reasoning. You are recom-
> mending it. But if you're just checking in that you are in the subway station
> X… I can guess that the majority of these people do that to somehow show
> off, like "Look, I'm in Paris. You are in K. and I am in Paris. Do you see the
> difference? (**SB12**)

This person discusses precisely the consumption posts which have no
other explanation than the expectation of being typified and the wish to
be typified in a particular way. With respect to this, the interviewee considers the author of the post attempts to translate the hierarchies of value
attributed to different restaurants, or to different cities, to herself and her
own social background. In his view, the practice of check-ins perfectly
illustrates the belief in the principle that we are what we have (or what we
consume). The relation between goods and identity has long been documented and theorized (McCracken 1988; Featherstone 1991; Lury 1996;
Leiss et al. 2005; Gabriel 2013). In this vein, consumption has been
regarded as a phenomenon of self-construction and expression, with different degrees of influence from social factors. Yet, besides the incontest-
able worth what we consume has for us personally and besides how much
that is shaped through supra-individual mechanisms, the relational element is still very strong. The interviewee does not read a check-in from
Paris as "I've always wanted to visit Paris and I am happy to finally do it",
or as "Paris is a great city", but as "I am in a better place than you". The
vertical organization is constantly there at the interpersonal level. Any
expression of the self is not thrown into a void, but into a social world,
and it is envisioned as "landing" on those with whom one has contact.
One imagines appearing cool, fashionable, rich, and classy *to their peers*
by Facebooking about their presence in Paris. And we must not forget

these peers are not an abstract entity. They are the people that user will meet at work the following week, the next door neighbors and the old mates. Thus, beyond self-expression with its originality or conformity to collective meaning structures, there are ties which make it directly significant one way or the other.

At the same time, this fragment, as well as many similar others which refer to check-ins in particular, but also to other posts where location is central, points to the importance of spatiality in understanding consumption within the system of meanings in which it is rooted. In this respect, the analysis of Facebook practices may benefit from insights from tourism studies. The widely cited works of Urry (1990, 1995) reveal both the literal and the symbolic dimensions of consuming places. However, given the increased frequency of trips in the contemporary world, as well as the growing likelihood of long-term mobility and the geographical spreading of people's networks, the symbolic dimension has changed. As I have pointed out above, the system of meanings with which the goods that we consume are endowed is intertwined not only with situational (inter)actions and identities, but also with durable bonds. In this respect, besides a trip to Paris being meaningful in the context of (a) the significance of Paris in relation to other cities and (b) the significance of such trips for the identity of the traveler, it is meaningful in the context of the traveler's bonds. In order for this latter meaning to be fulfilled, the practice of place consumption must necessarily be related with the practice of making that consumption visible. This need for consumption visibility is combined with one's geographically scattered network of ties and with the usually limited copresence of other ties at the same bar or the same hotel as the poster. Then, social networking comes historically as the continuation of, firstly, practices of place consumption which were physically accessible to others (e.g. going to a terrace in one's hometown where they can be seen by most people they know) and, secondly, face-to-face narratives, sometimes aided by pictures, which describe to others the consumption of a distant space (e.g. telling copresent people about the restaurant where one went over the weekend). Social networking allows place consumption to become integrated in the shaping of social relations even when those relations are quite weak and physically distant.

The meanings of visiting Paris may be associated with a particular economic and human capital pointing towards a certain class belonging. The very familiarity with this widely accepted meaning may be enough for one to embark on a trip to France. Their socialization into and embracement of this system of significance may make them genuinely happy to go, even if nobody else ever knows about it. It may also make them evaluate their own status in a more favorable light. However, status is also relational, as it refers to one's own standing with respect to others. Others are either imagined communities, or even imagined social fields, or vague multiplications of the generalized other; but first and foremost, they are the others in one's life. In this sense, the full social significance of consumption practices can only be seen in its engulfment into bonds. The improvement of the standing one has in their own network is at stake when the practice of consumption is accompanied by the practice of consumption sharing.

Interestingly, this is the aspect the majority of users pick when discussing Facebook non-interactional consumption-related posts. They insist more on the display of consumption than on the consumption itself. If we compare the interview excerpt where the interviewee talked about music consumption, and the excerpt where the informant tells me his opinion about place consumption, the emphasis is different. In the former, the actual taste was the main criterion for making sense of the other and estimating the potential bond. In the latter, the poster's choice of going to Paris on vacation is not the main interest. Rather, their choice of posting about it is more interesting to him. The meaning of the display, the "showing off" can also be read in structural terms, as an indicator of where one stands in a Bourdieusian social space.

Online Privacy: Performing Versus Stating Upper-Class Status

Continuing the discussion on check-ins leads us to a paradoxical point. The very information which is symbolically valuable and which can improve one's social standing and thus unleash bonding potential which was previously locked is also the one which the user is socially penalized for sharing. Furthermore, the meaning of posting overrides the meaning of consumption. It does not matter that you are in Paris. It does not even matter if I find that impressive in a different context. You posted about it, which not only annulled its value, but your action of posting has been a social disservice to you. The topic of boasting is present in most interviews, as is the quasi-universally critical attitude towards food sharing and check-ins.

Yet, before proceeding with the discussion on boasting and the structural component of Facebooking styles rather than contents, one other issue must be addressed. It is not accidental that the person judging music taste was evaluating the taste itself and the person judging restaurant posts is evaluating the very fact that the user decided to share that information. Here, the key is the difference between sharing consumption exclusively as status indicator and sharing consumption as experience. SB12 clearly explains he views the idea of sharing the experience of being in a good restaurant as acceptable. So, a post containing music/food/ books someone likes, ideally accompanied by a statement which highlights the experience of consuming that good over the structural implications embedded in the meaning of that good, is preferred. Of course, as discussed in the previous chapters, the actual sharing of experience at a distance requires an imaginary about the absent other, which is typically built with the help of online information combined with information obtained through other channels. Thus, if the bond is weak enough, vivid details will be missing and, very likely, so will the incentive of reconstructing the experience of the other. In this sense, the "shared experience" will be equivalent to the experience of reading about an empty check-in. However, it will constitute a different discursive frame. The author of the post would not really share her experience, but she would signal to the others her social adeptness in displaying status in a relatively subtle way. From here, it follows consumption of music, movies, books, which is the consumption of experience per excellence, would be deemed more acceptable or more "postable" than the consumption of material goods (unless framed carefully).

In contrast to the experiential frame, boasting represents the unapologetic and unrestrained declaration about one's own social status. Check-ins are good examples of such transparent claims of privileged lifestyles, as they lack any other justifying umbrella, but they are not the only types of contents readable as unequivocal status affirming. The negative interpretation of boasting is something about which I also openly asked Facebook users. My interest was on how this attitude was generated and what is it exactly that makes a post displaying one's own capital(s) intolerable. I was assured it was not primarily the lack of credibility of the author, nor the fact that the content itself was not a meaningful indicator of status. It was simply the violation of a social norm, something "you don't do". But familiarity with that norm is also a strong indicator of social status, perhaps even stronger than the actual content which is shared, since it is less affected by intentional control. In their study about the survival of the ideal type of the English gentleman, Miles and Savage (2012) point out "modesty about one's achievements and a studied vagueness about one's social position and class identity" (Miles and Savage 2012, p. 595) as some of the defining characteristics of the English upper class which have persisted over time and are still active today. While their argument is focused on a narrow cultural setting, the view about modesty as virtue is one that is generally accepted beyond cultural boundaries, and one that is very compatible with the narratives Facebook users have presented to me. The gentlemanly ethic of unstated superiority and the ability to differentiate from others without having to do so overtly—these are the markers of social status which come across from refraining from posting content about oneself. The other aspect Miles and Savage (2012) discuss and which is very helpful for understanding the mechanisms of social stratification in social networking practices is the culture of insider recognition. For instance, with respect to this, one user talks about the elements he notices when looking on an image on Facebook:

SB13: But if someone adds me and I already know that person, but not as much as I would like, I just take a quick look. For example, I look for the places. I don't know why I do that, but I take a look at the places.

INT: The places where the pictures are taken?

SB13: Yeah, the place… because people have some interesting pictures from places around the world.

INT: So what makes a good place and what makes a bad place?

SB13: A good place to me… I don't know; it's complicated. It's also related to the quality of the picture.

INT: So the quality of the picture is also important?

SB13: To me, yes. I really love that people spend time to upload pictures on their Facebook. To me, sometimes it's like when I see a good a picture, I enjoy it even if it's taken here in X, in front of the building that we are in or it is taken in the other part of the world, but the originality, to be creative, this sort of thing (…). (**SB13**)

This person describes the understated indicators of social class, the cues that make the other an insider or an outsider to the interviewee's "caste" from a structural perspective, before the possibility of a stronger actual bond is even considered. The quality of the image and the originality differentiate the author of the post and give suggestions about status without blatantly claiming it. What is also interesting is the fact that the user approaches these issues starting from a conversation about hierarchies of place. When asked about how places rank in systems of meaning, he helps me get a more accurate understanding of how the meanings around a particular post are constructed, by (1) bringing the focus back on the person who posted (e.g. how original they are, as opposed to how impressive the place is) and (2) by linking the declared marker of the photographer's social standing (where they traveled) to the tacit ones (like the quality of the picture). Furthermore, towards the end of the excerpt, the interviewee renounces the relevance of where the picture was taken altogether. In other words, irrespective of the openly displayed indicators of status, it is still the insider recognition based on quality and creativity which matters. At the same time, even the places where the author of the post traveled are not the same type of direct display of status as consumption of goods. The trip is, once again, framed more like an experience, so that it does not contrast the ethics of demure performance of social refinement.

While this user is particularly eloquent in explaining how social stratification is reflected in practices of posting on Facebook, his view is not uncommon. Critical and ironical memes have been created and circulated especially for establishing the practices of consumption sharing as unequivocally undesirable. Phrases like "Did you know you can actually enter an airport without checking in on Facebook?" and "Facebook, or it didn't happen" highlight the value placed on subtle and implicit status performances as opposed to open displays of wealth, education, courage, or any other virtue apparently associated with social prestige. In this respect, Facebooking style and decisions about which practices get shared from one's everyday life become definite indicators of social stratification. The same logic of structure lies behind the preference for posts without a focus on the poster. Besides the experientially framed posts, another category which does not collide with one's status building is that of posts which are not in first person. From images of random pets to freshly released gadgets and from political articles to health advice, none of the users with whom I have talked had a negative attitude towards it. Of course, many users were critical of the content of the posts (e.g. the health advice given on Facebook came from an unreliable source and was written with grammar mistakes). However, there was no negative comment about the decision to post, no questioning of the motives behind it, and no claim of inappropriateness. These posts can also be understood as symbolic markers of social structure, but they are not direct statements about one's own status. Interestingly, in these cases, the actual practice of sharing becomes negligible and attention paid to content is restored. In other words, it is only the explicit breaking of the fundamentally aristocratic norm of public modesty about one's own achievements which inverses the relevance between what is being shared and the practice of sharing.

In the end, this way of making sense of social networking practices in structural terms encourages impersonal posts; it encourages the circulation of various public online materials; it encourages news or videos "going viral". At the same time, it constructs self-referential posting as inelegant, unsophisticated, lower class, bragging. With this in mind, I believe the stratified take on practices of sharing announces a tendency towards a re-privatization and withdrawal of the self from social networking. The relational implications of online re-privatization are important. On the one hand, first-person narratives go back to the realm of close bonds, through face-to-face interaction and, at a distance, phone calls and chatting (note the increase in popularity of apps like WhatsApp over the last few years). Weak ties get relegated back to the periphery of access to personal information.

The person above, who was critical towards check-ins from various cities, metro stations, and restaurants, acts this re-privatized trend through his own posting practices:

INT: Can you think about the last two or three things you posted on Facebook? Or maybe your activities, not necessarily posts… maybe you shared or you commented…

SB12: Yeah, I shared first a link of a movie blog that I liked a lot, second… it was also a link to a blog, just one post in the blog which I thought was funny and the third one, I don't actually remember. No, I don't remember.

INT: Why did you post these things? Why did you feel the need to share them?

SB12: Hmmmm… good question (laughs). Yes, I thought that it's the thing that my friends probably do not know, so I decided to share it. Sometimes I am also sending links directly in a message. If I know that this person likes cinema and I for example find a nice article about cinema, sometimes I post it on their Facebook, sometimes I send it to the friend. Actually I am not sure about the decision process of how I will share it, but the main thing behind sharing is to let people know about interesting stuff.

Once more, the sharing practice is linked to the bond he has with others. He thinks of his friends when he posts, of their taste and their consumption practices, of the likelihood of them not having read the given blogs. In this sense, it is important to note only strong ties are relevant; weak ones do not even cross his mind. At the same time, the open self-reference is lacking. One may argue it is implicit, as it is blog content the interviewee himself read and found interesting enough to tell others about it. These aspects are telling about the educational capital, the taste and hobbies, the more general habitus of the user. Nevertheless, the factual information about his life events, the pictures about what he might look like nowadays, where he lives and works, whether he often goes to parties, and so on are missing. And if we think of what was of interest for weak ties, it was precisely this type of information. The information which gets revealed is still valuable, but it is limited to what can be shared with very weak bonds. The principle of the lowest common denominator is applied. Thus, while they are meant for close ties, posts like sharing blog articles are regarded as content which one does not mind random others reading. More importantly, this is content which does not have a typically lower-class statement about oneself incorporated within. The action of posting cinema reviews follows the exigency of performing a particular habitus without explicitly claiming that habitus. This mechanism (which is at its core a handbook case of distinction mechanism) rekindles early modern privacy rules of those with a high social status (Sennett 1992) and puts weak ties right back outside of the information-sharing circle. An often quoted affirmation made in 2010 by Facebook founder Mark Zuckerberg was that according to which privacy was no longer a social norm. While there may have been some truth to that several years ago, the relevance of performing privacy for social hierarchies is catching up with social networking. In the fragment quoted above, the information shared online had a rather impersonal character. Even so, the user concludes by saying he would sometimes send the link to the blog to a friend or two privately, which ultimately underscores the increasing withdrawal from the public eye.

However, it must be said the tendency towards re-privatization is not mainly privacy-driven. Rather, the re-appearance of privacy performance as a marker of social class is primarily a reaction to users' personal posts in non-interactional instances. The "knowing of the other" which I analyzed in the early chapters of this book, the resulting typifications, and the lack of the shared experience have stripped self-referential posts of any other social relevance than their status claims. The fact that everyone expects to be typified according to what they share translates any first-person phrase into a possibly deliberate and not very discrete attempt at establishing a favorable social evaluation for oneself. This is what is then regarded as an indicator of lower class. So, it is not the actual publication of particular information about oneself, or the uncontrolled sharing with too weak bonds, but the fact that Facebook's design only allows it to be blatantly shared that matters. As there are very few ways of posting publicly something about oneself without making it a status statement, many users choose to refrain from the practice altogether. To illustrate, one may talk about being vegetarian in a face-to-face conversation for a variety of reasons (e.g. it came up in a conversation about animal rights, it became obvious when choosing a restaurant to dine with friends, it was a topic used to fill an awkward silence, etc.); yet, a Facebook post mentioning the user is a vegetarian will typically be read as a status claim, whether it is one or not. One informant experienced this himself when he was publicly questioned by his friends about why he posted his decision to stop eating meat on Facebook. The possibility of the post being an open status claim and thus marking low-class belonging induces the user's silence about themselves. In other words, the constant suspicion about others setting themselves up for favorable evaluations regarding their success, power, balance, or happiness largely as a result of public exchanges being non-interactional by design has led to reluctance in posting about oneself and to re-privatization.

Social Structure in Online Interaction

Besides the non-interactional exchanges, ranging from consumption displays and status statements, to individual performances of social ideal types, interactions are also marked by a similar symbolic order. Regarding this aspect, popularity is of particular importance, as it reveals something about the user's social standing outside of whichever efforts they themselves may make to appear in a certain way. In the subchapter about the uses of the public character of online interaction, I quoted an interview fragment where the informant explained why she is impressed when posts have more likes and comments. She reads that as an indicator of the poster's popularity. And while she does not mention the role of who those people are, other respondents also talk about that. The face-giving process (Ivana 2016) through which someone with a well-established social prestige gives feedback to a user is emblematic in this sense. Then, the actual performance or claim of status is validated by someone who has the credibility, authority, or charisma to distinguish.

In interaction, the relational character of power is also apparent in other ways. Users constantly giving feedback to those of whom they think highly or who they consider powerful is a common occurrence. Furthermore, subtle interactional cues, like time taken for responses or imbalanced conversations where one person writes long messages or very elaborated formulations and receives back two words, clearly reveal the structure of power. Unanswered public comments have a similar meaning. In these cases, power is mostly embedded in network relations. However, these hierarchies within networks often largely, although certainly not always, overlap with macro-structural categories. In other words, the person who is popular and powerful enough within an informal network to not respond to comments, for instance, is very likely to also have a variety of other capitals and a performance of status, both on- and offline which makes them socially privileged in relation to others in the network.

Also arising from the upper-class taboo of promoting one's own achievements is the value of tags. Several interviewees have discussed the fact that it is preferable for the same content to be posted by someone else rather than by the user herself. This applies particularly to posts about the user (e.g. pictures from a highbrow event she attended). The fact that someone else made the information public means that one avoids the risk of "distasteful" status statement, but still allows the message to reach those in her network. Additionally, this occurrence is especially convenient because the subject herself does not need to perform status in any way to get it across. These are occurrences which I call third person status statements. Alternatively, public discussions about consumption practices or other status markers function towards similar outcomes. These interactional status performances also help users out of self-display, as they imitate acceptable face-to-face conversation.

This approach to social hierarchies and distinctions on Facebook is not only empirically sound, but also theoretically informed. In his work on the importance of consumption in the sociology of the past century, Warde (2002, 2014) discusses three main approaches. One is the macro-sociological economism of the 1960s, another is the cultural turn which started in the 1970s, and the third is the current practical turn. This approach, which came as a response to the cultural turn, draws on previous insights, while also highlighting the limitations of an excessive focus on culture. Namely, the lack of interest in embodiment, performance, and the overestimation of agentic deliberation have been signaled as causes for concern. In the loosely related field of tourism, a similar performance turn has also been noted (Rakic 2012; Edensor 1998, 2001; Haldrup and Larsen 2010), as the accent has shifted from meanings to doings and enactments. My current argument also follows these developments. By focusing on social status as not only a system of meanings, but also a set of performative practices, I reveal the ways in which particular advantages within the social field are not only interpreted, but also actualized and constantly reconstructed in the concrete process of Facebooking. This is a particularly important point to make, especially in the online environment, where deliberation does often precede decision making, and where the lack of copresence makes many traditional forms of social performance impossible. Yet, even so, online social performances function in their own right, while at the same time drawing from more general social norms. So, it is within these performances, with their practical and symbolic components, that this chapter has analyzed the interplay between structure (understood mainly as symbolic order) agency and network of ties.

References

Adams, Matthew. 2006. Hybridizing Habitus and Reflexivity: Towards an Understanding of Contemporary Identity? *Sociology* 40 (3): 511–528.

Anderson, Benedict. 1983. *Imagined Communities: Reflections on the Origin and Spread of Nationalism*. London and New York: Verso Books.

Barnett, George A., and Grace A. Benefield. 2017. Predicting International Facebook Ties Through Cultural Homophily and Other Factors. *New Media & Society* 19 (2): 217–239.

Bottero, Wendy. 2009. Relationality and Social Interaction. *The British Journal of Sociology* 60 (2): 399–420.

Bottero, Wendy, and Nick Crossley. 2011. Worlds, Fields and Networks: Becker, Bourdieu and the Structures of Social Relations. *Cultural Sociology* 5 (1): 99–119.

Bourdieu, Pierre. 1984. *Distinction: A Social Critique of the Judgement of Taste*. Cambridge, MA: Harvard University Press.

———. 1986. The Forms of Capital. In *Handbook of Theory and Research for the Sociology of Education*, ed. John G. Richardson, 241–258. New York: Greenwood.

Bryson, Bethany. 1996. 'Anything But Heavy Metal': Symbolic Exclusion and Musical Dislikes. *American Sociological Review* 61 (5): 884–899.

Collins, Randall. 2004. *Interaction Ritual Chains*. Princeton, NJ: Princeton University Press.

Crossley, Nick. 2008. (Net)Working Out: Social Capital in a Private Health Club. *The British Journal of Sociology* 59 (3): 475–500.

De Nooy, Wouter. 2003. Fields and Networks: Correspondence Analysis and Social Network Analysis in the Framework of Field Theory. *Poetics* 31 (5–6): 305–327.

DiMaggio, Paul. 1982. Cultural Capital and School Success: The Impact of Status Culture Participation on the Grades of U.S. High School Students. *American Sociological Review* 47 (2): 89–201.

Edensor, Tim. 1998. *Tourists at the Taj*. London: Routledge.

———. 2001. Performing Tourism, Staging Tourism: (Re) Producing Tourist Space and Practice. *Tourist Studies* 1 (1): 59–81.

Elder-Vass, Dave. 2007. Reconciling Archer and Bourdieu in an Emergentist Theory of Action. *Sociological Theory* 25 (4): 325–346.

Featherstone, Mike. 1991. *Consumer Culture and Postmodernism*. London: Sage.

Gabriel, Rami. 2013. *Why I Buy: Self, Taste, and Consumer Society in America*. Intellect Books Ltd.

Haldrup, Michael, and Jonas Larsen. 2010. *Tourism, Performance and the Everyday: Consuming the Orient*. London: Routledge.

Ivana, Greti-Iulia. 2016. Face and the Dynamics of Its Construction: A Relational and Multilayered Perspective. *Symbolic Interaction* 39 (1): 106–125.

King, Anthony. 2010. The Odd Couple: Margaret Archer, Anthony Giddens and British Social Theory. *The British Journal of Sociology* 61 (1): 253–260.

Lazarsfeld, Paul F., and Robert K. Merton. 1954. Friendship as a Social Process: A Substantive and Methodological Analysis. In *Freedom and Control in Modern Society*, ed. M. Berger, 18–66. New York: Van Nostrand.

Leiss, William, et al. 2005. *Social Communication in Advertising: Consumption in the Mediated Marketplace*. 3rd ed. New York: Routledge.

Lizardo, Omar. 2006. How Cultural Tastes Shape Personal Networks. *American Sociological Review* 71: 778–807.

Lury, Celia. 1996. *Consumer Culture*. Cambridge: Polity.

McCracken, Stephen D. 1988. *Culture and Consumption: New Approaches to the Symbolic Character of Consumer Goods and Activities*. Bloomington: Indiana University Press.

McPherson, Miller, et al. 2001. Birds of a Feather: Homophily in Social Networks. *Annual Review of Sociology* 27 (1): 415–444.

Miles, Andrew, and Mike Savage. 2012. The Strange Survival Story of the English Gentleman, 1945–2010. *Cultural and Social History* 9 (4): 595–612.

Peterson, Richard A., and Andy Bennett. 2004. Introducing the Scenes Perspective. In *Music Scenes: Local, Trans-Local and Virtual*, ed. A. Bennett and R.A. Peterson. Nashville: Vanderbilt University Press.

Peterson, Richard A., and Roger M. Kern. 1996. Changing Highbrow Taste: From Snob to Omnivore. *American Sociological Review* 61 (5): 900–907.

Puetz, Kyle. 2015. Consumer Culture, Taste, Preferences, and Social Network Formation. *Sociology Compass* 9 (6): 438–449.

Rafieian, Shahram, and Howard Davis. 2016. Dissociation, Reflexivity and Habitus. *European Journal of Social Theory* 19 (4): 556–573.

Rakic, Tijana. 2012. Philosophies of the Visual [Method] in Tourism Research. In *An Introduction to Visual Research Methods in Tourism*, ed. T. Rakic and D. Chambers, 17–32. New York: Routledge.

Sennett, Richard. 1992. *The Fall of the Public Man*. New York: WW Norton Publishing.

Singh, Sourabh. 2016. What Is Relational Structure? Introducing History in the Debates on the Relation between Fields and Social Networks. *Sociological Theory* 34 (2): 128–150.

Straw, Will. 1991. Systems of Articulation, Logics of Change: Communities and Scenes in Popular Music. *Cultural Studies* 5 (3): 368–388.

Tavory, Iddo. 2010. Of Yarmulkes and Categories: Delegating Boundaries and the Phenomenology of Interactional Expectation. *Theory and Society* 39 (1): 49–68.

Urry, John. 1990. *The Tourist Gaze: Leisure and Travel in Contemporary Societies*. London: Sage.

———. 1995. *Consuming Places*. London: Routledge.

Vaisey, Stephen, and Omar Lizardo. 2010. Can Cultural Worldviews Influence Network Composition? *Social Forces* 88 (4): 1595–1618.

Warde, Alan. 2002. Changing Conceptions of Consumption. In *The Changing Consumer*, ed. A. Anderson, K. Meethan, and S. Miles, 10–24. London: Routledge.

———. 2014. After Taste: Culture, Consumption and Theories of Practice. *Journal of Consumer Culture* 14 (3): 279–303.

Wimmer, Andreas, and Kevin Lewis. 2010. Beyond and Below Racial Homophily: ERG Models of a Friendship Network Documented on Facebook. *American Journal of Sociology* 116 (2): 583–642.

8

Conclusions

My argument so far has been aimed at understanding the meanings inculcated in the exchanges of information on Facebook and the ways in which those meanings are intertwined with relatively stable ties. In order to achieve this aim, I have established certain understandings for social interactions, for meaning construction based on experience, for ties, and for Facebook as a social space generated by its users through the actualization of a given set of potentialities. Starting from there, I went on to discuss the specificities of exchanges of information occurring on Facebook and the distinction users make between Facebook and real life. Afterwards, the relation between meaning construction and underlying ties has been approached from several angles. Firstly, I explored users' narratives about posting and overviewing, with no reference to instances of interaction. Within this thematic sphere, the interrelation between the significance of overviewing and tie strength remained a central focus. Secondly, building upon the mechanisms observed in non-interactional contexts, I shifted the emphasis towards the analysis of how meaning endowment in public social interactions emerges from and is assimilated to different ties. The importance of publicness in interpretative processes has also been touched upon. In the last section of that chapter, meaning

© The Author(s) 2018
G.-I. Ivana, *Social Ties in Online Networking*, Palgrave Studies in
Relational Sociology, https://doi.org/10.1007/978-3-319-71595-7_8

construction in private interactions and its variety in respect to tie strength has been looked into. The significance with which Facebook contents are endowed in the context of the underlying bonds between users is shaped by a variety of coordinates. In both non-interactional overviewing and interactional exchanges, I highlighted the importance of previous tie strength and relational normativity. Having said this, social networking actions make sense for the users especially when regarded through the relations they have with those in their circle. And those relations involve a major emotional component. Consequently, I have also dedicated a chapter of the book to the often underestimated emotions intersecting Facebook use. In this respect, pride and shame, need for support, belonging, anger, and emotions connected to romance have been tackled. Last but not least, the links between underlying bonds and Facebook exchanges also have a macro-structural component. Bearing this in mind, one chapter is focused on homophily manifests itself in the network, as well as how negotiations of social status unfold, aided by particular static indicators and dynamic performances.

This research has been designed to capture the multiplicity, variation, and color of the relation between meaning constructions in Facebook exchanges and bonds, rather than proposing a monolithic answer to a research question. Nevertheless, within this diversity that the fieldwork has helped me illustrate, there are some threads ensuring the unitary aspect of the argument. One of them is the focus on the hermeneutic approach. The entire line of thought that has been followed in the course of the book was centered on the issue of interpretative processes, more specifically, how Facebook users construct their understanding of and emotions around the information shared/exchanged. The actions and interactions, the unfolding of certain episodes that the interviewees talk about, the out-of-the-ordinary practices, as well as the routinized habits have been explored through the lens of the meaning constructions and the interpretations they have been given by the subjects. At this point it must be highlighted that throughout this book, meaning has been regarded as holistic, rather than cognitive. Thus, a Facebook post is meaningful for the user who shares/receives it, not only through reflection upon it, but also through experience (sometimes with a particular level of embodiment) and emotions it evokes. In this respect, the distinctions between interactional and non-interactional exchanges, the analysis of first-hand experiences of togetherness in "being with the other", and the discussion about emotions are examples of instances where the book focuses on that which is significant without being primarily cognitive. In the same vein, the focus on bonds, on projections and expectations about how they may evolve, the relational contextualization of dispersed Facebook posts contributes to capturing meaning in all its dimensions. Thus, the other thread that is present throughout the argument is the focus on the tie framing the interpretation of contents communicated through Facebook. While the interpretation of the shared information itself has been briefly touched upon in several instances, the main topic remained the relation between the significance of social networking actions and the underlying tie, rather than with the contents themselves. For instance, when analyzing how one user makes sense of a vacation picture published by another user, I focused more on the type and strength of tie between the author of the post and the interpreter, than on what was in the picture. Furthermore, when discussing what was in the picture, the emphasis was still relational (e.g. what the user intended to communicate/what was received/how that relates to various ties, etc.). The reason for doing so is that, based on the interviews, the tie constantly appears as a key factor for meaning construction. Who the other is, how long I have known him/her, how much shared experience we have, how close to him/her I find myself or wish myself to be—all these aspects are part of the bond which is conditioned by, but perhaps to a greater extent conditioning of, the meaning construction around what takes place on Facebook. Moreover, there has been another thread stemming from the emphasis on meaning construction, but also from the importance given to the actual experience of sharing information and interacting on Facebook. Namely, I am referring to the norms which structure both what is shared in online networking and how it is read. Regarding this topic, the insights are multiple, as we can speak of widely accepted social norms regulating general behavior (like the range of acceptable dressing styles), a particular informal bond normativity (what friends are expected to do for each other), interaction normativity (such as when one is obliged to answer to another), emotional normativity (what is legitimate for one to feel and when), and structurally differentiated normativity (like what is acceptable for certain strata of the social structure, but not for others). All these aspects of normativity have been discussed in relation to Facebook posts at different points throughout the book.

While these threads give unity to the approach, they also point towards variety in findings. Different ties favor different mechanisms of meaning making, just as different interactions are experienced by the subjects under different flows, depending on both the setting and the tie. They also have different potentials of contributing to a reshaping of that tie. Some patterns have indeed been identified and certain mechanisms of meaning construction emerged as correlated with particular contextual elements. However, given the limited resources and small scale of my research, I am reluctant in claiming the elaboration of generalizable patterns for meaning attribution in exchanges on Facebook. What I will say is that this research describes variation in the mechanisms of meaning attribution around exchanges occurring on Facebook in relation with different types of underlying ties and with contextual elements in the exchange (interactional vs. non-interactional, public vs. private). I believe the discussion about the mechanisms people employ to make sense of what they experience directly or know of is very revealing for an interpretative social scientist irrespective of whether it leads to generalizations or not. Yet, many of the mechanisms of meaning construction, as well as their variation, have been very similarly represented by most of the interviewees. So, one user might read a post from a strong tie very differently than the same post from a weak tie, but he might read it very similarly to how another user reads his posts from his/her strong ties. As a consequence, I believe this homogeneity supports the assumption of a level of generality. More extensive research might investigate whether my depiction of the mechanisms of meaning attribution in relation to different types of underlying ties is applicable on a different scale.

Before, I mentioned that outside of the question of generalizability, I view the issue of making sense of one another as a very fruitful object of study. Coming to the case of the current research, I consider it fruitful because it sheds light on the exchanges happening under conditions that by default make the other less accessible than face to face. The current research is an attempt to get as close as possible to how subjects live their experience of Facebooking and how they make sense of it, while keeping in mind that despite being apart when they browse or interact, they carry their bonds within them. This contributes to a deep understanding of the practices occurring on Facebook, but it also expands outside of it, into the study of other interaction/tie contexts.

Leaving aside the specificity of some of the arguments related to Facebook (such as the existence of a world within reach for one interactant that is inaccessible to the other, the possibilities of monitoring without the other acknowledging it, or the deliberation necessary prior to an interaction), there are a series of aspects that are lend themselves to analyses of social interactions and ties in general. An example is the fact that people who are involved in a weaker tie with each other are more likely to look for indicators by which they typify each other, since they do not have a consistent enough previous shared experience. If that common past experience existed, and the tie were stronger, the need for an active reflection and for typification would fade away. On a different note, the adaptation of one's behavior not only to his/her own projections about the future of the tie but also to the imagined projection the other has about the tie is also something that occurs in various settings outside of Facebook. Thus, from this perspective, my research provides insights into the connection between various ties and meaning constructions in social interactions, two issues that have often been analyzed separately (e.g. conversation analysis for interactions and social capital literature for ties), despite their obvious link.

Directions for Future Research

One of the topics I have touched upon is the temporal anchoring of meaning construction especially in relation to ties (as emerging from past shared experiences or from projections about future togetherness). Regarding temporality, an interesting direction for future research would be a longitudinal study capturing the fluctuations in ties and their correlation with changes in interactions, as well as the changes in meaning attributions over time.

Furthermore, not only ties and interactions change constantly, but social networking does too. Towards the end of the book, one idea

I mentioned is the tendency of re-privatization of the self in social networking. It is my firm belief that this tendency is central for the direction in which the reshaping of social networking is heading. Many of my long discussions with Facebook users began with their first social networks, with Hi5, AOL, MySpace and Fotolog. The popularity of these networks has fluctuated significantly over time. If there is a common element in how the decline in interest came about, it is the Bourdieusian process through which they went before being rendered "uncool". In this respect, Facebook as a whole does not appear to be following the same pattern. However, particular practices and some commonly used features of public display do. So, a reorientation of Facebook away from the private sphere, and with it, a reshaping of social networking, is highly likely.

Following the narratives of my interviewees, I regard social networking as having had three distinct phases. The first one, the precursor to online networking, were the chatting rooms of the 1990s, which included connection and communication with strangers and anonymity. The second were the abovementioned pre-Facebook social networking sites, where the user's identity was public and connections with strangers continued. The third, represented predominantly by Facebook, but to certain extent also by Twitter, was already a step closer to privatization, as users had control over who can see what they post and it became normalized that unknown people would be kept out. The fourth stage, which I argue has begun, is even less open with personal information. The structural explanations for re-privatization are accompanied by other processes. For instance, the bonds, for which I have argued throughout the book, become more and more important in establishing what is said and to whom online. In face-to-face bond normativity, there is a clear difference between what one shares with a close friend and what they share when they accidentally meet a schoolmate they previously had not seen in ten years. The more social networking has become part of our lives, the more online experience is assimilated with the offline world. What we would not tell the old mate when we meet them, we will be less and less willing to have them read on Facebook too. Furthermore, this tendency of mimicking the offline favors interactional settings, real-time responses over static statements and displays.

Bearing in mind these considerations, research into the current and particularly future shape of online networking is necessary. Facebook, and social networks in general, have had a tremendous role in rehabilitating old ties, in negotiating the strength of newer ones, in the ways in which people keep in touch and in the knowledge they get from each other's lives. As social networking is constantly changing, we know little about the shape and implications of these changes. It is my hope that these topics will be explored in future research and that this book represents an encouragement for social scientists to mobilize the resources of relational sociology in their explorations.

References

Aarseth, Espen J. 1997. *Cybertext: Perspectives on Ergodic Literature*. Baltimore and London: JHU Press.

Adams, Matthew. 2006. Hybridizing Habitus and Reflexivity: Towards an Understanding of Contemporary Identity? *Sociology* 40 (3): 511–528.

Adloff, Franc, and Steffen Mau. 2006. Giving Social Ties, Reciprocity in Modern Society. *European Journal of Sociology* 47 (1): 93–123.

Aguirre, Alwin C., and Sharyn Graham Davies. 2015. Imperfect Strangers: Picturing Place, Family, and Migrant Identity on Facebook. *Discourse, Context & Media* 7: 3–17.

Ahmed, Sara. 2001. The Organisation of Hate. *Law and Critique* 12 (3): 345–365.

Alduiza, Eva, Camilo Cristancho, and Jose M. Sabucedo. 2014. Mobilization through Online Social Networks: The Political Protest of the Indignados in Spain. *Information, Communication & Society* 17 (6): 750–764.

Anderson, Benedict. 1983. *Imagined Communities: Reflections on the Origin and Spread of Nationalism*. London and New York: Verso Books.

Andrejevic, Mark. 2006. The Discipline of Watching: Detection, Risk, and Lateral Surveillance. *Critical Studies in Media Communication* 23 (4): 391–407.

Argyle, Michael, and Monika Henderson. 1984. The Rules of Friendship. *Journal of Social and Personal Relationships* 1 (2): 211–237.

© The Author(s) 2018   **205**
G.-I. Ivana, *Social Ties in Online Networking*, Palgrave Studies in
Relational Sociology, https://doi.org/10.1007/978-3-319-71595-7

Auter, Zachary J., and Jeffrey A. Fine. 2017. Social Media Campaigning: Mobilization and Fundraising on Facebook. *Social Science Quarterly*. First published 28 February 2017.

Azarian, Reza. 2010. Social Ties. Elements of a Substantive Conceptualization. *Acta Sociologica* 53 (4): 323–338.

Bakardjieva, Maria. 2003. Virtual Togetherness: An Everyday-life Perspective. *Media, Culture & Society* 25 (3): 291–313.

———. 2005. *Internet Society: The Internet in Everyday Life*. London: Sage.

Baker, Andrea. 2008. Down the Rabbit Hole: The Role of Place in the Initiation and Development of Online Relationships. In *Psychological Aspects of Cyberspace: Theory, Research, Applications*, ed. A. Barak, 163–184. Cambridge: Cambridge University Press.

Barassi, Veronica. 2013. Ethnographic Cartographies: Social Movements, Alternative Media and the Spaces of Networks. *Social Movement Studies* 12 (1): 48–62.

Barbalet, Jack. 1998. *Emotion, Social Theory, and Social Structure: A Macrosociological Approach*. Cambridge: Cambridge University Press.

———. 2002. Why Emotions are Crucial. In *Emotions and Sociology*, ed. J. Barbalet, 1–9. Oxford: Blackwell Publishing.

Barnett, George A., and Grace A. Benefield. 2017. Predicting International Facebook Ties Through Cultural Homophily and Other Factors. *New Media & Society* 19 (2): 217–239.

Bateman, Patrick J., Jacqueline Pike, and Brian Butler. 2010. To Disclose or Not: Publicness in Social Networking Sites. *Information Technology & People* 24 (1): 78–100.

Baym, Nancy K. 2010. *Personal Connections in the Digital Age*. Cambridge: Polity Press.

Baym, Nancy K., and danah boyd. 2012. Socially Mediated Publicness: An Introduction. *Journal of Broadcasting & Electronic Media* 56 (3): 320–329.

Ben-Ze'ev, Aaron. 2004. *Love Online: Emotions on the Internet*. Cambridge: Cambridge University Press.

Berger, Peter, and Thomas Luckman. 1966. *The Social Construction of Reality*. Harmondsworth: Penguin Books.

Bergson, Henri. 1910. *Time and Free Will. An Essay on the Immediate Data of Consciousness*. Trans. F.L. Pogson. London: George Allen & Unwin.

Beyer, Jessica L. 2014. The Emergence of a Freedom of Information Movement: Anonymous, WikiLeaks, the Pirate Party, and Iceland. *Journal of Computer-Mediated Communication* 19 (2): 141–154.

Birnbaum, Matthew Gardner. 2008. *Taking Goffman on a Tour of Facebook: College Students and the Presentation of Self in a Mediated Digital Environment.* Tuscon: The University of Arizona.

Blumer, Herbert. 1969. *Symbolic Interactionism: Perspective and Method.* Englewood Cliffs, NJ: Prentice-Hall.

Booth, Alan, and Elaine Hess. 1974. Cross-Sex Friendship. *Journal of Marriage and the Family* 36 (1): 38–47.

Borup, Jered, Richard E. West, and Rebecca Thomas. 2015. The Impact of Text Versus Video Communication on Instructor Feedback in Blended Courses. *Educational Technology Research and Development* 63 (2): 161–184.

Bottero, Wendy. 2009. Relationality and Social Interaction. *The British Journal of Sociology* 60 (2): 399–420.

Bottero, Wendy, and Nick Crossley. 2011. Worlds, Fields and Networks: Becker, Bourdieu and the Structures of Social Relations. *Cultural Sociology* 5 (1): 99–119.

Bourdieu, Pierre. 1984. *Distinction: A Social Critique of the Judgement of Taste.* Cambridge, MA: Harvard University Press.

———. 1986. The Forms of Capital. In *Handbook of Theory and Research for the Sociology of Education*, ed. John G. Richardson, 241–258. New York: Greenwood.

———. 1989. Social Space and Symbolic Power. *Sociological Theory* 7 (1): 14–25.

boyd, danah. 2010. Social Network Sites as Networked Publics: Affordances, Dynamics, and Implications. In *Networked Self: Identity, Community, and Culture on Social Network Sites*, ed. Zizi Papacharissi, 39–58. London: Routledge.

boyd, danah, and Nicole B. Ellison. 2007. Social Network Sites: Definition, History, and Scholarship. *Journal of Computer-Mediated Communication* 13 (1): 210–230.

Boym, Svetlana. 2001. *The Future of Nostalgia.* New York: Basic Books.

Bryant, Erin, and Jennifer Marmo. 2012. The Rules of Facebook Friendship: A Two-Stage Examination of Interaction Rules in Close, Casual, and Acquaintance Friendships. *Journal of Social and Personal Relationships* 29 (8): 1013–1035.

Bryson, Bethany. 1996. 'Anything But Heavy Metal': Symbolic Exclusion and Musical Dislikes. *American Sociological Review* 61 (5): 884–899.

Bucher, Taina. 2012. Want to be on the Top? Algorithmic Power and the Threat of Invisibility on Facebook. *New Media & Society* 14 (7): 1164–1180.

————. 2017. The Algorithmic Imaginary: Exploring the Ordinary Affects of Facebook Algorithms. *Information, Communication & Society* 20 (1): 30–44.

Burke, Peter J., and Jan E. Stets. 2009. *Identity Theory.* Oxford: Oxford University Press.

Chauhan, G.S., and T. Shukla. 2016. Social Media Advertising and Public Awareness: Touching the LGBT Chord! *Journal of International Women's Studies* 18 (1): 145–155.

Chaulk, Kasey, and Tim Jones. 2011. Online Obsessive Relational Intrusion: Further Concerns About Facebook. *Journal of Family Violence* 26 (4): 245–254.

Christiansen, Martha Sidury. 2017. Creating a Unique Transnational Place: Deterritorialized Discourse and the Blending of Time and Space in Online Social Media. *Written Communication* 34 (2): 135–164.

Cohen, Dov, and Richard Nisbett. 1994. Self-Protection and the Culture of Honor: Explaining Southern Violence. *Personality and Social Psychology Bulletin* 20 (5): 551–567.

Collins, Randall. 1990. Stratification, Emotional Energy, and the Transient Emotions. In *Research Agendas in the Sociology of Emotions*, ed. T.D. Kemper, 27–57. Albany: State University of New York Press.

————. 2004. *Interaction Ritual Chains.* Princeton, NJ: Princeton University Press.

Cooley, Charles. 1964. *Human Nature and the Social Order.* New York: Schocken Books.

Couldry, Nick. 2008. Mediatization or Mediation? Alternative Understandings of the Emergent Space of Digital Storytelling. *New Media & Society* 10 (3): 373–391.

Cross, S.E., A.K. Uskul, B. Gercek-Swing, Z. Sunbay, C. Alözkan, C. Günsoy, B. Ataca, and Z. Karakitapoğlu-Aygün. 2014. Cultural Prototypes and Dimensions of Honor. *Personality & Social Psychology Bulletin* 40: 232–249.

Crossley, Nick. 2008. (Net)Working Out: Social Capital in a Private Health Club. *The British Journal of Sociology* 59 (3): 475–500.

Dehghani, Milad, and Mustafa Turner. 2015. A Research on Effectiveness of Facebook Advertising on Enhancing Purchase Intention of Consumers. *Computers in Human Behaviour* 49 (1): 597–600.

De Nooy, Wouter. 2003. Fields and Networks: Correspondence Analysis and Social Network Analysis in the Framework of Field Theory. *Poetics* 31 (5–6): 305–327.

DeNora, Tia. 1999. Music as a Technology of the Self. *Poetics* 27 (1): 31–56.

DiMaggio, Paul. 1982. Cultural Capital and School Success: The Impact of Status Culture Participation on the Grades of U.S. High School Students. *American Sociological Review* 47 (2): 89–201.

———. 1987. Classification in Art. *American Sociological Review* 52 (4): 440–455.

Dimmick, John. 2003. *Media Competition and Coexistence: The Theory of the Niche*. Mahwah, NJ: Lawrence Erlbaum Associates.

Dimmick, John, and A.B. Albarran. 1994. The Role of Gratification Opportunities in Determining Media Preference. *Mass Communication Review* 21: 223–235.

Dimmick, John, John Christian Feaster, and Artemio Ramirez. 2011. The Niches of Interpersonal Media: Relationships in Time and Space. *New Media & Society* 13 (8): 1265–1282.

Donath, Judith, and danah boyd. 2004. Public Displays of Connection. *BT Technology Journal* 22 (4): 71–82.

Donati, Pierpaolo. 2015. Manifesto for a Critical Realist Relational Sociology. *International Review of Sociology* 25 (1): 86–109.

Duffett, Rodney Graeme. 2015. The Influence of Facebook Advertising on Cognitive Attitudes Amid Generation Y. *Electronic Commerce Research* 15 (2): 243–267.

Edensor, Tim. 1998. *Tourists at the Taj*. London: Routledge.

———. 2001. Performing Tourism, Staging Tourism: (Re) Producing Tourist Space and Practice. *Tourist Studies* 1 (1): 59–81.

Elder-Vass, Dave. 2007. Reconciling Archer and Bourdieu in an Emergentist Theory of Action. *Sociological Theory* 25 (4): 325–346.

Elias, Norbert. 2001. *The Society of Individuals*. New York: Continuum Publishing.

Ellison, Nicole B., Rebecca Gray, Cliff Lampe, and Andrew T. Fiore. 2014. Social Capital and Resource Requests on Facebook. *New Media & Society* 16 (7): 1104–1121.

Ellison, Nicole B., Rebecca Heino, and Jennifer Gibbs. 2006. Managing Impressions Online: Self-Presentation Processes in the Online Dating Environment. *Journal of Computer-Mediated Communication* 11 (2): 415–441.

Ellison, Nicole B., Cliff Lampe, and Charles Steinfield. 2009. Social Network Sites and Society: Current Trends and Future Possibilities. *Interactions* 16 (1): 6–9.

Ellison, Nicole B., Charles Steinfield, and Cliff Lampe. 2007. The Benefits of Facebook "Friends": Social Capital and College Students' Use of Online Social Network Sites. *Journal of Computer-Mediated Communication* 12 (4): 1143–1168.

Emerson, Richard M. 1972. Exchange Theory Part: 2 Exchange Relations and Networks. *Sociological Theories in Progress* 2: 58–87.

Emirbayer, Mustafa. 1997. Manifesto for a Relational Sociology. *American Journal of Sociology* 103 (2): 281–317.

Emirbayer, Mustafa, and Jeff Goodwin. 1994. Network Analysis, Culture, and the Problem of Agency. *American Journal of Sociology* 99 (6): 1411–1454.

Farnsworth, Jacob, and Kenneth W. Sewell. 2012. Fearing the Emotional Self. *Journal of Constructivist Psychology* 25 (3): 251–268.

Farquhar, Lee. 2013. Performing and Interpreting Identity through Facebook Imagery. *Convergence: The International Journal of Research into New Media Technologies* 19 (4): 446–471.

Featherstone, Mike. 1991. *Consumer Culture and Postmodernism*. London: Sage.

Felmlee, Diane, et al. 2012. Gender Rules: Same- and Cross-Gender Friendships Norms. *Sex Roles* 66 (7–8): 518–529.

Flam, Helena. 2005. Emotions' Map: A Research Agenda. In *Emotions and Social Movements*, ed. H. Flam and D. King. London: Routledge.

Foot, K.A., B. Warnick, and S.M. Schneider. 2005. Web-based Memorializing after September 11. *Journal of Computer-Mediated Communication* 11 (1): 72–96.

Foucault, Michel. 1995. *Discipline and Punish: The Birth of the Prison*. New York: Vintage Books.

Gabriel, Rami. 2013. *Why I Buy: Self, Taste, and Consumer Society in America*. Intellect Books Ltd.

Gamson, William A. 1992. The Social Psychology of Collective Action. In *Frontiers in Social Movement Theory*, ed. A.D. Morris and C. Mueller, 53–76. New Haven, CT: Yale University Press.

Garcia, Angela Cora, and Jennifer Baker Jacobs. 1999. The Eyes of the Beholder: Understanding the Turn-Taking System in Quasi-Synchronous Computer-Mediated Communication. *Research on Language and Social Interaction* 32 (4): 337–367.

Garcia Gomez, Antonio. 2010. Disembodiment and Cyberspace: Gendered Discourses in Female Teenagers' Personal Information Disclosure. *Discourse and Society* 21 (2): 135–160.

Garde-Hansen, J., A. Reading, and A. Hoskins, eds. 2009. *Save As… Digital Memories*. Basingstoke: Palgrave Macmillan.

Goffman, Erving. 1959. *The Presentation of Self in Everyday Life*. New York: Doubleday.

———. 1967. *Interaction Ritual: Essays On Face-to-Face behavior*. New York: Anchor Books.

———. 1971. *Relations in Public: Microstudies of the Public Order*. Berkeley: University of California Press.

———. 1983. The Interaction Order: American Sociological Association, 1982 Presidential Address. *American Sociological Review* 48 (1): 1–17.

Grabe, Shelly, Janet Shibley Hyde, and Sarah M. Lindberg. 2007. Body Objectification and Depression in Adolescents: The Role of Gender, Shame, and Rumination. *Psychology of Women Quarterly* 31 (2): 164–175.

Granovetter, Mark. 1983. The Strength of Weak Ties: A Network Theory Revisited. *Sociological Theory* 1: 201–233.

Günsoy, Ceren, Susan E. Cross, Adİl Sarıbay, Irmak Olcaysoy Ökten, and Meltem Kurutaş. 2015. Would You Post that Picture and Let Your Dad See It? Culture, Honor, and Facebook. *European Journal of Social Psychology* 45 (3): 323–335.

Haldrup, Michael, and Jonas Larsen. 2010. *Tourism, Performance and the Everyday: Consuming the Orient*. London: Routledge.

Hansson, Mats G. 2008. *The Private Sphere. An Emotional Territory and Its Agent*. Dordrecht: Springer.

Harrigan, Nicholas, and Janice Yap. 2017. Avoidance in Negative Ties: Inhibiting Closure, Reciprocity, and Homophily. *Social Networks* 48 (1): 126–141.

Hepp, Andreas. 2013. The Communicative Figurations of Mediatized Worlds: Mediatization Research in Times of the 'mediation of everything'. *European Journal of Communication* 28 (6): 615–629.

Hess, Andreas. 2007. Against Unspoilt Authenticity: A Re-appraisal of Helmuth Plessner's The Limits of Community (1924). *Irish Journal of Sociology* 16 (2): 11–26.

Heyman, Rob, and Jo Pierson. 2013. Blending Mass Self-communication with Advertising in Facebook and LinkedIn: Challenges for Social Media and User Empowerment. *International Journal of Media & Cultural Politics* 9 (3): 229–245.

Higonnet, Anne. 1998. *The History and Crisis of Ideal Childhood*. London: Thames and Hudson.

Hiller, Harry H., and Tara M. Franz. 2004. New Ties, Old Ties and Lost Ties: The Use of the Internet in Diaspora. *New Media & Society* 6 (6): 731–752.

Hilsen, Anne Inga, and Tove Helvik. 2014. The Construction of Self in Social Medias, such as Facebook. *AI & Society* 29 (1): 3–10.

Hochschild, Arlie Russell. 1979. Emotion Work, Feeling Rules, and Social Structure. *American Journal of Sociology* 85 (3): 551–575.

———. 2012. *The Outsourced Self: Intimate Life in Market Times*. New York: Metropolitan Books.

Hogan, Bernie. 2010. The Presentation of Self in the Age of Social Media: Distinguishing Performances and Exhibitions Online. *Bulletin of Science Technology* 30 (6): 377–386.

Holdsworth, Amy. 2011. *Television, Memory and Nostalgia*. Basingstoke and New York: Palgrave Macmillan.

Holmes, Mary. 2014. *Distance Relationships: Intimacy and Emotions Amongst Academics and their Partners in Dual-Locations*. Basingstoke: Palgrave Macmillan.

Homans, George Caspar. 1950. *The Human Group*. New York: Harcourt, Brace.

———. 1961. *Social Behavior: Its Elementary Forms*. London: Routledge & Kegan Paul.

Huck, Steffen, and Jean-Robert Tyran. 2007. Reciprocity, Social Ties, and Competition in Markets for Experience Goods. *Journal of Socio-Economics* 36 (2): 191–203.

Innes, Joanna, Steven King, and Anne Winter. 2013. Introduction: Settlement and Belonging in Europe, 1600–1950: Structures, Negotiations and Experiences. In *Migration, Settlement and Belonging in Europe, 1500–1930s: Comparative Perspectives*, ed. S. King and A. Winter, 1–28.

Irwin, Melissa D. 2015. Mourning 2.0—Continuing Bonds Between the Living and the Dead on Facebook. *OMEGA—Journal of Death and Dying* 72 (2): 119–150.

Ito, Mizuko, Heather A. Horst, Matteo Bittanti, danah boyd, Becky Herr Stephenson, Patricia G. Lange, C.J. Pascoe, and Laura Robinson. 2008. *Living and Learning with New Media: Summary of Findings from the Digital Youth Project in The John D. and Catherine T. MacArthur Foundation Reports on Digital Media and Learning*. Cambridge, MA: MIT Press.

Ivana, Greti-Iulia. 2013. A Postmodern Panopticon: Lateral Surveillance on Facebook. *Global Media Journal: Mediterranean Edition* 8 (1): 1–14.

———. 2016a. Face and the Dynamics of Its Construction: A Relational and Multilayered Perspective. *Symbolic Interaction* 39 (1): 106–125.

———. 2016b. Present Contemporaries and Absent Consociates: Rethinking Schütz's "We Relation" Beyond Copresence. *Human Studies* 39 (4): 513–531.

Jameson, Fredric. 1991. *Postmodernism or, The Cultural Logic of Late Capitalism*. Durham, NC: Duke University Press.

Johnston, Hank. 2009. *Culture, Social Movement and Protest*. Aldershot: Ashgate.

Johnston, Kevin, Maureen Tanner, Nishant Lalla, and Dori Kawalski. 2013. Social Capital: The Benefit of Facebook 'Friends'. *Behaviour and Information Technology* 32 (1): 24–36.

Kang, Seok. 2007. Disembodiment in Online Social Interaction: Impact of Online Chat on Social Support and Psychosocial Well-being. *CyberPsychology & Behavior* 10 (3): 475–477.

Kasket, Elain. 2012. Continuing Bonds in the Age of Social Networking: Facebook as a Modern-Day Medium. *Bereavement Care* 31 (2): 62–69.

Kaun, Annee, and Fredrik Stiernstedt. 2014. Facebook Time: Technological and Institutional Affordances for Media Memories. *New Media & Society* 16 (7): 1154–1168.

Kaur, Puneet, Amandeep Dhir, Sufen Chen, and Risto Rajala. 2016. Flow in Context: Development and Validation of the Flow Experience Instrument for Social Networking. *Computers in Human Behavior* 59: 358–367.

Kebadayi, Sertan, and Katherine Price. 2014. Consumer—Brand Engagement on Facebook: Liking and Commenting Behaviors. *Journal of Research in Interactive Marketing* 8 (3): 203–223.

Keller, E., and B. Fay. 2012. *The Face to Face Book: Why Real Relationships Rule in a Digital Marketplace*. New York: Free Press.

Kemper, Theodore D. 1978. *A Social Interactional Theory of Emotions*. New York: John Wiley.

———. 1990. *Research Agendas in the Sociology of Emotions*. New York: State University of New York Press.

———. 1991. An Introduction to the Sociology of Emotions. *International Review of Studies on Emotion* 1: 301–349.

———. 2011. *Status, Power and Ritual Interaction—A Relational Reading of Durkheim, Goffman and Collins*. Farnham: Ashgate.

Kincaid, James R. 1992. *Child-Loving: The Erotic Child and Victorian Culture*. New York and London: Routledge.

King, Anthony. 2010. The Odd Couple: Margaret Archer, Anthony Giddens and British Social Theory. *The British Journal of Sociology* 61 (1): 253–260.

Knautz, Kathrin, and Katsiaryna Baran. 2016. *Facets of Facebook: Use and Users*. Hawthorne, NJ: Walter de Gruyter.

Konecki, Krzysztof. 2008. Touching and Gesture Exchange as an Element of Emotional Bond Construction. Application of Visual Sociology in the Research on Interaction between Humans and Animals. *Forum: Qualitative Social Research* 9 (3): 1–46.

Kwak, K.T., S.K. Choi, and B.G. Lee. 2014. SNS Flow, SNS Self-disclosure and Post Hoc Interpersonal Relations Change: Focused on Korean Facebook User. *Computers in Human Behavior* 31: 294–304.

Kwon, Seok-Woo, Colleen Helfin, and Martin Ruef. 2013. Community, Social Capital and Entrepreneurship. *American Sociological Review* 78 (6): 980–1008.

Lambert, Alexander. 2016. Intimacy and Social Capital on Facebook: Beyond the Psychological Perspective. *New Media & Society* 18 (11): 2559–2575.

Lawler, Edward J. 2001. An Affect Theory of Social Exchange. *The American Journal of Sociology* 107 (2): 321–352.

———. 2009. The Power Process and Emotion. In *Power and Interdependence in Organizations*, ed. D. Tjosvold and B. van Knippenberg, 169–185. New York: Cambridge University Press.

Lawler, Edward J., Shane R. Thye, and Jeongkoo Yoon. 2008. Social Exchange and Micro Social Order. *American Sociological Review* 73 (4): 519–542.

Lazarsfeld, Paul F., and Robert K. Merton. 1954. Friendship as a Social Process: A Substantive and Methodological Analysis. In *Freedom and Control in Modern Society*, ed. M. Berger, 18–66. New York: Van Nostrand.

Ledbetter, Andrew. 2009. Measuring Online Communication Attitude: Instrument Development and Validation. *Communication Monographs* 76 (4): 463–486.

Leiss, William, et al. 2005. *Social Communication in Advertising: Consumption in the Mediated Marketplace*. 3rd ed. New York: Routledge.

Levine, Donald. 1985. *The Flight from Ambiguity/Essays in Social and Cultural Theory*. Chicago: University of Chicago Press.

Lizardo, Omar. 2006. How Cultural Tastes Shape Personal Networks. *American Sociological Review* 71: 778–807.

Lohmeier, Christine, and Christian Pentzold. 2014. Making Mediated Memory Work. Cuban-Americans, Miami Media and the Doings of Diaspora Memories. *Media, Culture & Society* 36 (6): 776–789.

Louch, Hugh. 2000. Personal Network Integration: Transitivity and Homophily in Strong-tie Relations. *Social Networks* 22 (1): 45–64.

Lury, Celia. 1996. *Consumer Culture*. Cambridge: Polity.

Lyndon, A., J. Bonds-Raacke, and A. Crattty. 2011. College Students' Facebook Stalking of Ex-partners. *Cyberpsychology, Behavior and Social Networking* 14 (12): 711–716.

Manago, Adriana M., L. Monique Ward, Kristi M. Lemm, Lauren Reed, and Rita Seabrook. 2015. Facebook Involvement, Objectified Body Consciousness,

Body Shame, and Sexual Assertiveness in College Women and Men. *Sex Roles* 72 (1–2): 1–14.

Marshall, Tara C. 2012. Facebook Surveillance of Former Romantic Partners: Associations with PostBreakup Recovery and Personal Growth. *CyberPsychology, Behavior & Social Networking* 15 (10): 521–526.

May, Vanessa. 2017. Belonging from Afar: Nostalgia, Time and Memory. *The Sociological Review* 65 (2): 401–415.

Mazur, Allen, and Theodore A. Lamb. 1980. Testosterone, Status, and Mood in Human Males. *Hormones and Behavior* 14 (3): 236–246.

McAndrew, Francis T., and Hye Sun Jeong. 2012. Who Does What on Facebook? Age, Sex, and Relationship Status as Predictors of Facebook Use. *Computers in Human Behavior* 28 (6): 2359–2365.

McCracken, Stephen D. 1988. *Culture and Consumption: New Approaches to the Symbolic Character of Consumer Goods and Activities*. Bloomington: Indiana University Press.

McKenna, K.Y.A., et al. 2002. Relationship Formation on the Internet: What's the Big Attraction? *Journal of Social Issues* 56 (1): 9–31.

McLaughlin, Caitlin, and Jessica Vitak. 2011. Norm Evolution and Violation on Facebook. *New Media & Society* 14 (2): 299–315.

McLuhan, Marshall. 1964. *Understanding Media: The Extensions of Man*. New York: McGraw-Hill.

McPherson, Miller, et al. 2001. Birds of a Feather: Homophily in Social Networks. *Annual Review of Sociology* 27 (1): 415–444.

Mead, George H. 2015. *Mind, Self, and Society. The definitive edition*. Chicago: University of Chicago Press.

Micalizzi, Alessandra. 2014. In Search of a Lost Identity. In *Identity Technologies: Constructing the Self Online*, ed. A. Poletti and J. Rak. Madison, WI: University of Wisconsin Press.

Miles, Andrew, and Mike Savage. 2012. The Strange Survival Story of the English Gentleman, 1945–2010. *Cultural and Social History* 9 (4): 595–612.

Miller, Vincent. 2011. *Understanding Digital Culture*. London: Sage Publications.

Miller, Daniel, and Don Slater. 2000. *The Internet: An Ethnographic Approach*. Oxford: Berg Publishers.

Molm, Linda D. 1994. Is Punishment Effective? Coercive Strategies in Social Exchange. *Social Psychology Quarterly* 57 (2): 75–94.

O'Meara, Donald. 1989. Cross-sex Friendship: Four Basic Challenges of an Ignored Relationship. *Sex Roles* 21 (7–8): 525–543.

Papacharissi, Zizi. 2002. The Virtual Sphere: The Internet as a Public Sphere. *New Media & Society* 4 (1): 9–27.

————. 2011. *A Networked Self: Identity, Community, and Culture on Social Network Sites*. New York: Routledge.

Parsons, Talcott. 1951. *The Social System*. London: Routledge.

Pauwels, Luc. 2005. Websites as Visual and Multimodal Cultural Expressions: Opportunities and Issues of Online Hybrid Media Research. *Media, Culture & Society* 27 (4): 604–613.

Pentzold, Christian. 2009. Fixing the Floating Gap: The Online Encyclopaedia Wikipedia as a Global Memory Place. *Memory Studies* 2 (2): 255–272.

Peterson, Richard A., and Andy Bennett. 2004. Introducing the Scenes Perspective. In *Music Scenes: Local, Trans-Local and Virtual*, ed. A. Bennett and R.A. Peterson. Nashville: Vanderbilt University Press.

Peterson, Richard A., and Roger M. Kern. 1996. Changing Highbrow Taste: From Snob to Omnivore. *American Sociological Review* 61 (5): 900–907.

Phua, Joe, et al. 2017. Uses and Gratifications of Social Networking Sites for Social Capital: Comparing Facebook, Twitter, Instagram, and Snapchat. *Computers in Human Behavior* 72: 115–122.

Pickering, Michael, and Emily Keightley. 2006. The Modalities of Nostalgia. *Current Sociology* 54 (6): 919–941.

Powell, Christopher, and François Depleteau. 2013. *Conceptualizing Relational Sociology: Ontological and Theoretical Issues*. New York: Palgrave Macmillan.

Puetz, Kyle. 2015. Consumer Culture, Taste, Preferences, and Social Network Formation. *Sociology Compass* 9 (6): 438–449.

Pullen Mark, J., and Charles Snow. 2007. Integrating Synchronous and Asynchronous Internet Distributed Education for Maximum Effectiveness. *Education and Information Technologies* 12 (3): 137–148.

Putnam, Robert. 2000. *Bowling Alone: The Collapse and Revival of American Community*. New York: Simon & Schuster.

Quinn, Diane M., Rachel W. Kallen, and Jean M. Twenge. 2006. The Disruptive Effect of Self-objectification on Performance. *Psychology of Women Quarterly* 30 (1): 59–64.

Radden, Jennifer. 2000. *The Nature of Melancholy: Readings on Melancholy, Melancholia and Depression from Aristotle to Kristeva*. Oxford: Oxford University Press.

Rafieian, Shahram, and Howard Davis. 2016. Dissociation, Reflexivity and Habitus. *European Journal of Social Theory* 19 (4): 556–573.

Rakic, Tijana. 2012. Philosophies of the Visual [Method] in Tourism Research. In *An Introduction to Visual Research Methods in Tourism*, ed. T. Rakic and D. Chambers, 17–32. New York: Routledge.

Ralon, Laureano, and Marcelo Vieta. 2011. McLuhan and Phenomenology. *Explorations in Media Ecology* 10 (3–4): 185–206.

Rawls, Anne W. 1987. The Interaction Order Sui Generis: Goffman's Contribution to Social Theory. *Sociological Theory* 5 (2): 136–149.

Resnick, Paul. 2001. Beyond Bowling Together: Socio-technical Capital, HCI in the New Millennium. In *Human-Computer Interaction in the New Millennium*, ed. J.M. Carroll, 647–672. New York: ACM Press.

Rodogno, Raffaele. 2012. Personal Identity Online. *Philosophy and Technology* 25 (3): 309–328.

Rosenfeld, Michael J., and Reuben J. Thomas. 2012. Searching for a Mate: The Rise of the Internet as a Social Intermediary. *American Sociological Review* 77 (4): 523–547.

Saarikallio, Suvi. 2011. Music as Emotional Self-regulation Throughout Adulthood. *Psychology of Music* 39 (3): 307–327.

Scheff, Thomas J. 1990. *Microsociology: Discourse, Emotion, and Social Structure.* Chicago: The University of Chicago Press.

———. 2005. Looking-Glass Self: Goffman as Symbolic Interactionist. *Symbolic Interaction* 28 (2): 147–166.

———. 2014. The Ubiquity of Hidden Shame in Modernity. *Cultural Sociology* 8 (2): 129–141.

Schiermer, Bjørn, and Hjalmar Bang Carlsen. 2016. Nostalgia, Irony and Collectivity in Late-modern Culture. *Acta Sociologica* 60 (2): 158–175.

Schütz, Alfred. 1967. *The Phenomenology of the Social World.* Evanston, IL: Northwestern University Press.

———. 1970. In *Alfred Schütz on Phenomenology and Social Relations*, ed. Helmut R. Wagner. Chicago: University of Chicago Press.

———. 1976. *Collected Papers II: Studies in Social Theory.* The Hague: Martinus Nijhoff.

Schwartz, Ori. 2011. Who Moved My Conversation? Instant Messaging, Intertextuality and New Regimes of Intimacy and Truth. *Media Culture & Society* 33 (1): 71–87.

Schwartz, Raz, and Germaine Halegoua. 2014. The Spatial Self: Location-based Identity Performance on Social Media. *New Media & Society* 17 (10): 1643–1660.

Sennett, Richard. 1992. *The Fall of the Public Man.* New York: WW Norton Publishing.

Silverstone, Roger. 2002. Complicity and Collusion in the Mediation of Everyday Life. *New Literary History* 33 (4): 761–780.

Simmel, Georg. 1950. *The Sociology of Georg Simmel*. Ed. and Trans. Kurt H. Wolff. New York: The Free Press.

———. 2009. *Sociology: Inquiries into the Construction of Social Forms. Vol. I and Vol. II*. Eds. and Trans. Anthony J. Blasi, Anton K. Jacobs and Mathew Kanjirathinkal. Boston: Brill.

Singh, Sourabh. 2016. What Is Relational Structure? Introducing History in the Debates on the Relation between Fields and Social Networks. *Sociological Theory* 34 (2): 128–150.

Smith-Doerr, Laurel, and Walter W. Powell. 2005. Networks and Economic Life. In *Handbook of Economic Sociology*, ed. N.J. Smelser and R. Swedberg, 2nd ed., 379–402. Princeton, NJ: Princeton University Press.

Steinfield, Charles, Nicole B. Ellison, and Cliff Lampe. 2008. Social Capital, Self-esteem, and Use of Online Social Network Sites: A Longitudinal Analysis. *Journal of Applied Developmental Psychology* 29 (6): 434–445.

Stets, Jan E., and Michael J. Carter. 2012. A Theory of the Self for the Sociology of Morality. *American Sociological Review* 77 (1): 120–140.

Strano, Michele M., and Jill Wattai Queen. 2012. Covering Your Face on Facebook: Suppression as Identity Management. *Journal of Media Psychology* 24 (4): 166–180.

Straw, Will. 1991. Systems of Articulation, Logics of Change: Communities and Scenes in Popular Music. *Cultural Studies* 5 (3): 368–388.

Stryker, Sheldon. 2004. Integrating Emotion into Identity Theory. In *Theory and Research on Human Emotions*, ed. J.H. Turner, 1–23. Emerald Group Publishing Limited.

Tavory, Iddo. 2010. Of Yarmulkes and Categories: Delegating Boundaries and the Phenomenology of Interactional Expectation. *Theory and Society* 39 (1): 49–68.

Thayer, Robert E., Robert J. Newman, and Tracey M. McClain. 1994. Self-regulation of Mood: Strategies for Changing a Bad Mood, Raising Energy, and Reducing Tension. *Journal of Personality and Social Psychology* 67 (5): 910–925.

Tönnies, Ferdinand. 1957. *Community and Society*. East Lansing, MI: Michigan State University Press.

Trepte, Sabine, and Leonard Reinecke, eds. 2011. *Privacy Online: Perspectives on Privacy and Self-Disclosure in the Social Web*. Dordrecht: Springer.

Tufekci, Zeynep. 2008. Grooming, Gossip, Facebook and Myspace. *Information, Communication & Society* 11 (4): 544–564.

———. 2015. Algorithmic Harms beyond Facebook and Google: Emergent Challenges of Computational Agency. *Journal on Telecommunications & High Technology Law* 13: 203–445.

Turkle, Sherry. 2011. *Alone Together: Why We Expect More from Technology and Less from Each Other.* New York: Basic Books.

———. 2015. *Reclaiming Conversation: The Power of Talk in a Digital Age.* New York: Penguin Press.

Urry, John. 1990. *The Tourist Gaze: Leisure and Travel in Contemporary Societies.* London: Sage.

———. 1995. *Consuming Places.* London: Routledge.

Vaccari, Cristian. 2017. Online Mobilization in Comparative Perspective: Digital Appeals and Political Engagement in Germany, Italy, and the United Kingdom. *Political Communication* 34 (1): 69–88.

Vaisey, Stephen, and Omar Lizardo. 2010. Can Cultural Worldviews Influence Network Composition? *Social Forces* 88 (4): 1595–1618.

van Dijck, Jose. 2013. *The Culture of Connectivity: A Critical History of Social Media.* New York: Oxford Scholarship Online.

van Doorn, Niels. 2011. Digital Spaces, Material Traces: How Matter Comes to Matter in Online Performances of Gender, Sexuality and Embodiment. *Media, Culture & Society* 33 (4): 531–547.

Vannini, Phillip, and Alexis Franzese. 2008. The Authenticity of Self: Conceptualization, Personal Experience, and Practice. *Sociology Compass* 2 (5): 1621–1637.

Walther, Joseph B., Brandon Van Der Heide, Kim Sang-Yeon, David Westerman, and Stephanie Tom Tong. 2008. The Role of Friends' Appearance and Behavior on Evaluations of Individuals on Facebook: Are We Known by the Company We Keep? *Human Communication Research* 34 (1): 28–49.

Warde, Alan. 2002. Changing Conceptions of Consumption. In *The Changing Consumer*, ed. A. Anderson, K. Meethan, and S. Miles, 10–24. London: Routledge.

———. 2014. After Taste: Culture, Consumption and Theories of Practice. *Journal of Consumer Culture* 14 (3): 279–303.

Waskul, Dennis D. 2002. The Naked Self: Being a Body in Televideo Cybersex. *Symbolic Interaction* 25 (2): 199–227.

———. 2005. Ekstasis and the Internet: Liminality and Computer-mediated Communication. *New Media & Society* 7 (1): 47–63.

Weber, Max. 1978. *Economy and Society: An Outline of Interpretive Sociology.* Berkeley: University of California Press.

Wegerif, Rupert. 2013. *Dialogic: Education for the Internet Age.* London: Routledge.

Wellman, Barry, Anabel Quan Haase, James Witte, and Keith Hampton. 2001. Does the Internet Increase, Decrease, or Supplement Social Capital? *Social Networks, Participation, and Community Commitment* 45 (3): 436–455.

Werking, Kathy. 1997. *We're Just Good Friends: Women and Men in Nonromantic Relationships.* New York: The Guilford Press.

West, Anne, Jane Lewis, and Peter Currie. 2009. Students' Facebook 'Friends': Public and Private Spheres. *Journal of Youth Studies* 12 (6): 615–627.

White, Michele. 2006. *The Body and the Screen: Theories of Internet Spectatorship.* Cambridge, MA: MIT Press.

White, Harrison. 2008. *Identity and Control: How Social Formations Emerge.* Princeton, NJ: Princeton University Press.

Wimmer, Andreas, and Kevin Lewis. 2010. Beyond and Below Racial Homophily: ERG Models of a Friendship Network Documented on Facebook. *American Journal of Sociology* 116 (2): 583–642.

Wolfe, Alvin. 1970. On Structural Comparisons of Networks. *Canadian Review of Sociology* 7 (4): *226–244.*

Yap, Janice, and Nicholas Harrigan. 2015. Why does Everybody Hate me? Balance, Status, and Homophily: The Triumvirate of Signed Tie Formation. *Social Networks* 40: 103–122.

Yngvesson, Barbara. 2010. *Belonging in an Adopted World: Race, Identity, and Transnational Adoption.* Chicago: University of Chicago Press.

Yoon, Jeongkoo, Shane Thye, and Edward J. Lawler. 2013. Exchange and Cohesion in Dyads and Triads: A Test of Simmel's Hypothesis. *Social Science Research* 42 (6): 1457–1466.

Young, Alyson Leigh, and Anabel Quan-Hasse. 2013. Privacy Protection Strategies on Facebook. The Internet Privacy Paradox Revisited. *Information, Communication & Society* 16 (4): 479–500.

Young, Garry, and Monica T. Whitty. 2010. In Search of the Cartesian Self: Intentional Disembodiment within 21st Century Communication. *Theory & Psychology* 20 (2): 209–229.

Yuval-Davis, Nira. 2006. Belonging and the Politics of Belonging. *Patterns of Prejudice* 40 (3): 196–213.

———. 2007. Intersectionality, Citizenship and Contemporary Politics of Belonging. *Contemporary Review of International Social and Political Philosophy* 10 (4): 561–574.

Zhao, Shanyang. 2004. Consociated Contemporaries as an Emergent Realm of the Lifeworld: Extending Schütz's Phenomenological Analysis to Cyberspace. *Human Studies* 27 (1): 91–105.

―――. 2005. The Digital Self: Through the Looking Glass of Telecopresent Others. *Symbolic Interaction* 28 (3): 387–405.

―――. 2007. Internet and the Lifeworld: Updating Schütz Theory of Mutual Knowledge. *Information, Technology & People* 20 (5): 140–160.

Index[1]

A

Ahmed, S., 21n1, 141
Anger, 45, 160–164, 198

B

Barbalet, J., 100, 141
Baym, N. K., 46, 68, 94
Belonging, 14, 47, 144, 157–160,
    175, 179, 184, 191, 198
Berger, P., 116, 126
Bergson, H., 38, 129
Body, embodiment, 39, 65, 75, 148,
    154, 192, 198
Bond
    bond potential, 11, 15, 17–19,
        96–97, 101, 131, 180–181,
        184

friendship, 9, 11, 16, 93
new bonds, 28, 87, 94–100, 103,
    106, 108, 181
old bonds/ties/contacts, 7, 28,
    87–94, 102, 108, 136, 159,
    183, 202, 203
romantic partnership, 2, 5, 10,
    11, 16, 33, 63, 79, 83–86, 95,
    108, 124, 127, 164–167, 173
strong/close bond/closeness, 12, 13,
    15–17, 19, 45, 56, 74–76, 78,
    80, 81, 83, 85, 86, 88–91, 93,
    95, 96, 98, 100, 105, 106, 108,
    112–127, 133–138, 145, 146,
    156, 157, 175, 189, 200, 201
weak/distant bond/distance, 3,
    12–19, 53, 55, 74, 75,
    86–108, 112–114, 116, 117,

[1] Note: Page numbers followed by 'n' refer to notes.

© The Author(s) 2018
G.-I. Ivana, *Social Ties in Online Networking*, Palgrave Studies in
Relational Sociology, https://doi.org/10.1007/978-3-319-71595-7

Bond (*Cont.*)
    122, 125–127, 135–138, 145,
        157, 159, 163, 177, 181,
        184–191, 200, 201
Bourdieu, P., 12, 174, 175, 178
boyd, d., 3, 28, 46

C

Collins, R., 8, 10, 141, 161, 162,
        166, 178
Cooley, C., 10, 104, 142, 143, 166
Copresence, 34, 37, 38, 40, 130,
        183, 193
Crossley, N., 175, 178

D

Dimmick, J., 38, 133
Disembodiment, 32, 39, 47, 53, 64

E

Elias, N., 1–3
Ellison, N. B., 3, 28, 94, 96
Emotion, 7, 14, 17, 21n1, 47, 54,
        55, 77, 78, 99, 100, 107,
        141–167, 198, 199
Exchange of information
    being with the other/experiencing
        the other, 62, 68, 73, 199
    knowing of the other, 62, 68, 73,
        106, 190
Expectation, 4, 8–10, 14, 15, 17, 27,
        40, 54, 62, 69, 74, 78, 82, 90,
        105, 115, 116, 141, 144, 148,
        152, 153, 162, 164, 165, 167,
        182, 199

F

Facebook news feed, 73–74, 91, 102,
        107, 156
Facebook Wall, 77, 95, 97, 98, 106,
        120, 126, 137, 142, 149, 151,
        164
Feedback
    comment, 20, 34, 68, 111, 112,
        114, 117, 119, 125
    like, 34, 68, 111, 120, 179
    share, 111, 117, 135, 144, 153
Flow, 38–40, 64–67, 79, 80, 121,
        124, 129, 130, 132, 145, 200

G

Goffman, E., 7, 9, 11, 15, 121, 142,
        143, 149, 166
Group size
    dyad, 35, 158
    triad, 158

H

Harrigan, N., 11, 12
Hochschild, A. R., 1, 13
Holmes, M., 63
Homophily, 12, 174–177, 198

I

Institutionalization, 84, 116–119,
        121, 124–126, 137, 138
Interaction, 5, 8–11, 14–17, 19, 20,
        27, 28, 31–40, 45, 46, 48, 53,
        54, 56–58, 61–69, 77, 81, 83,
        84, 86, 87, 96, 99, 101,
        103–105, 111–138, 141, 142,

148–150, 152, 153, 163, 173, 178, 179, 181, 188, 191–193, 197–201

Ivana, G., 13, 14, 35, 149, 191

K

Kaun, A., 39, 64
Kemper, T., 147, 150, 152, 161

L

Lawler, E., 158
Life course/life trajectory, 7, 27, 89–92, 101, 107, 108, 145, 173
Lived durée/first hand experience, 2, 9, 17, 37, 39, 56, 57, 64–67, 73, 123, 132, 138, 157, 199
Lizardo, O., 178
Luckman, T., 116, 126
Lury, C., 182

M

May, V., 157
McLuhan, M., 29
McPherson, M., 174
Mead, G. H., 104, 142, 143, 166
Mediation, 27, 28, 69
Mediatization, 28, 45, 52, 53, 55, 69
Melancholy, 154, 155
Miles, A., 186

N

Non-interactional exchange, 8, 62, 100, 113, 131, 178, 191, 199

Norm/normativity, 5, 8, 10, 12–15, 18, 50, 52, 74, 80, 90, 91, 93, 100, 119, 120, 141, 143, 144, 147, 148, 153, 154, 158, 159, 161, 163–166, 186, 188, 190, 193, 198–200, 202
Nostalgia, 154–157

O

Online debate, 118, 119, 128–132, 137, 138, 161, 163, 174
Overviewing, 73–108, 122, 137, 138, 163, 197, 198

P

Papacharissi, Z., 46, 52
Pentzold, C., 154, 155
Power, 8, 94, 122, 142, 147–150, 152, 163, 191, 192
Pride, 7, 21, 142–152, 154, 159, 177, 198
Public, publicness, 2, 6, 9, 11, 20, 30–32, 34, 35, 38–40, 46–52, 55, 56, 61, 67, 68, 73–86, 88, 90, 92–96, 98, 99, 101, 104–106, 108, 111–117, 119–134, 137, 138, 142, 143, 145, 146, 148–150, 162–167, 181, 188, 190–192, 197, 200, 202
Puetz, K., 178

R

Re-privatization, 188, 190, 191, 202

S

Scheff, T., 141–143
Schütz, A., 15–17, 21n1, 29, 32, 33, 56, 77, 129
Sennett, R., 47, 154, 190
Shame, 106, 121, 142–151, 154, 165, 198
Shared experience, 8, 13, 14, 27, 63, 76, 78, 82, 84, 87, 89, 92, 96, 97, 99, 103, 107, 112, 118, 122–125, 178, 185, 190, 199, 201
Simmel, G., 8, 12, 16, 158
Singh, S., 175, 176
Social class, 7, 21, 187, 190
Stalking, 5, 20, 97, 103–108, 136
Stets, J., 160
Stryker, S., 144
Symbolic order, 176, 178, 180, 191, 193

T

Tie, *see* Bond

Togetherness, 4, 13, 16, 17, 20, 21, 35, 56, 61–69, 78, 90, 129, 132, 138, 157, 158, 173, 199, 201
Tufekci, Z., 5, 29
Turkle, S., 4, 54, 62
Typification, 15, 55, 76, 79, 89, 90, 96–100, 102, 107, 108, 122, 129, 131, 138, 145, 181, 190, 201

W

Weber, M., 8, 10, 30
Wellman, B., 3, 175
White, H., 8–10, 19, 175
Wolfe, A., 8

Y

Yuval-Davis, N., 158

Z

Zhao, S., 32

Printed by Printforce, the Netherlands